Our Common
History
as Christians

Our Common History as Christians

ESSAYS IN HONOR OF ALBERT C. OUTLER

Edited By
John Deschner,
Leroy T. Howe,
and Klaus Penzel

New York
Oxford University Press
1975

PREFACE

The possibility of a *Festschrift* for Albert C. Outler was first entertained several years ago by several members of the Perkins School of Theology faculty. Initially the project took shape at the hands of Professors John Deschner and Klaus Penzel, under the leadership and with the constant encouragement of Dean Joseph D. Quillian, Jr.; the undersigned writer joined them at the stage of preparing the manuscript for publication.

Throughout the volume the central emphasis—one of several that might have been selected in view of the many-faceted character of Albert Outler's interests—is his work as a historian of the Christian tradition, or, in the words of Perkins church historian William S. Babcock, of "the complex and mysterious human processes in which the Christian community seeks, from time to time, to define and to achieve its Christian identity."

The Editors have solicited contributions that would bear most specifically upon the theme of "our common history as Christians," one on which Mr. Outler had brooded for decades and one which, in the judgment of the Editors, has called forth some of his most significant work. The first group of essays reflects recent ecumenical discussion and represents something of the context within which the theme itself has become cogent. The second group may be understood as probing diverse historical periods, with "common Christian history" as a regulative ideal. The third group suggests some of the theme's import for understanding various fields of theological inquiry—e.g., biblical, historical, and systematic theology.

The splendid cooperation of all the contributors, and of Oxford University Press, in bringing the book to completion is itself eloquent testimony to the esteem in which Mr. Outler is everywhere held. The Editors are especially appreciative of the tireless efforts of Mrs. Bonnie Jordan, who prepared the manuscript so patiently and competently, and attended to many details pertaining to the project.

Originally this volume was envisioned as a gesture of appreciation to be presented to Albert Outler upon his retirement from Perkins School of Theology. But now a new occasion has happily presented itself: Mr. Outler's decision to remain at Perkins as Research Professor of Theology. We wish him many fruitful years in this capacity as scholar-teacher and, more personally, as colleague and friend.

LEROY T. HOWE

September 1, 1974

CONTENTS

ALBERT COOK OUTLER

A BIOGRAPHICAL MEMOIR

John Deschner

Albert Outler could have disposed of my undergraduate enquiry with a line or two, but he didn't. He typed two solid pages. I had to lead worship at that 1943 student conference, and my idea was to cite passages from his address in the worship service that followed. So I wrote in advance for some quotations. His response, then as so many times afterward, was to make my question a wedge for teaching something else: I received not only the key lines of his coming address but also a quick course in what worship ought to be.

When he actually turned up—and especially afterward, when he consented to ride as far as Dallas with the University of Texas delegation, hunched up against a blue Texas norther under a flapping tarp on the back of a truck—I decided that this Duke theologian came human end foremost. And while succeeding years have brought changing, deepening relations between us—from teacher at Yale to ecumenical co-worker, guide, and colleague at Perkins—I have always known that my truest perception of this man was my first. He is a remarkable friend, reckless in his self-giving, who immediately saw into, admonished, enjoyed, enabled the

---

The author is Professor of Theology at Perkins School of Theology, Southern Methodist University.

answering friendship of that passing student. And the same
sure touch has continued for thirty years.

Albert Cook Outler is the son of a Southern Methodist
parsonage. Born November 17, 1908, in Thomasville, Georgia,
to John and Gertrude Outler, his roots lie deep in the
piety and style of that home, tradition, and region. It was
a region in which homogeneity of community, church, and
family was still very real, and gracious living not yet a
synonym for affluence. Southern Methodism had from its
beginnings—and certainly this was true at the turn of the
century—a stronger sense than its northern counterpart of
tradition and constitution. Georgia Methodism had only
recently been shaken by the "holiness" controversies, and the
Wesleyan themes and impulses were matters of explicit and
cultivated attention. Albert's undergraduate education at
Wofford provided the liberal education for which this
Southern Methodist civilization still had an honored place. In
all three respects—tradition, Wesleyanism, liberal studies—the
stamp of the future theologian's work was given by Southern
Methodist culture in a moment of equilibrium. He later
wrote:

> If one may speak in terms of "atmospheres" rather than calendar
> dates, it would then be true to say that I was born and reared in the
> eighteenth centruy—in a parsonage-home of warm-hearted piety and
> in a college still devoted to a classical curriculum.[1]

After receiving his A.B. degree in 1928, he taught English
and took a pastorate—Baxley Circuit in southern Georgia—for
two years. About this he gently said, "Many have come
farther but few have come from farther back." From 1930 to

---

1. The principal sources of materials quoted in this memoir are
Outler's essay, "How My Mind Has Changed," in the book of the same
title, ed. Harold E. Fey (Cleveland: World Publishing Co., 1961), pp.
40–54; and *The Perkins Journal* 27, 3 (Spring 1974), containing several
articles honoring Outler and a comprehensive bibliography of his
writings.

1933 he studied for his B.D. at Emory University, writing as his senior thesis "Psychotherapy and Pastoral Care." Simultaneously he served student pastorates at Pineview (1930–32) and Gordon (1932–34). On December 18, 1931, he married his old college sweetheart, Carlotta Grace Smith, to whom—it is rumored—he had proposed a month after they met. Two children, Frances and David, and two grandchildren have completed this close and lively family circle.

This Emory period produced also the first of many proposals for practical church reform, in an article in the *Wesleyan Christian Advocate* on "A New Deal for Presiding Elders." This was his proposal: less emphasis on their role as visiting preachers and routine administrators, and more on their role as personnel directors and pastors to pastors. Later efforts to upgrade Methodist Boards of Ministry are already prefigured here.

Of the seven years in pastorate and seminary he later wrote that it "marked a brief but exciting passage into and through the nineteenth century—with a conversion to 'liberalism' at the very time when its first effective critiques were being noticed in this country." In 1935, after a year as Associate Pastor at Mulberry Street in Macon, he began doctoral studies at Yale University, where, as he recalled, he was "thrust into the twentieth century." His field of specialization was historical theology, and his interests and studies were then as always far-ranging.

> I read Irenaeus and Barth the same semester. While I was being immersed in Plato and Augustine I was also being agitated by the early Niebuhrs, A. J. Ayer, and T. S. Eliot. I read a bit of Kierkegaard and Jaspers, I heard exciting but vague talk of Heidegger and Bultmann and I actually *met* Paul Tillich. There were seminars in psychology at the Institute of Human Relations and a dissertation on Origen that had to satisfy Robert Calhoun, Roland Bainton, and Erwin Goodenough. What a jumble it all was—and what an adventure!

Duke University made the new doctor an Instructor in Theology (1938–39), and in short order Assistant Professor

(1939–41) and Associate Professor (1941–45). Establishing oneself as a teacher of theology is always more exhausting than any non-teacher will ever imagine; yet these were also years of intensive study and scholarly activity. There were the patristic studies "Origen and the *Regulae Fidei*" and "The Platonism of Clement of Alexandria," as well as characteristic essays on the relation of patristics to contemporary issues and themes. Of particular importance to Outler himself was a substantial essay on "A Christian Context for Counseling" (1945), the first fruit of a life-long interest in the relation between psychology and theology, an interest that had begun in his early clinical training and was later to result in the work *Psychotherapy and the Christian Message.*

Yale called, and in 1945 Outler returned to New Haven as Associate Professor of Theology, to be appointed full Professor in 1948 and holder of the Timothy Dwight Chair in Theology. Concerned for "my double involvement in *Academia* and *Ecclesia*," he also asked for and received appointment to the Methodist Church at nearby Wallingford (Connecticut), which he served for two years along with his Yale post, preaching, pastoring, and even burning the mortgage! As one of his Yale students, I can bear witness to the high interest in his lectures, to the contagiousness of his ecumenical commitment, and to the helpfulness of his personal counseling for many. Outler quickly became one of the important faculty figures for us at Yale.

These Yale years (1945–51) made heavy demands on the new professor for leadership in the general enterprise of religion in higher education. Typical was the Hazen Foundation's program; his reflections and recommendations were published in *Colleges, Faculties and Religion: An Appraisal of the Program of Faculty Consultation on Religion in Higher Education, 1945–48.* And there was a steadily growing list of scholarly reviews and essays resulting from his more strictly scholarly activities. His participation in the Duodecim, for example—that archetype of theological discussion groups—produced as his contribution to the Augustine volume[2] what one scholar called "the best publication on Augustine's Christology available in English today." And the worktable was strewn with several patiently maturing manuscripts.

Outler's move to Texas and Southern Methodist University in 1951—leaving a historically distinguished chair for a professorship in a denominational Southern seminary of middle rank—astonished his friends and acquaintances. For Outler, however, it was a typically foresighted step. He knew that S.M.U. had recently received the handsome J. J. Perkins benefaction and a new seminary campus. He knew also that a number of faculty appointments would soon need to be made. He had helped recruit a vigorous new dean, Merrimon Cuninggim, and knew his determination to create a front-rank theological school in the Southwest. Most of all, it was the same hunger for *"Academia* and *Ecclesia"* marking his work from student pastorate to Wallingford that now attracted him to the one large university still closely identified with the Methodist Church. As he wrote:

> Like many another Southerner who had left home, I was feeling a stronger pull to return—to share in the development of theological education in a region where Protestantism is still a major cultural factor and to work more closely with the churches through a university set down in their midst.

Perkins was to become his permanent base, and the setting of his major accomplishments as teacher, academic statesman, scholar, churchman, and ecumenist.

First there was the reshaping of the theology school. From revising admission procedures to designing a fresh curriculum and recruiting a faculty to reach it—and, not least, persuading

---

2. "The Person and Work of Christ," in ·*A Companion to the Study of St. Augustine,* ed. by Roy W. Battenhouse (New York: Oxford University Press, 1955).

Methodists to accept the changes—Outler's contribution as leading member of the faculty and counselor to the new dean was always impressive and often decisive. That Perkins has an important place in American theological education today may be laid in no small measure to his faculty leadership during the 1950s.

His teaching likewise took on bellwether importance, not only because it spread into several fields—those of systematic theology, church history, pastoral care—but as much because of its example for others. "I would rather be remembered as a teacher than almost anything else," he once remarked.

In the larger university also, Outler soon became a pervasive influence as adviser to a new president, as senator and as committee man. It was basically his idea to have a campus "Festival of the Humanities" as a means of generating university-wide dialogue. He also proposed and guided the development of a Council on the Humanities as a means for funding the research of younger faculty members and establishing regular interdisciplinary dialogue among them. In 1962–63 Outler was chairman of the committee that drafted S.M.U.'s Master Plan for the ensuing decade and created the university's interdisciplinary University College to which all students belong during their freshman and sophomore years. Shortly thereafter, he had a crucial part in stimulating and guiding a series of doctoral programs at S.M.U. and chairing the Graduate Council of the Humanities (1960–63), and himself producing the design for the now well-established Graduate Program in Religion. While this side of his work is not widely known outside the university, few professors on any campus have been as effective in planning and inspiring academic life and strategy, both officially and unofficially, or have left as deep a mark on a single university.

Along with all this extracurricular activity went a steadily increasing flow of scholarly production. In fact, the move to Texas seems to have been favorable to scholarly activity, and, as his bibliography in this volume will attest, his Perkins years have seen the appearance of eight major works: editions of

Augustine and Wesley, two volumes on ecumenics, and theological essays on psychotherapy, tradition, providence and history, and Wesleyan evangelism. And that is not to mention scores of scholarly essays, papers, addresses, reviews, plus more than thirty lectureships, many of them based on book-length manuscripts still awaiting revision and publication at this time. The fuller bibliography of Outler's writings contain 244 published items, 208 of them appearing after 1951.

Even so, it may be maintained that Outler's major contribution during these years—or certainly until very recently—lies in his work as churchman and ecumenist. As churchman, it is not simply that he clearly stands in the front rank of the self-consciously Methodist theologians of this century, and is accepted to a remarkable degree by that denomination as a representative theologian. Beyond his labors as a theologian lies a prodigious activity, both official and unofficial, in ecclesiastical conferences, boards, and commissions. Throughout the Perkins years, he has been a highly active member of the North Texas Annual Conference, serving for several years as chairman of its Board of Ministry. He has been a delegate to every one of the quadrennial General Conferences since 1960. He helped create the United Methodist Commission on Ecumenical Affairs, and he was chairman of the denomination's Theological Study Commission on Doctrine and Doctrinal Standards whose report, adopted by the General Conference in 1972, is the first offical clarification in this century of American Methodism's doctrinal heritage and its contemporary uses.

But it has been as ecumenist that the various aspects of Outler's work are most nearly brought together and most widely known.

His earlier ecumenical work had its setting primarily within the Faith and Order Commission of the World Council of Churches. As a Methodist delegate to the Third World Conference on Faith and Order (Lund, 1952), he advanced a proposal for an ecumenical attempt to write "our common history as Christians," and was soon participating in both the standing Faith and Order Commission and its executive Working Committee. His best-known Faith and Order contribution was made through his chairmanship (1953–63) of the American Section of the Theological Commission on Tradition and Traditions—K. E. Skydsgaard chaired the parallel European Section—in which was developed an understanding of scripture, Tradition, and traditions that broke new ground in the ecumenical discussion, and was subsequently widely used in other contexts (e.g., in the theological work of the Consultation on Church Union). His least-known contribution was his influence on the text that became the New Delhi statement on "the unity we seek" (1961), surely the single most famous paragraph in the World Council's history. Outler was himself a Methodist delegate to the WCC Third Assembly at New Delhi. Along the way, he was a leading participant in the North American Conference on Faith and Order at Oberlin in 1957, in preparation for which he wrote his book on tradition. This Faith and Order activity culminated in his service as Vice Chairman of the Fourth World Conference on Faith and Order at Montreal in 1963.

By the early 1960s he was also deep in theological preparations for the Consultation on Church Union. His touch can be discerned not only in the drafts on scripture and tradition, but especially in the difficult probings of the critical issue: a more adequate COCU understanding of ministry. Outler never tired of exploring the possibilities of the New Delhi approach: a mutual recognition of members and min-stry as the actual "unity we seek"; and impulses from his addresses, e.g., his Atlanta ministry (1968) on "The Mingling of Ministries," persist in the creative work of COCU today.

But Outler's most famous ecumenical work was surely his participation as Methodist delegate-observer in all four sessions of the Second Vatican Council (1962–65). Although he is one of the master teachers of conciliar history, his preparations for this role assumed the proportions of a major scholarly project. And his collection of documents and books, including a voluminous personal diary of each day's Council action as he observed it happening, constitutes a valuable non-Roman archive of this historic event. This expertise did not go unappreciated in Rome. Counseling drafters of documents; addressing Council members and *periti*; taking a prominent part in Pope Paul's concluding worship service with the delegate-observers; accepting a position on the board of the new Institute for Ecumenical Research at Tantur (near Jerusalem), Outler was at the Council's close one of the leading non-Roman figures of the Council. Moreover, his official role has continued since the Council in his leadership in both the national and international bilateral conversations between Roman Catholics and Methodists; and unofficially he is a respected interpreter of the Council and Pope Paul's postconciliar policy to both Catholics and non-Catholics. The appreciative echo among American Roman Catholics has been wide and persistent. For a while one read more about Outler in the Roman Catholic press than in the Methodist. That the University of Notre Dame conferred an honorary doctorate upon him and that he was elected president of the American Catholic Historical Association (1971–72) are only two of the many signs of Catholic appreciation.

Since Vatican II, Outler has turned increasingly toward strengthening the ecumenical and evangelical foundations in Methodism itself. His chief instrument in so doing has been his mastery of both the Methodist and the Evangelical United Brethren traditions, and especially that of the Wesleys. For many years he had required of his students a serious exploration of Methodism's constitutional and doctrinal history, with the consequence that Perkins became a center for the study of Methodist theological history. And there is a direct line from that teaching to the main positions of the 1972 General Conference report on standards of doctrine. Also important, though less widely known, is his work at the

1968 and 1970 General Conferences. At Dallas (1968), he preached the sermon for the uniting service and prepared for the Commission on Ecumenical Affairs a resolution on "The United Methodist Church and the Cause of Christian Unity. That resolution, which was unanimously adopted by the General Conference, may be the most substantial ecclesiological statement ever officially made by that body. This was followed at St. Louis in 1970 by another Outler-initiated resolution from the same Commission, again unanimously adopted. Without rescinding any of our Articles of Religion, this resolution made it clear how Methodism relates to the anti-Roman elements in that historical tradition in an age of ecumenical convergence. The resolution, presented and received at the Vatican, stands as an example of how ecumenically creative the responsible re-reception of tradition can be.

During this period there were also new initiatives in the ecumenical and theological education of the Methodist laity. With his sure sense for where the laity's thinking is and could be, Outler has always been one of the most sought-after—and understood!—speakers and preachers in United Methodism. In 1966 his book *That the World May Believe* was published—to become a widely used manual for Methodists on the ecumenical movement and Methodism's role in it. In 1972, Outler, sensing the rising tide of conservative evangelicalism, published his *Evangelism in the Wesleyan Spirit*, which has since become for the new conservatives a link to their Wesleyan inheritance. Outler is widely welcomed today as speaker and consultant in Methodist and other neo-conservative circles.

Most recently his energies have been poured into a Wesleyan labor of love, one that may become his most enduring achievement as a scholar: his critical edition of the Wesley *Sermons* for the Wesley Works Project. In the early 1960s Outler was one of the initiators of the Oxford University Press project to publish a complete critical edition of the entire Wesley corpus in more than thirty volumes. His *John Wesley* of 1964 had been a kind of trial run at editing

Wesley. Now it fell to him to edit the first four or five volumes in this joint British-American effort. Strengthened by the expertise of an irreplaceable team of assistants, Wanda Smith, Kate Warnick, and his own librarian-wife Carla, Outler expects to complete it in his new post-retirement appointment as Research Professor of Theology at Perkins.

Painstaking labor at home and in England has enabled him to reconstruct the first rigorously critical version of these much-abused texts. Wesley's maddening habit of not referring to his abounding sources by name has been countered by an organized team effort at "finding another footnote." As preparation for his introductions and interpretations, Outler has mastered seventeenth- and eighteenth-century English history, secular as well as religious, as have few other investigators of Methodism. He has, for example, repeatedly visited the British Museum to familiarize himself, so far as possible, with every book listed in Wesley's careful, continuing lists of his own reading. In 1964 Outler had already opened up a new vein of Wesley interpretation by pointing out the large influence of the Greek Fathers upon Wesley's theology.[3] There is little doubt that his *Sermons* will set a standard for other editors and scholars, not simply in its meticulous critical work, but in its historical interpretation of this eighteenth-century "folk-theologian." After an over--emphasis on Wesley as evangelist and organizer, Outler is showing us Wesley as theologian, and not least as ecclesiologist and ecumenical pioneer. A first installment on this interpretation was given in his Fondren Lectures of 1974, "Theology in the Wesleyan Spirit," shortly to be published separately.

Much more should be mentioned: his participation and, often, leadership in learned and professional societies and academies, his numerous honorary degrees and the reasons for them. Particularly interesting, though little known, is his

---

3. *John Wesley*, ed. by Albert C. Outler (New York: Oxford University Press, 1964).

initiative in the organizing of a post-doctoral Seminar on the Development of Catholic Christianity which includes professors of religion from many Texas colleges and seminaries, and covers the spectrum from Roman Catholics to Southern Baptists and the Church of Christ. About thirty-five participants have worked together on a bi-monthly basis for seven years on problems of second-century ecclesiastical, theological, and exegetical history, and despite serious proposals to the contrary, refuse to terminate the seminar.

Space prevents a more thorough assessment of this many-sided career—still to all appearances in mid-flight—as pastor, counselor, preacher, teacher, historian-scholar, systematic theologian, academic statesman, Methodist, Church leader, ecumenist. As Church theologian, he is one of the few truly representative voices in the American Methodist tradition. As theological educator, he has exercised a lasting influence on Perkins and Southern Methodist University. As historian-scholar he has written more than his share of permanently valuable books, and is primarily responsible for a new awakening of non-Methodist (as well as Methodist!) interest in Wesley as theologian. As systematic theologian, he has steadily unfolded his sense of the providential and salutary continuity of Christian history amid all the discontinuities of place and period and person, and his vision of the mystery of God's love at the basis of real syntheses of faith and reason, church and society, theology and culture. It is as systematic theologian and believer that Albert Outler counts himself a man of the university. As teacher, apart from his impact on curricula and pedagogy, he is the gladly-remembered mentor of (by now) thousands of working preachers, and the continuing tutor, counselor, and mark-setter for scores of teachers and professors. As ecumenist, he is one of the genuinely creative spirits and minds of his generation, and surely a prophet—yet to be fully appreciated—of the growing convergence between catholicism (both Roman and Eastern Orthodox), main-line protestantism, and conservative evangelicalism.

And yet the most impressive thing about this theological career is not its variety but its creativity, its imaginative sense of strategy, its quality, and its exemplary demonstration of how theology can relate to church and culture. It has been a sustained contribution of high quality and relevance, wherever he has been at work, with ample time or without it.

It is my good fortune to be able to say to him on behalf of many: Thank you—for the insight and guidance, for the example, the instruction, and the stimulation, for the humor, and most of all for the friendship so freely given, without calculation, to so many. Many know that friendship as a decisive element in their lives—and among them I am certainly and gratefully among the first.

I

CONTEMPORARY ISSUES

THE FLAMING CENTER
Or THE CORE OF TRADITION

K. E. Skydsgaard

I

Few items of theology have been so intensively studied in the last thirty years—exegetically, historically, and systematically—as the concept of tradition.

In the ecumenical movement, the Third World Conference on Faith and Order at Lund in 1952 was an important starting point for the exploration of this crucial and disputed word. In the report of this conference the word "tradition" itself is not found (except three times in a less technical sense), but the matter is clearly indicated in Chapter 3 "Continuity and Unity II." The following resolution was offered:

> We propose the establishment of a Theological Commission to explore more deeply the resources for further ecumenical discussion to be found in that common history which we have as Christians and which we have discovered to be longer, larger and richer than any of our separate histories in our divided Churches. Such a study would focus not only on the hard cores of disagreement between us, but also on the positive discoveries there to be made of the various levels of unity which underlie our diversities and dividedness.[1]

The author is Emeritus Professor of Theology, University of Copenhagen.

The expression "common history," which, so far as I know, was first proposed by Albert Outler, is another expression for the reality of the word "tradition." The "common history which we have as Christians" and "the separate histories of our Churches" correspond to the later expression "Tradition and traditions."

At the Working Committee meeting of Faith and Order, held at Château de Bossey in 1953, we find the explicit expression "Tradition and Our Traditions" as the heading of a Memorandum prepared by Professor Florovsky and Professor Outler. Here we are at the center of the problem. "The term 'tradition' is a divisive theological concept," as we read in the Minutes, "but no Christian can escape it, simply because Christianity is a historical religion."[2] Here something important and, in the perspective of Protestant theology, new is stated: tradition and history are two converging realities. It is typical that in the subject index of The Symbolical Books of the Evangelical Lutheran Church (ed. 1967) the word *traditio* does not occur, but *traditiones* does—and here we are referred to *Menschensatzungen*, human inventions and rules![3] As a theological concept the word *traditio* exists only as a polemical notion, to be rejected. Today, partly because of biblical exegesis and partly because of the ecumenical movement, this situation has changed completely: Christianity is a historical religion, not only because it was founded at a definite point in history, not only because it has a history, but because it *is* a history. The Gospel is not a manifesto settled once-for-all, but a living proclamation, a handing over in space and time of a *kerygma* that will have to be delivered, received, understood in every new historical situation, and handed on to new generations.

There is a genuine, common Christian Tradition, and there are different traditions; but the different traditions may be regarded as specific, variegated expressions of the same

Tradition. We are confronting the problem of theological pluralism. The crucial question is, Whether this pluralism has to be a cacophony of differently tuned instruments in a great orchestra, or whether it cannot rather be a symphony in which the very different instruments form an ensemble. An orchestra must be pluralistic in order to produce the richness of sound the composer had in his ears.

Some concrete questions were formulated at the meeting in 1953. Thus, "Is there a describable common *traditio* in all existing communities which call and profess themselves Christian?" "When and how do additions to or deviations from the primitive or initial *traditio* alter the character and import of faith and order?" "How far can we recognize the essential complex of *kerygma* and *paradosis* in Christian communities *other* than our own?" (pp. 32, 33). "It is not enough to compare blocs of doctrines, *as they exist*; comparison is valuable if it is historical comparison. We can meet together only because we are united in a common tradition."[4] Common history is the same as common tradition. And presumably it is possible to have a clear conception of what this common tradition or history is. Professor Outler was not present at that meeting, but through his cooperation with Professor Florovsky he contributed greatly to the vivid discussion, which resumed in the following years.

During the same year (1953) it was decided to initiate an "Enquiry into Tradition and the Traditions." A group of seven persons should study "the problem of Tradition in its biblical and historical aspects, paying particular attention to the problem as it has been put before us in recent literature, in order to bring out the importance and need of such a study for ecumenical understanding."[5] The following year, at the meeting of the Working Committee at Evanston in 1954, it was decided to set up a "Theological Commission on

Tradition and Traditions," which should normally operate in two sections, one European, the other American, in close collaboration. Professor Outler was to serve as co-chairman of the American section, the author of this essay as co-chairman of the European section.[6] This recommendation was the starting point for a not always easy but nevertheless fruitful project on both sides of the Atlantic, on two different plans but with the same goal: to reconsider the necessity and theological significance of the word "tradition" or *paradosis*, a word that very often has been the fundamental scandal for theologians descended from the Reformation.

Now, it is not the purpose of this article to pass a judgment on the value of the work of these two groups. I want only to stress two points: first, that by this work on both sides a serious attempt was made to revaluate the importance of tradition in its historical, ecumenical, and systematic aspects. The old opposition between scripture and tradition was seen in a new light, through both the more sociological and historical approach of the American group and the more systematic work done by the European group. The affirmation that, rightly understood, "Christianity is a religion of Tradition" is today regarded as a matter of course; but it was not very obvious to dogmatic theologians at that time, although this way of thinking had been long taken for granted in biblical studies.

Second, I avail myself of the opportunity to thank and honor the man to whom this book is dedicated, for his enthusiasm and indefatigable zeal for this common work and for his inspiring cooperation.

The work of these two groups found its provisional conclusion at the Third World Conference of Faith and Order at Montreal in 1963. Here the problem "Scripture, Tradition, and Traditions" was taken up for a fresh, independent, original investigation which, as far as I see, can be regarded as a milestone in Protestant theology. This work was completed at almost the same time as the Second Vatican Council made its contribution to this crucial problem, issuing two years later, in 1965, in the "Dogmatic Constitution on Divine Revelation," which begins with the phrase, "Hearing the word of God with reverence. . . ."

It is not my task for the moment to compare these two documents from Montreal and Rome. There are considerable diversities and still much that is theologically explosive in these two papers, but they also form a fruitful springboard for further ecumenical and theological investigation in this extremely important field. Only one thing should be mentioned. Perhaps it is only an accidental coincidence, but nevertheless a significant and promising one. The Montreal document in its important report, "Scripture, Tradition, and Traditions," ends, after a serious attempt to scrutinize the problem of scripture and tradition, with a reference to *Tradition*. It is "the Church's great commission to transmit the Tradition, the word of grace and hope, to men in this new global culture, as in the past it was preached to Jerusalem, to Hellas, to Rome and Gaul and to the uttermost parts of the earth."[7] The Roman Catholic document "Dogmatic Constitution on Divine Revelation" ends with an allusion to the *Bible*.

In this way, therefore, through the reading and study of the sacred books, let "the word of the Lord run and be glorified" (2 Th. 3:1) and let the treasure of revelation entrusted to the Church increasingly fill the hearts of men. Just as the life of the Church grows through persistent participation in the Eucharistic mystery, so we may hope for a new surge of spiritual vitality from intensified veneration for God's word, which "lasts forever" (Isa. 40:8; cf. 1 Pet. 1:23-25).[8]

A comparative study of these two documents will certainly show significant diversities and controversial points. Nor can it be denied that the Roman Catholic document suffers from an inner ambiguity, due to divergent opinion within Roman Catholicism concerning the relation between scripture and tradition. On the Protestant side certain points were also unclear. Yet in the spirit and intention of the two statements we find a clear, common tendency: it is as impossible to say *scriptura sola*, as it is to say *traditio sola*. The two concepts are inseparable.

The two statements agree further that in the juxtaposition of scripture and tradition the word "scripture" does have a definite emphasis. The unclarity will press for further studies.

II

Although only a short stretch of years has passed since Montreal 1963 and Rome 1965, a very decisive, radical, all-embracing evolution has taken place, one that also affects the problem of tradition.

First, some words about our situation today. What is happening today has happened for centuries—more or less under the surface—and even broke forth in powerful and radical spiritual movements and in individual leaders who personalized and also canalized the revolutionary tendencies of the time. I think of the frequently violent explosions of emancipation from the Christian Church and the established society of the Western world, explosions that frightened and alarmed both Church and society. What formerly erupted as an "exception to the rule," however, has now reached a state of permanence and almost universal legitimacy. Through a very slow but inevitable process, Western culture has dissociated itself from its Christian origins and from close connection with the Christian churches. The Christian Occident (*das christliche Abendland*) is disappearing; a "new world" is coming. What this "new world" holds in store for us has not yet been disclosed, but we are able to see rather sharp outlines of it.

In general the churches regarded themselves as a bulwark against this evolution and in favor of established society. From the other side the churches were accused of reaction, immobility, and a strong conservatism, as the great obstacle to human liberty and progress. It is true that there was a rather close liaison between the Church and Western civilization. They were, so to speak, interdependent. The churches clung to a cultural, political, and social pattern of life formed across the centuries and in no small degree influenced by Christian faith and thought. Together Church and Occident formed a rather strong synthesis, and it is this synthesis that is now openly disintegrating. Perhaps the Christian churches today are passing through one of their greatest crises precisely because the liaison between Church and Western culture was so close. Very often the churches of the West were virtually identified with this Christianized Occident, although their common history also shows great tensions. In the main, however, this Christain Occident consolidated and secured the churches both spiritually and economically. In this atomosphere they were regarded as the chief factor insuring order and peace, not to speak of the guarantee of the grace of God and everlasting life.

Today the churches are more and more compelled to find their way in the midst of a world that no longer recognizes them as representatives of truth and humanity, but, on the contrary, as relics of the past, without significance for the evolution of mankind toward a more humanized world. The modern world regards the churches with the utmost skepticism, if it regards them at all. The churches realize for their part that the modern world is able to find its way without their message and existence.

The question is whether the churches will be able to find

and enter into a relation with this "new" world, in which they have to live and in which they are called to be witnesses of Christ. They will certainly be forced to leave their solid, thick-walled buildings and live in more modest quarters—if they are to have any permanent domicile at all. It is not possible within the framework of a short article to describe this situation in detail. Many Christians today—ministers, bishops and other church leaders, theologians, and a great many of the congregations—are aware of this situation, its complexity and dangers. Some of them see also the great promise for the Church in the midst of this "new" world.

One thing has been obvious to all who are capable of observing the signs of the times: namely, that an "old world" is now after a long struggle for life disappearing, and a "new age" after a long time of preparation is now entering the scene of human history. This situation has caused something like a schism among the churches, a line of demarcation between Christians which cuts across all other divisions, thereby completely changing the old ecumenical pattern.

The earlier ecumenical movement did its work in relatively quiet surroundings. The churches had this in common, that their relations with the world were almost identical. The world had not yet confronted the churches with a problem that prevented their struggling against each other in natural competition. Their ecumenical efforts were sincere and also necessary, but they had time to discuss and were able to do this "in peace." Without saying one word against the ecumenical endeavor of former times, I think we must admit that today we are compelled to rethink the problem of ecumenism.

The new situation creates great tension in the churches. This tension arises because of a new and different view of the world, completely "liberated" not only from the churches but also from the foundation which in spite of all their diversity the Christian churches had in common. There are Christians who believe that the clear intention of more progressive Christians to reconsider in a radical way their view of our world and its stormy history is an utterly dangerous tendency toward heresy and apostasy. This "new" spirit is seen as the sign of a deadly crisis of faith, of obedience, and of authority in the churches.

The Church, so it is said, finds its identity along the lines of tested orthodoxy. A readjustment (*aggiornamento*) is, of course, necessary, but within the pattern of the tradition, which has its clear signs and distinctive marks, whether the shibboleth is "scripture alone" or "tradition and scripture." A deviation from this way with its clear *yes* and *no* will ultimately turn out to be not only the end of the Church but also the end of "Christianity itself." This point of view is traditional in the sense that the Church has its specified way to go, a way sufficiently indicated and elucidated in the past.

This view involves also a clear conception of the world. The Church is "the ark of salvation" in the world. The Church, for instance, cooperates with the state in order to create tolerable conditions of life, to defeat negative insurrections against the established order, and to organize works of help and mercy toward those who need support, even though its main, and God-given, task is the salvation of man's soul. On the other hand, we also meet today an attitude characterized by sympathetic openness toward the world, a serious sense of responsibility for mankind in order to create a human world fit for human beings created by God. A new theology of creation and its salvation is coming into being. The word "salvation" signifies not only—not even primarily—salvation of man's soul from sin and death; it means also the restoration of the whole man, body and soul, thus necessarily including the political aspect.

In the New Testament the word "to save" has a twofold

meaning which nevertheless forms a unity. The word signifies the proclamation of forgiveness, or redemption from death and judgment, and in the same breath a curing of bodily diseases, of demonic obsession and all evils that destroy human life. Nietzsche accused Christians of being "Platonists," because they neglected and despised the earthly material life, thereby separating two things that belong together, matter and spirit. In short, the Kingdom of God means the new world in which the whole human being—body and spirit—by the powerful grace of God has been brought back to its Creator and Redeemer. In this view Christianity must be "revolutionary," not identifying itself with specific political movements but keeping a vigilant watch for all destructive powers that threaten human life. The Christian must look forward because the Kingdom of God is coming. The Kingdom can never be absorbed by religion or by institutionalized churches or by certain types of piety. The Kingdom of God is the flaming, warming, but also burning and consuming, fire.

As an attempt to understand our situation, I draw attention to the play of Jean Paul Sartre, *Le Diable et le bon Dieu*. Three persons appear. First the priest, the traditionalist. He is quite bound to the past, and cannot get rid of it; he tries, but the more he exerts himself the more he is clutched by the past. Unavoidably he is a prisoner of the past. His opposite party is the prophet, who believes fanatically in the future and energetically rejects the past. If man constantly denies the past with its tyranny and alienating power, says this prophet, the kingdom of perfection and intimacy will reign, in which all bondage to the external and "objective" will be overcome.

These two—the priest bound to the past and the prophet turned to the future—are now defeated by a third person, a soldier, the leading character in the drama and the spokesman for the author. He hates the past and its restraints and tradition. Therefore he simply kills the priest. On the other hand, he does not at all agree with the prophet and his hopes for the future. For him the only acceptable position is to stick to the *present*. Only he who accepts himself in the autonomous decision of each moment gains himself and keeps his human identity. In three words: restoration, revolution, and autonomy; or the past, the future, and the present; or in still other terms: the "traditionalist," the "futurist," and the "existentialist." All three types are to be found in the churches today, and represent the actual situation much more precisely than such previous character- izations as conservative, moderate, liberal, or modernist.

The relation between these two attitudes is often extremely difficult, apparently with no possibility of finding a common way between them. And thus a new and sharp, but also fruitful ecumenical front has been opened in the churches, one that cuts across all previous fronts, and to no small degree changes the older, more dogmatic divisions.

In the two "camps" just described, the word "tradition" has a different sound. In the older type, tradition plays an important role, even if the word itself, possibly for dogmatic reasons, is not explicitly used. The Church has, so to speak, its "fixed" image. The word does mean different things for the different churches; yet beneath all the divergencies there is a common ground: the Church is the people of God, in the world but not of the world. It is a holy people, and hence separated from the world. This image may be obscured, and thus it must be the Church's ongoing task to renew this image, by keeping it free from "the spirit of the world." Church and world belong together, but the Church may not lose herself in the world. The world is the realm into which the Church is sent in order to bring salvation through Word and Sacrament, and through the holy life of the believers.

The Church always needs renewal, but within the pattern of the true tradition.

In the second "camp" (whether Protestant or Catholic), the word "tradition" has an undertone of rigidity and stagnation. Tradition implies stiffness, because it binds us to the past and thereby prevents our advance into the future. God is the God of history, not only understood as the past but including the future as well. God is creating new things, even today. "Future" is the great watchword; and here the Church must be together with the world, which, in its best and most creative aspirations, is open to the future—that is, to a new, humanized world, a good dwelling for mankind. The Church has its existence for the sake of the world as created and redeemed by God.

III

We now come to the crux of the matter: To what extent does this new situation, roughly outlined above, influence the problem of tradition and of scripture and tradition? Does a new situation in the life of the churches serve as some sort of hermeneutic principle for the word "tradition" and the expression "our common history"? Are we able to come to a deeper understanding of "tradition" and "our common history"?

It seems to me that the answer must be affirmative. Are we not today compelled to raise questions that did not seem to be relevant or even possible within the framework of our established Churches but now have come to the fore with almost irresistible force?

First a few words about the word *traditio*. It has various meanings, positive and negative. Let me try to rough out a positive and deeply human meaning for the word. *Tradition* ordinarily has a connotation of something unchangeable in the midst of the disorder and fluctuations of human history. Tradition has a certain authority, an indisputable strength. It comes from the deepest sources of human life, as a mysterious guide for truth and knowledge in the turmoil of history. This is the case, for instance, in Plato and in not a few modern philosophers. Tradition and history are two opposite but nevertheless interdependent realities in human existence: history understood as the unquiet, steadily changing, contingent element in human existence; tradition seen as the constant, abiding, and uniting factor, without which human history would be split into non-cohesive fragments that would effectively disintegrate human existence.

But the concept of tradition I have in mind is fundamentally different from traditionalism, which means immobility and stagnation. Traditionalism is a caricature of tradition, although a very frequent one, a shadow that always accompanies the real figure. Tradition as a genuinely human phenomenon is a personal acceptance, a spiritual adaptation, a truthful handing-over to others for their free reception, a spiritual process presupposing the human person as a responsible and free entity. This understanding of the word "tradition" should be absolutely maintained, for the reason that it touches the foundation of human existence. *Traditio* is an *existentiale humanum*. Even Sartre's prophet and soldier cannot exist without tradition in this sense. By denying it they defeat true human existence. On the other hand, the priest in the play completely misunderstands tradition, which he cannot get rid of because he certainly confounds tradition and traditionalism.

"Tradition" thus explained, however, does not exclude that the very same word can cover totally different contents. How is this possible? The subject of tradition is man himself, and this subject is not a "pure" one but a man who has the will to put his own stamp upon all that he thinks and does.

He not only receives and adapts; he also tries to master what he receives. Tradition is an anthropological concept. It deals with the problem of man and his history.

Who is this subject of tradition? According to the Christian understanding, man is an ambiguous entity. A creature completely dependent upon God, he is also inclined to act as sovereign lord, to be aggressive when he meets the surrounding world, to choose the better part for himself, to place himself in the center. Man wishes to control what he receives and what he hands over. Quite unconsciously he tends to form the tradition in his own image. Tradition has in itself a power to convince, but all too often it cannot preserve its purity against man's will. Tradition participates in the ambiguities of human nature. Therefore the word "tradition" is not a "pure" word, but contaminated by the sinfulness of human nature. To sin is precisely to deviate from the true destiny of man, to miss the goal.

Human tradition always involves a fatal bias toward the stabilization of man himself. It becomes a defense of man's desire to exist in his own way. And because others wished to exist according to *their* self-understanding, different traditions clashed. The fantastic story of the Tower of Babel recurs. A new tradition, or a new variant of the older one, was founded. Theologically expressed: man was created in the image of God, to be open for God, to dialogue with God, to receive what God delivered to him—in short, to live "in God's tradition." But he also hears the voice of temptation: You shall be as God! This word is not wholly false: God's will *is* to make man godlike—in Jesus Christ; but in the mouth of the adversary this word meant rebellion, usurpation. And usurpation vis-à-vis God means distortion of essential humanity and of true tradition. Man is a split personality: on the one hand able to transcend himself toward an open or secret dialogue with God, on the other hand constantly seeking to possess himself in proud and vain isolation.

So too, "tradition" is an ambiguous word—and this should not be forgotten, even when we speak of Christian tradition, which too can be subject to temptation and fall, as the history of our churches proves abundantly. Thus, at certain moments of its history the Christian Church has been asked very serious questions concerning her tradition. Christian tradition is not a harmonious organic evolution, a quiet growth in wisdom and insight, like a seed that grows slowly and finally comes to fruition. Its way has been a very stormy and often humiliating one. The problem of unity and disunity is not so easy to understand as we think and wish. The guidance of the Holy Spirit toward fullness of truth goes through fire and great extremes. But a bit of tradition, as a straight and unbroken line, often dazzled the churches—both leaders and, under their authority, the so-called laity. For long periods the ambiguity of tradition was seen by only very few, and they often suffered from the blindness and traditionalism of authorities and lay people. The truth, however, could not be kept down. A renewal, often through painful travail, took place.

In this "history of the tradition" the specific situations played an important role. At the Working Committee meeting at Geneva 1953 it was stated that

> there is a tendency to minimize the meaning of Christian history and to regard every development as a kind of "accretion." This tendency also can be described as an attempt to deny any authoritative significance to any historical development which takes us beyond the primitive *kerygma* and order. (p. 32)

Without commenting on this statement for the moment, I wish only to underline a highly interesting and, in its consequences, rather revolutionary point in it. Here, at any rate in principle, it is admitted that history plays a role in tradition. To extrapolate from this text—it seems to me that one is justified in holding that a historical moment can play a decisive role as a hermeneutic factor in the understanding of the Christian Gospel. History really plays a role in the understanding of the Christian tradition.

Here again the question is raised: To what extent can our situation in the world today, at this peculiar point in the Christian tradition, contribute to our seeing something that was not sufficiently understood or even recognized at previous stages of Christian theology and Christian practice, even though it certainly never disappeared but time and again broke forth with irresistible force? It seems to me that our time in particular has a character of *kairos* for Christian dogmatics and preaching, because of the very strong emphasis given to the true humanity of Christ, the Messiah of God, the incarnate Word. No situation is without danger and temptation. This situation also runs the risk of minimizing other aspects, of overlooking vital biblical points of view. But this does not gainsay that an absolute, necessary, and inescapable Christian truth is brought to light here, often in a most provocative manner, thereby helping us to a richer and more adequate understanding of the essence of the Christian tradition.

This emphasis on the humanity of Christ helps us to correct the understanding of "our common history" by pointing to a reality which lies *before* this common history and without which we will certainly misunderstand "our initial tradition." In the ecumenical document just quoted we read: "The Church had a common history for many centuries, and this common history is a common background for all existing denominations, at least it should be so." What is meant by "our common history" or by the expression on the following page, "the primitive or initial *tradition*" which certainly corresponds to "our common history"?[9]

I do not think it unfair to say that these expressions refer to that concept of Christianity which had its starting point in the Apostolic witness, especially in the Christological and Trinitarian fragments of dogmatic and liturgical character in the New Testament, and which were formulated and authorized in the different symbols of the first four centuries as the result of penetrating scrutiny by the Fathers. The linguistic shape of these thoughts and their dogmatic implications were taken from current and available philosophy and its language. It is, indeed, a great mistake to neglect or look superciliously at this tremendous theological effort of the first Christian centuries. To forget that is, as Karl Barth once said, "a theological barbarism." It is, however, exactly at this point that a fundamental question does arise and must be raised. Is this "common history" really "the initial tradition"? The very weak point of the Trinitarian view, if I may use this summary expression, consists in a rather obvious shortcoming concerning the real history and radical historicity of our salvation in Christ.

The Christian tradition has two dimensions, which actually are only *one*: the Christological-Trinitarian and the biblical-historical. Between these two there is a relation of mutuality and interdependence. It must not be forgotten, however, that the foundation of Christian tradition is not a dogmatic statement, but a living historical person as we know him through the faithful remembrance of the first generation, the witness of the Apostles.[10] Without this historical-biblical picture of Jesus—so different from the "liberal" picture of Jesus—there is no real Christain tradition, but merely an abstract Christological speculation. It is true that we know the man Jesus only through interpretation. This is inevitable.

We do interpret Jesus from the Christian tradition. But we also go the opposite way—that is, the biblical-historical Jesus, pictured in faith by disciples who had been with him in his earthly life and now knew him as the risen Lord, *this* man is the flaming center, the core of tradition, and therefore necessarily the hermeneutic principle of every later Christian tradition. This interpretation of Jesus Christ is "the initial tradition."

Let me briefly mention some main features of this biblical figure: Jesus of Nazareth, son of Mary, baptized by John the Baptist together with obvious sinners; tempted, not once but throughout his whole life; preaching the Kingdom of God with its claims sharpened to the point of impossibility of fulfillment, and with its message of unconditional forgiveness. He was in "the tradition of his Father" (Matt. 11:27), a tradition he would hand over to his disciples. Whence his extremely difficult "seminars" with them, slowly drawing them out of their inherited bondage to authorities of quite another kind—secular and especially religious—in order to open their hearts and thoughts for him and *his* understanding of the Kingdom of God *and* of himself. We must mention also his absolute freedom, his life in the midst of people who were despised and overlooked—the prostitutes, the lepers, and many others—his radical love for man, his intransigent struggle unto death with the church authorities of his time. Through all this he lived his life in total obedience to his Father, thus radically breaking "the tradition of Adam," a tradition characterized by Adam's will to live his life on his own, although he never got rid of God his creator. As the second Adam, Jesus fulfilled the destiny of the obedient Servant of the Lord, the man of sorrows, who ended his life without any form of glory as one shipwrecked, bankrupt, deserted, betrayed to the enemy by his friends, crucified as a political rebel. "Tradition" or *paradosis* means both to hand over *and* to betray! Shortly after his death it was proclaimed that on the third day this man rose from the dead and that he was exalted to the right hand of God. He was adored as *kyrios*.

This biblical Jesus is a real man, having a real history, remembered in faith and worship, a remembrance that could not be put into abstract philosophical terms but was preached in the form of narratives containing human words, deeds, and symbols.

Of course this figure, its life, death, and resurrection, also challenged the intellect and called for "theology." But this initial *fides quaerens intellectum* was never allowed to leave the historical plane and wander from the point, absorbed in speculation. More, the Trinitarian thought was imbued with history.

This man had an existence of his own, but always exclusively *in* God. This is the truth of the doctrine of *enhypostasia*. When he was total man, he was total God. In the deepest abyss of human life he was most God. In him God himself was present on earth. This biblical-historical Jesus Christ is the Lord of tradition: he who castigates the tradition of his people, who also has the right to break such a tradition—be it ever so old—when it deviates from the right line, who is the renewer and fulfiller of tradition. This flaming center alone is the core of tradition. He is, *sit venia verbo*, the only permanent "hermeneutical principle" for true tradition.

This is, it seems to me, in a few words the contribution of our time to the "doctrine of tradition." Not something new but nevertheless something that needed to be said and heard. I wonder whether this theological insight is not clearer for us today than it was twenty years ago.

NOTES

1. *Report of the Third World Conference on Faith and Order, Lund, 1952,* Faith and Order Commission Papers No. 15 (London: SCM Press, 1953), p. 15.

2. *Minutes of the Working Committee of the Commission on Faith and Order, Château de Bossey, 1953,* Faith and Order Commission Papers No. 17 (Lausanne: Imprimerie La Concorde), p. 33.

3. *Die Bekenntnisschriften der Evangelisch-Lutherischen Kirche,* 5th ed. (Göttingen: Vandenhoeck & Ruprecht, 1967). English trans.: *The Book of Concord,* ed. Theodore G. Tappert (Philadelphia: Fortress Press, 1959).

4. *Minutes of the Working Committee of the Commission on Faith and Order, Château de Bossey, 1953,* pp. 32f.

5. Ibid.. p. 36.

6. *Minutes of the Commission and Working Committee, Evanston and Chicago, 1954,* Faith and Order Commission Papers No. 21 (Lausanne: Imprimerie La Concorde).

7. *Report of the Fourth World Conference on Faith and Order, Montreal, 1963,* ed. P. C. Rodger and L. Vischer, Faith and Order Commission Papers No. 42. (London: SCM Press, 1964), p. 60.

8. Walter M. Abbott, ed., *The Documents of Vatican II* (New York: Guild Press—America Press—Association Press, 1966), p. 128.

9. *Minutes of the Working Committee of the Commission on Faith and Order, Château de Bossey, 1953,* pp. 32f.

10. I shall not tackle here the crucial problem concerning the relation between the "historical" Jesus and the "kerygmatic" Christ. I wish only to refer to the biblical witness to the historical Jesus, pictured in faith by the first disciples.

WHAT METHODIST THEOLOGY HAS TO LEARN FROM ECUMENICAL THEOLOGY

Rupert E. Davies

It is widely believed that Methodists are short on theology, long on good works. When Methodists have begun to recover from the sense of outrage (or, in some cases, of pride) created by this opinion, they are bound to ask how far it is true, and then to admit that there is a measure of truth in it. Color is certainly lent to it by the vision—no doubt quite unrelated to fact—of Methodist ministers and people in the United States incessantly engaged in furthering, by finance and feverish activity, every good cause in sight, while their theologians are hidden away in universities and seminaries where their learning is taken up and lost in the vast treasure house of American scholarship. And there is the equivalent vision—not by any means unfounded in fact—of Methodist theologians in Britain so completely occupied in teaching future ministers and other students that they have no time to pursue their theological interests, while the ministers themselves, and therefore their people, have to make do with what they learned in college many years ago from those same over-worked theologians or their predecessors.

But there *is* such a thing as Methodist theology, both in

The author is Emeritus Principal, Wesley College, Bristol (England).

Britain and the Methodist Churches of British origin, and in America and the Methodist Churches of American origin. We must distinguish these two traditions because there are significant differences as well as significant similarities between them; but both stem from John Wesley, and can trace a continuous development from his Sermons and Notes on the New Testament. This essay will concern itself chiefly with the "British" tradition, because of the limitations of the author's knowledge and experience. But if it be true, as is often alleged, that American Methodist theology has tended to swing between the two poles of undue concern for individual salvation and excessive preoccupation with social and political matters, whereas British Methodist theology has avoided extremes and sought to take refuge in a sensible, but sometimes uneasy, compromise between the two, this fact is in itself an indication of a basic identity of purpose, as well as of a difference of approach. Methodist theologians, wherever they are found, do not greatly contribute to metaphysical speculation on the being of God, or to the higher flights of Christology. It is their métier to follow John Wesley both in his exploration of the "way to heaven,"[1] which he held to be the prime subject of theology and preaching, and in his incessant down-to-earth application of the Second Great Commandment to every situation of human need.

Methodist theology is not in itself very complex, even though, like any other theology, it raises complex issues. It is even inclined to make a virtue of simplicity, sometimes to the scorn of German dialecticians and American wielders of the devastating polysyllable. This simplicity sometimes conceals an unwillingness to get to grips with abstruse but searching problems, excused—when it is brought to light—on the flimsy ground that "life is more than logic." But it sometimes shows that the heart of the matter can best be reached by stripping a problem of its encrusted ambiguities, and asking directly:

What is the biblical view on this subject? Here also the authority of John Wesley may be adduced:

> I design plain truth for plain people: therefore, of set purpose I abstain from all nice and philosophical speculations: from all perplexed and intricate reasonings; and, as far as possible, from even the show of learning, unless in sometimes quoting the original Scripture.[2]

and he notes later: "I have accordingly set down in the following sermons what I find in the Bible concerning the way to heaven."[3]

Methodist theology, then, as it is understood by the generality of its teachers and preachers in the British tradition, can be described with full use of contemporary terminology (which some would call jargon) as Christocentric evangelicalism, humanized and partly demythologized. In its own simple terms it confesses its faith that God is creator, sovereign, and father; that man is intended to be a child of God but is estranged from him and therefore from himself by selfishness of heart and by sinful action; that Jesus Christ, who shares the being of God, has redeemed all men by his life, death, and resurrection, offering them forgiveness and reconciliation between God and man and between man and man; that the Holy Spirit, who is one with the Father and the Son in the unity of the Trinity, gives new life, guides the Church and its members into the truth which is in Christ, assures the children of God of their acceptance by God, binds them together in fellowship, and enables them to grow into the maturity of perfect love; that the Church is the family of God wherever it is found; that the two sacraments of the Gospel convey the grace of God to those who receive them—the one a sign of entry into the Church and of the washing away of sin, the other a sign of union with Christ in his death and resurrection, and of incorporation into his

Church; and that the free gift of God is eternal life through faith in Jesus Christ.

It is not, of course, to be assumed that any part of Christian faith as usually accepted but here omitted is not believed by Methodists. But some of the omissions are significant. Belief in the devil, belief in hell as a place or state of punishment, belief in substitutionary theories of the atonement, belief in the doctrine of the Virgin Birth as integral to the faith, belief in the verbal inspiration and infallibility of the Scriptures, belief in a visible Second Coming, belief in the physical resurrection of Jesus from the tomb, are no longer prescribed even for ministers and local preachers, still less for lay people. Certainly there are many Methodists, ordained and lay, who hold such beliefs; but no one who rejected or questioned them in whole or in part would be regarded as in any way apostate or heretical.

Of course there are theologians of a traditionalist frame of mind who regard as a betrayal of essential Methodism the relegation to the status of the optional of doctrines held firmly by John Wesley. But this view does not prevail; it is rather the general opinion that modern Methodist theology, as it is given above, preserves the core of Wesley's own theology, while relieving his successors of the obligation to retain elements in his thought which he accepted from the past but which we can no longer accept in the light of recent additions to our knowledge and understanding.

This theology of which we speak is held and expounded— at least in British Methodism—in a characteristically open and tolerant manner. The validity of the word "characteristically" will be questioned by many. It is true that from time to time Methodist theology has passed through a rigid and dogmatic phase, but a strong tendency to pluralism has never been entirely absent, and has often been dominant.[4] It can be traced to Wesley's own distinction, in his sermon "A

Catholic Spirit," between "opinions" and "the main branches of Christian doctrine."

> A man of catholic spirit is one who . . . gives his hand to all whose hearts are right with his heart; one who knows how to value and praise God for all the advantages he enjoys with regard to the knowledge of the things of God . . . ; one who retaining these blessings with the strictest care, keeping them as the apple of his eye, at the same time loves—as friends, as brethen in the Lord, as members of Christ, and children of God, as joint partakers now of the present kingdom of God and fellow-heirs of his eternal kingdom—all, of whatever opinion or worship or congregation, who believe in the Lord Jesus Christ, who love God and man, who . . . are careful to abstain from evil and zealous of good works.[5]

Whether Wesley would have allowed this breadth of doctrinal affirmation within the Methodist Societies themselves is open to question; but in the period since those Societies took on the role and acquired the attributes of a Church, his successors have more and more taken his words to apply there also, though sometimes they have not openly admitted this fact.

It can be safely said, therefore, that within the ranks of Methodist theologians over the whole world there are to be found great variations in the interpretation of Methodism's basic theology, and articulate exponents of points of view which those who do not hold them certainly call "extreme." And almost *all* extremes are represented in this way, whether they be of the left or of the right, as well as the schools of thought which tend towards left or right without reaching the extremes. In fact, there seem to be only two operative disqualifications for Methodist teachers and preachers: disbelief in the objective existence of God, which may, at least in Britain, become the basis of a charge of heresy, and lead to exclusion; and refusal to recognize the right to remain in the

Church's ministry of those who have different views (or "opinions," in Wesley's sense) from one's own—in which case the exclusion from the ranks of the ministry is self-induced.

Most of the ordained ministry in Britain do not opt for any of the extremes but remain in the central area of Methodist theology as it is sketched above, with, perhaps, occasional excursions into disputed territory under the impact of new ideas or fashions of thought. John Robinson's *Honest to God* impelled many in the direction of advanced immanentist theology and persuaded them to locate God in the depths of their being, in accordance with the new mythology that he suggested. But by now they have usually returned to a more traditional concept of God—though not, one may hope, without the reservations and reformulations that Robinson's book showed to be urgently necessary. This residence in a central area both reasonably spacious and believed to be in conformity with the intentions of John Wesley for his preachers—if they are properly understood—gives them the security of mind that is provided by other means in the more authoritarian Churches. It has to be acknowledged, however, that there is a recurrent plea in some circles that a larger dose of authoritarianism would be salutary. This plea comes sometimes from High Church Methodist circles, sometimes from Conservative Evangelicals, and sometimes from those who fear that the constant admission of exceptions to this or that doctrinal or disciplinary requirement erodes the very foundation of the whole structure; and this view must be respected, and taken into account when making any general judgment on the present and future of Methodism.

The fairly simplistic "scheme" of Methodist doctrine outlined above does not here need to be defended or even amplified. Suffice it to say that with varying emphases it has provided the staple diet of Methodist congregations since their inception, and therefore must have played a considerable part in determining their ethos and their characteristic views about man and God. It is probable—though difficult to prove—that most Methodist theologians and teachers, at least in Britain, would acknowledge that its acceptance by the Methodist Church as a whole is the main reason why they remain Methodists: and many of those who criticize it at various points, and even at times appear to reject it completely, would concede that they remain Methodists because Methodism provides a stable background for their own more daring speculations,[6] and a kind of haven to which they can return if their speculations leave them unsatisfied.

But it is the main contention of this essay that during the present century contact and comparison with other versions of Christian doctrine, and especially with the developing methods and achievements of ecumenical theology, have revealed serious defects that had previously gone unnoticed. These defects, it will be seen, apply much more to the way in which Christian doctrines are approached and handled than to the doctrines themselves, though sometimes the distinction is hard to maintain. And they have become much more apparent in the last twenty years or so than they were in the early days of the ecumenical movement. Here the Third World Conference on Faith and Order, in Lund in 1952, furnishes a watershed. Up to the time of that Conference, and in the preparation for it, it was expected of the participating confessions and communions that each of them should present in the clearest possible light its own doctrinal position on the matters at issue. They were not asked, of course, to defend those positions, still less to claim for them any superiority over others. They were asked to present them in an unadulterated state, in a form uninfluenced by relations with other churches (as, indeed, they *were* for the most part uninfluenced). This they gladly did; and the age of "comparative ecclesiology" and comparative theology was a long and peaceful one. But at Lund this age was brought to an end; and thereafter, because of the findings of that Conference, the churches embarked on the much more intricate task of digging together for the common roots of their faith. The whole situation thereupon became more fluid, and the confessions of each Church more vulnerable.

For now each Church had to ask questions about itself as it set its hand to the common task. "We have always held this view," its theologians had to say; but this was in isolation. Now we have to see whether what we derive from our tradition will stand up to criticism (even unspoken) from other communions; and can it find its place in the catholic wholeness which we seek? It still remains ecumenical bad manners to condemn or harshly criticize the tenets of other Churches; theologians plainly trying hard to abstain from this are a pleasant sight at ecumenical conferences. But this fact makes it all the more inevitable that each Church should scrutinize itself in this particular era of ecumenism.

Methodists have engaged in this exercise with no greater enthusiasm than others, and sometimes with less. And the fact points to the *first* serious defect of Methodist theology: its parochialism (which could also be called provincialism). The question is asked about every Methodist minister in Britain in the course of the meeting of the May Synod of every District: "Does he believe and preach our doctrines?" Historically considered, this is a highly understandable question. It goes back, of course, to Wesley's time; and presumably in his mind when he framed it was the desire to know whether "his" preachers were loyal to the Christian faith as he and his colleagues proclaimed it; that is, whether they announced the doctrines about personal and social religion which he had restored to the teaching of the Church, in addition to the common body of teaching that the Church declared. To him they were *doctrines;* we should more naturally call them *emphases.*

To ask if the authorized preachers of a Church continue to believe and uphold its teaching is a harmless enough thing to do, though it must strike the outsider as quaint; and it may be that the annual repetition of the question tends to blunt its usefulness. But the form in which the question is put, though it has perfectly good historical justification, has tended to influence the spirit in which it is answered. It has helped Methodists to think—though who shall say whether they would have thought in that way in any case?—that they have a set of doctrines which are in some sense their personal property, and have to be held close to Methodist bosoms, in case any ill-disposed persons should seek to snatch them away, and claim them as their own. Perhaps it is the word "our" that is most to blame in this matter. It *means*, historically, "reclaimed by Mr. Wesley from oblivion"; it has come to mean, in the course of time, "held and valued by Methodists, and probably by no one else."

This proprietary attitude towards certain elements in the Christian faith has spread to other areas of Christian life and theological understanding. It is even to be found when certain institutions are spoken of, as when we sometimes say "our Kingswood School," "our Church," and even—blasphemy of blasphemies—"our John Wesley" (a phrase that causes Anglicans when speaking of Wesley sometimes to omit his Methodist connections altogether), and, often, "our Methodism."

Because of the insidious prevalence of this spirit, Methodist theology becomes a kind of enclave in the general territory of Christian Doctrine; and Methodist theologians and others become inordinately preoccupied with *Methodist* origins, *Methodist* sacramental doctrine, *Methodist* history, *Metho-*

dist social witness, etc., etc. No one can object to a decent, seemly, and scholarly interest in Methodist antiquities, and in the *minutiae* of Methodist historical development, and in the Methodist contribution to this or that area of human life and thought. The definitive edition of Wesley's Works now in preparation has a necessary place in modern theological scholarship. So far, so good. But no other denomination spends so much time and energy in extolling its own virtues and elucidating its distinctive contributions! There seems to be a nagging fear that they will be overlooked or rejected. Only in recent years have the quinquennial conferences of the World Methodist Church begun to turn away from the almost exclusive consideration of Methodism. No less than nineteen addresses and lectures on aspects of Methodism, theological and other, were delivered at the Ninth World Methodist Conference at Lake Junaluska, North Carolina, in 1956—and delivered to an assembly composed of Methodists who knew a large amount about the subjects already from the many previous addresses about them which they had heard or delivered up and down the world.

It is not hard to give historical and psychological reasons for this parochialism so far as Britain is concerned. Methodism there has always had to fight for its existence: at first for its spiritual and institutional existence—this battle has been won long since; and then for its theological and cultural existence, against the ingrained belief of the British people that the Established Church—in England the Church of England and in Scotland the Church of Scotland—has a monopoly of Christian culture, intelligent theology, and properly conducted ritual. According to this belief, in England even atheists and agnostics are Anglican (or sometimes Roman Catholic) atheists and agnostics, and in Scotland they are Presbyterian atheists and agnostics: it follows *a fortiori* that believers fall into the same classes. Methodists do not belong anywhere on this reckoning, or think they do not. They are often regarded as admirable people, since everyone in Britain, except the Government of the day, loves a nonconformist who is decent in his protests; but this does not apply to their culture or their theology. Hence the well-known "consciousness of effortless superiority" ascribed to the Church of England; and the equally well-known inferiority complex of the Methodists, resulting in excessive self-appreciation.

The reasons for the same phenomenon, so far as it exists, in the United States and elsewhere are not so obvious, but no doubt they also lie deep in social and cultural history: perhaps in the identification of the Methodists in the past with sections of the community which were not culturally and socially acceptable to the governing classes and the intellectual élite.

But historical reasons do not wholly excuse theological narrowness in the past; still less do they justify its continuance in the present and into the future. The results of the failure of Methodists to transcend it are with us in Methodism itself. Many theologians of Methodist origin find themselves compelled to break away completely from the trammels of their past and assert their non-Methodism, sometimes losing connection with the genuine roots of their theological understanding. Those who remain within the Methodist tradition develop a love-hate relation to it, decrying it in private, often with bitterness—and sometimes also in public—in order to declare their emancipation from its prejudices, while remaining inwardly loyal to its claims upon them and continuing to exhibit its ethos in their style of life and thought.

The *second* serious defect of Methodist theology is an inveterate tendency to pietism. The last word requires definition, lest it be confused, even unconsciously, with piety. Pietism means the limitation of the Christian religion, and therefore of Christian theology, to spiritual concerns. But the word "spiritual" is itself obscure; we here take it to mean "relating to the inward contact of the soul with God." So pietism is that form of Christianity which is primarily concerned with the inner life of the soul, and with other matters only as an appendix or practical consequence. In practice it seems usually to concentrate on the *individual* and his spiritual development. But in theory this need not be so, since there can be a group of people, in a monastery or on retreat, who cultivate together their corporate spiritual life. Indeed, at least in early Methodism, and to some extent since, this has been precisely one of the aims of the "class meeting." Yet it is hard to resist the conclusion that even when this aim is being pursued, emphasis tends quickly to shift from the spirituality of the group to that of the individual. And in much pietistic spirituality this emphasis is unabashed.

Of course pietism has a long and honourable history in the Christian Church. The Johannine writings in the New Testament give ample justification for it, and quotations from the Pauline corpus can be adduced in its support. From time to time it has served as a very important counteraction to the deadness of orthodox, institutional Christianity. Its classical form, a revolt against high-and-dry Lutheranism, emerged in eighteenth-century Germany. Its contribution has always been to deepen the spiritual life, and to send its adherents back to the divine source of renewal, conversion, and growth. It is often dismissed out of hand as otherworldly. But this term again is ambiguous; if it implies preoccupation with the life to come to the exclusion of terrestrial interests, then it is unbiblical; and there are intermittent examples of this throughout church history. But if it simply implies an interest in a world other than that revealed by the senses, who can deny that such an interest is germane to biblical Christianity?

Nor are its contributions to human physical and mental welfare inconsiderable. The University of Halle, the orphan houses set up by A. H. Francke, and the hospital-community of Bethel (in Bielefeld, Germany) created and built up by Von Bodelschwingh more recently in the same tradition, are sufficient evidence of the benefits conferred on the world by German Pietism. And if it be said that these are works of charity, and do not assist the radical transformation of society for which Christians ought to pray and work, this is true; and yet these earlier Pietists did at least see further into human needs than their Christian contemporaries. If it be said that these works of charity could have been done just as effectively without Christian motivation, and are in no sense a logical implicate of pietistic theology, this also may well be true. But they were done for Christian reasons, and it is better that they should have been done on imperfect theological grounds than omitted altogether, as they were by those with a fuller theology as well as by those who rejected theology and religion altogether.

Now, Wesley's own theology was to a large extent pietistic in the sense defined.[7] It was concerned with the "way to heaven" of the individual soul, and is explicated in terms that refer almost solely to spiritual realities. And Wesley's instructions to his preachers included the words, "You have nothing to do but to save souls." Nor, granted that his mission was "to spread Scriptural holiness throughout the land" and reform the Church of England, could anything be expected but this.

But his theology ceases to be pietistic at a very important point, and that is the point of "perfect love." No doubt this concept is for the most part expounded in spiritual terms. In what still remains the magisterial account of the various

notions of perfection held in the history of the Christian
Church, R. N. Flew's *The Idea of Perfection*, it is rightly
pointed out that the first distinguishing mark of Christian
perfection according to Wesley is that "the goal is uninter-
rupted communion with God." Flew continues: "It is also
described as Love, including both love to God and love to
man."[8] To the modern Christian one of the disappointing
features of the history of Christian perfection is the almost
universal preoccupation of the mystics, and others who figure
in Flew's book, with their inward spiritual states, and their
comparatively little interest in its ethical outworkings.
Besides, the ethical outworkings that do come into the
picture are often limited in their scope to purely personal
relations. Modern Methodists are inclined to feel this about
Wesley not least.

But Wesley does in fact break out of this mold to a greater
degree than Flew gives him credit for. His brother's hymns on
Christian holiness do little to reveal this break-out. The
emphasis is on such ideas as these:

> I would be thine; thou know'st I would,
>   And have thee all my own;
> Thee, O my all-sufficient Good,
>   I want, and thee alone.
>
> Thy name to me, thy nature grant,
>   This, only this, be given:
> Nothing beside my God I want
>   Nothing in earth or heaven.

But John's larger theology sometimes emerges:

> Thy mind throughout my life be shown,
>   While, listening to the sufferer's cry,
> The widow's and the orphan's groan,
>   On mercy's wings I swiftly fly.
> The poor and helpless to relieve,
>   My life, my all, for them to give.

For John had seen that the nature and the mind of God were shown not only in the forgiveness of sins and in the gift of regeneration but also in his care for the whole life of his creatures; and that if it was of the essence of Perfect Love that the nature of God was implanted in the believer, then, clearly, the Christian who aspired to Perfect Love was committed to works of compassion on an unlimited scale. When this is appreciated, the efforts of Wesley himself to relieve poverty and sickness, to obtain justice and liberty for the oppressed (most notably, the slaves), to offer education to all within his range, and to diminish vagabondage and smuggling, fall into place. And what he practised himself he commended to all his followers—indeed enjoined upon them: "Do all the good you can by all the means you can, in all the ways you can, at all the times you can, to all the people you can, as long as ever you can."

But later generations of Methodists have found it hard to follow out this consequence of their own theology. The Wesleyan Methodists of Britain in the nineteenth century certainly conceived holiness and love in far narrower terms, concerning themselves with their inward states and the cultivation of fellowship within their own society. Not that they abstained from works of charity for those outside their own ranks; but these were adjuncts to their faith, and valuable as such, but not integral elements in their faith. They could be omitted for apparently good reasons, and the man who omitted them was still a good Methodist. (He might well compound for his lack of compassionate activity by giving generously to a special collection on Sunday, especially for overseas missions.) The Primitive Methodists, however, being much more closely in touch with actual human need and desperation than the bourgeoisie of Wesleyan Methodism, were much more aware of "the social implications of the Gospel."

Political and economic events and theories, of course, have long ago overtaken the naïve belief of Wesley and his well-disposed contemporaries that charity on a large scale is the answer to all human material need (in fact, Wesley is often criticized for not having seen what it took another half-century of industrial development and the genius of Karl Marx to make clear). Yet we have seen that there was the germ of a radical approach to human society in Wesley theology at its very centre, the doctrine of God. This germ has not been fostered—indeed, has been allowed to atrophy. In Britain, F. D. Maurice and the Christian Socialists, Bishop Charles Gore and his disciples, and among Methodists Hugh Price Hughes, John Scott Lidgett, and in the present century Donald Soper, among others, have done their best to awaken the Christian conscience on social matters and to outline a non-pietistic theology. In America theological liberalism as understood by Methodists has done the same. But the whole of this effort was largely discredited after World War I by the Barthian critique of liberalism; and Methodist theology remains on the whole doggedly convinced that the word "salvation" in the New Testament has little to do with anything except the relation of the soul to God. One consequence of this is that the theological radicals in Britain and America have felt themselves forced into violent opposition to orthodox Methodist theology in order to make their point about Christianity and society, when all the time they could have drawn the conclusion they wanted from the depths of their own tradition.

If liturgy is the creator of theology, it may be that a phrase in the preface to the Intercessions in the New Sunday Service of British Methodism may be a pointer to the future: "God our Father, grant us the help of your Spirit in our prayers for the salvation of mankind"; prayers then follow for national, political, economic, and social life, as well as for the mission and unity of the Church. So "salvation" may at last have regained something of its deeper Scriptural content. But until this fuller understanding of salvation is widely accepted, pietism remains hard to eradicate.

The *third* serious defect in Methodist theology is a certain pseudo-historicism. It is part of our Christian faith that God works in history—however hard it may be from time to time to identify his activity—and that the Holy Spirit is at all times guiding the Church into all truth, as the truth is in Jesus. But when all the communions of Christendom have agreed on this common profession of faith, each of them proceeds to pick out the period of history where God is claimed to have worked hardest and the Holy Spirit to have been at his most illuminating. The Orthodox Churches select the period of the great Ecumenical Councils; Roman Catholics the High Middle Ages; Anglicans the first four centuries of Christian history, with a later outburst of heavenly activity during the period of the Caroline Divines; Lutherans the life and times of Martin Luther; and Methodists the eighteenth century. This becomes a form of surreptitious canonization, and the norms of thought and conduct for each denomination, though officially derived from the New Testament, turn out to have been fixed by the interpretation of the New Testament promulgated by the "canonical" periods and their writers. Methodism may be no worse than other communions in this respect, but it is certainly no better.

It cannot be wrong to attend most carefully to the utterances and examples of our "fathers in the faith," and to the basic teachings of that Church to which we owe, under God, our own knowledge of God and his ways. And of course it is not wrong—on the contrary, it is both right and necessary—to require of the ministers and other spokesmen, and even, to a smaller degree, of the members, of any communion that their views and message conform with the basic principles of that communion. We have said this before, and it really goes without saying.

But it is plainly absurd to suggest that God's work or revelation in one period of history takes precedence over what he does and says in other periods (except in the one case of the period of the Incarnation, where God, as we believe, acted once for all in Christ). The only way to make the suggestion less absurd is to hold the theory that the institution of the Papacy, or the possession of a particular succession of ministry through episcopal laying-on-of-hands, guarantees inerrancy, or particular reliability, at certain points of time declared by authority to be *the* points of time. But this whole concept is unacceptable to Methodists, and it is therefore very odd to find them canonizing the Sermons and Notes on the New Testament of John Wesley—and even odder for British Methodists to do the same to the doctrinal clauses of the Deed of Union of 1932, which brought together the Primitive, United, and Wesleyan Methodists. Yet these things happen.

The truth is that denominational loyalty, leading to the desire to preserve the faith and discipline of one's own Church, has come to obscure the fact that the Sermons and Notes and the Deed are historical documents—just as the Roman Catholic Church has taken four difficult centuries to see that the decrees of the Council of Trent are historical documents.

All documents are, of course, historical in a general sense. By a historical document here is meant one that is properly understood only if it is realized that it was written in a particular historical context, in answer to particular historical problems and under particular historical pressures. It is easy to recognize the context, the problems, and the pressures that helped to produce the writings of John Wesley, and not least those writings that have gained a position of authority.

Also, the circumstances attending and leading up to the signing of the Deed of Union in 1932 have been the subject of much enlightening research,[9] and may now be said to have been laid bare.

To say that we must look at these documents historically is not of course to say that we are now in a position to discredit them and to neglect the statements they make, even if this kind of conclusion is becoming common among sociologists. A clear distinction must be made in the case of any historical document between the form in which a statement is made, where the historical context is highly operative, and the content of the statement, where the historical context is still certainly operative but in a different way. Once this distinction is made—and it is not necessarily easy to make it in any given case—it becomes the business of the historian and the theologian to disentangle, first of all, the form and the content, and then within the content the relative and the absolute: that which belongs to the time of writing and that which is permanently true if it is true at all. Then, at last, the theologian is in a position to say that this or that is a fundamental tenet of the Methodist Church.

It cannot be said that Methodist theologians have done more than begin on this intricate and sometimes tiresome process; and meanwhile the rest are still guilty of attaching a wholly false mystique to the Methodists' part of the historical process.

The exposition of these three defects in Methodist theology, or rather in the approach of Methodists to their theology, has perhaps already revealed the conclusion to which this essay is rapidly proceeding. A much deeper commitment to and immersion in the ecumenical dialogue could do a great deal to remedy all three failings. It is of the nature of ecumenical thinking that anyone who takes part in it forgoes any claim to monopoly for his particular version of

Christian truth. In fact, anyone who considers himself bound to claim such a monopoly will never, if he is sensible, take part in any form of ecumenical conversation at all. The Orthodox Churches and the Roman Catholic Church have to go through a crisis of conscience before they can commit themselves wholeheartedly to ecumenism, since their claims for themselves are readily interpreted by them as a claim to the possession of the whole truth. Methodism has seen this point from the start. It now needs to grasp in its fullness the further fact that what each communion regards as its distinctive contribution is something it holds in trust for the whole Church and must be ready to submit to the criticism of the whole Church; and that the gaps in its own witness can best be filled, not by further cogitation on its own origins and traditions, but by learning from other communions what they have seen and Methodism has not. This realization is the antidote to parochialism.

The second defect could not have been cured by ecumenical theology itself while it remained somewhat exclusively Protestant, and, even more, while it remained the preserve of German and other neo-orthodox Western theologians. But now, first, a more corporate conception of salvation and of the whole range of Christian truth has entered the debate by way of the Catholic traditions. Yet something else in addition was also needed to counter pietism effectively, since Catholics are tainted with their own brand of pietism. And, second, the entry of the Catholics has been followed by that of the churchmen of the Third World, and, in their train, the theologians of liberation and revolution—an alarming phenomenon, perhaps, in the eyes of many people, but a necessary ingredient of the larger truth that needs to be uncovered.

Thus, for instance, "salvation" has come to be seen in a new light, and the theology of salvation to be re-formulated, with wide repercussions on the whole of the rest of theology. Christians have always known that God's purpose is the salvation of all men, and when it becomes apparent that this is intended to reach not just individual souls but every aspect of human life and every human relation as well, and that therefore God's purpose is not fulfilled until the whole created universe is redeemed, it becomes impossible to hold that any man is fully saved until God's salvation is complete; it becomes an untenable view that the only thing that really matters is that individual souls should be made ready for eternity. The rights of human beings to justice, freedom, health, the conservation of human resources, and the education of the whole personality are as truly part of the Gospel's content and the Church's mission as the doctrine of justification by faith and the resurrection of the dead. The healing of society is not an appendix to the Church's task; it is inherent in the task itself. There is not a spiritual Gospel forever in competition with a social Gospel; there is one Gospel comprising all the elements of God's saving purpose.

If this is a correct account of ecumenical theology as it is now conceived, it provides an atmosphere in which any pietism, and not just Methodist pietism, cannot survive. But also, lest it be forgotten, this is an atmosphere in which a merely political religion, or one that denies the value of prayer and worship, or of the believer's communion with God, is equally under condemnation.

Finally, we come to the therapeutic effect of ecumenical involvement on the defect of pseudo-historicism, of canonizing denominational history. Perhaps we here touch on the most speedily working effect of all. Only a little discussion with Christians of other communions is enough to convince the member of any communion that much of what he has previously held to be essential to his faith is culturally conditioned; indeed, there is danger at this point that the inexperienced ecumenist will rapidly conclude that *all* the distinctiveness of his denomination is the result of cultural development and therefore expendable, so that we may have the unattractive phenomenon of a Christian who belongs to no Church and simply calls himself an ecumenical Christian! But a more prolonged and mature involvement in ecumenical thinking overcomes this danger, and teaches the art of discernment between the transitory and the lasting constituents of confessional truth. And this art, as we have seen, is one that Methodism needs to learn—and not in the theological realm only. So Methodists will learn that their history and its documents, though invaluable, are not sacrosanct, or determinative for all time.

There are undoubtedly many in all the Methodist Churches who see a deep involvement in ecumenical theology as a threat to the existence of their Methodism. But the very fact that they have this anxiety is good evidence that Methodist theology needs to be held up to the light of ecumenism, so that its real worth may be seen and its weaknesses purged.

NOTES

1. "Preface to *Sermons on Several Occasions*," par. 5, in Albert C. Outler, ed., *John Wesley* (New York: Oxford University Press, 1964), 89.

2. Ibid., par, 3, p. 89.

3. Ibid., par. 6, p. 90.

4. The issue of "pluralism" has indeed been sharpened recently in British Methodism. A group of conservative ministers, objecting to the official toleration of "liberal" and "radical" ways of thinking, has hived off to the Free Methodist Church, which apparently, despite its name, insists on uniformity of theological outlook.

5. "A Catholic Spirit," III, 5, in Outler, ed., *John Wesley*, p. 103.

6. A notable example of this occurred recently in British Methodism,

when a minister who had publicly rejected the objective existence of God, and repudiated the whole corpus of Christian doctrine, still wished to remain a Methodist minister.

7. I have noted the strong resemblance between German Pietism (not only in its Moravian form) and Methodism in my *Methodism* (Harmondsworth: Penguin Books, 1963), p. 23.

8. R. Newton Flew, *The Idea of Perfection in Christian Theology* (London: Oxford University Press, 1934; reprinted 1968), p. 323.

9. See, for instance, J. H. S. Kent, *The Age of Disunity* (London: Epworth Press, 1966), pp. 1-44.

THE CRISIS IN
AMERICAN CATHOLICISM

George A. Lindbeck

The most widely discussed description of the current
Catholic crisis of which I know was written for the French
scene. A member of the Academy, one of the French
"immortals," himself not a Catholic, Maurice Druon, published an article in *Le Monde* for August 7, 1971, which
provoked innumerable replies. Let me quote the first two
paragraphs:

> From the outside at any rate, nothing threatened nor attacked.
> People no longer spat at priests: anticlericalism had been relegated
> to the museum. The question of the separation of Church and state
> had been settled and provided no pretext for combat. The Church,
> from the simple curate in his village to the Pope holding universal
> sway, had never enjoyed a more assured situation, a more general
> respect, a more unshakable prestige.

> And suddenly the Church begins to splinter, decline, and dissolve.
> Some say it is about to collapse. The priests reverse altars, sell the
> ornaments, remove the saints. They change the language, close the
> organs, welcome the guitars, and bless the wrecking crew. No rite
> remains, no rule is spared. The vaulting of dogmas cracks, and the
> house of the good God is opened to all the storms.

The author is Professor of Theology, Divinity School and Department of
Religious Studies, Yale University.

Perhaps an American Druon would have used, not the image of the collapsing cathedral, but that of the "One-Hoss Shay." The appropriateness of that poem for our theme is not accidental. Oliver Wendell Holmes intended it as an allegory for the sudden disintegration of old-time New England religion in the last century. Nevertheless, let us proceed non-allegorically.

On the eve of the Council, American Catholicism was more flourishing than it had ever been. The Roman Catholic constituency had become the largest and most powerful of American minorities, comprising a quarter of the population; and its proportionate strength was steadily increasing. The school system from the primary grades through graduate studies was expanding. New seminaries and convents dotted the countryside, and there was no shortage of new priests and nuns of fill them. Further, Catholicism had become part of the national Establishment. The first Catholic president was in the White House; and for the purposes of Hollywood, priests of the Father Flanagan-Spencer Tracy type and nuns of the Ingrid Bergman type were the quintessentially American religious figures.

Above all, Pope John XXIII, the most widely beloved father figure in recent history, was on the papal throne, and he had convoked a Council. Its purpose was the double one of *aggiornamento*—that is, updating or modernizing the Church—and *ressourcement*—that is, to give it a Protestant twist, re-Christianization by turning the Church back toward the sources of the faith in the Bible and the early Fathers.

For the overwhelming majority of observers, both Catholic and non-Catholic, the Council made an astonishingly good beginning. Secularists joined in acclaiming the *aggiornamento*, the new openness to the world; and Protestants enthusiastically greeted the passing of the Counter-Reformation, the concern for what Hans Küng called the legitimate demands of the Reformers, the return to the Bible. Almost everyone—not least Albert C. Outler and other Protestant observers at the Council (including myself)—forecast a great upsurge of Christian vitality and faithfulness within the Roman Catholic communion.

What has happened, however, is in many ways the reverse of this. The aftermath of Vatican II can be read as disastrous. Piety, at least in its more visible forms, has declined. Even the older generation now goes to church less frequently, and younger American Catholics, according to the most recent statistics, are no more faithful in attendance than their Protestant counterparts. Catholic schools, after reaching their high point a decade ago, are now rapidly contracting. Priestly and religious vocations have dropped drastically in quantity and, some say, in quality also. Further, the tiny trickle of those leaving their churchly callings a decade ago has now grown to a torrent. Unless the loss in manpower and womanpower is sharply reversed, the collapse of traditional institutional forms will be inescapable in a few decades. (France and Italy, it should be added, are in this respect much more seriously threatened than the United States.)

In addition, the Church that was once a paragon of apparent peace and obedience is now wracked by open dissension. Pope Paul's attempt to perpetuate the birth control ban has been flouted, not only by the silent practice of many Catholic couples but also publicly by theologians and even some bishops. Attacks on clerical celibacy and advocacy of intercommunion with non-Catholics and of women's ordination continue to grow, no matter what the hierarchy says or does. Most astonishing of all, perhaps, is the challenge to infallibility launched by Hans Küng, and the extraordinarily confused debate that this has generated. Other Christain denominations also have serious problems, but both the sharp contrast with the recent past and the sheer intensity make Roman Catholic difficulties seem far greater than those of other major Christian bodies.

Indeed, one suspects that no Protestant denomination could undergo such sudden and massive changes without total fragmentation. In worship, for example, the abandonment of medieval patterns, the modernization and the sources, has been in essence more radical than what was accomplished at the Reformation—and the Reformation format still prevails in Episcopalian, Lutheran, and Reformed churches. Further, nuns have suddenly emerged from the convents to participate in civil rights marches at Selma or be stoned by, of all people, Catholics in the streets of Chicago. Anti-war priests like the Berrigan brothers have been pursued by Jesuit-educated minions of the FBI with more ardor than was directed against all the hippies, yippies, and Weathermen of the nation combined.

Perhaps the FBI was right. Perhaps the Berrigans were the major symbolic threat to the war. Roman Catholicism, the supposed bastion of medieval reaction, has suddenly, even if reluctantly, become the major spawning ground of Christian theologians of liberation and even of violent revolution, such as the slain hero of the Colombian resistance, Father Camillo Torres. The claims to Catholic legitimacy made in his behalf may be awkward at times; but a decade ago before the Council they would have been inconceivable. Thus, developments greater than those that have occurred slowly and amorphously in a period of generations within Protestantism have been compressed into months and years. The center does not hold; all things dissolve.

It is not surprising, then, that some who would not have dreamed of doing so a few years ago are asking whether the Roman Catholic Church can long survive. Malachi Martin predicts that by the year 2000 it will have disappeared as an institution recognizably continuous with its past.[1] Dr. Martin, it should be noted, is not an ignorant outsider. For four years he was part of Cardinal Bea's unofficial conciliar task force. Monsignor George Higgins, a *peritus* at the Council and now a divisional director of the U.S. Catholic Conference, says that Martin, to whom he was "fairly close," was "privy to what Bea and Pope John were saying and doing behind the scenes as they prepared for the council."[2] In those days Martin was confident of the future of the Church.

This, to be sure, proves nothing regarding the quality of his prediction, but it is a symptom of the depth of the crisis as it is experienced by some people who are familiar with the centers of Roman Catholic power. Other more sober comments could be added. John Tracy Ellis, dean of American Catholic historians, has written that in the 183 years since the organization of the Church in this country, "it has never known anything to approximate its present dispiritedness and disarray."[3] We cannot, however, linger further on description. We must turn now to diagnosis of the causes.

It is difficult to do this without being partisan. As with most Protestants, my instinctive sympathies are with Catholic progressives such as Hans Küng, who blame the church authorities—the bishops and the Pope. It is their passivity or, even worse, reaction that has, Küng says, dissipated the "joy, trust, elan and eagerness to reform" characterizing the Church after the Council. One must have, he continues, "pity on the multitudes," for, as Jesus complained in his day, they have no shepherds to guide them, to lead them into the future. They have been frustrated on such urgent matters as mixed marriages, birth control, and the law of celibacy. Gradualism is good and necessary in some matters, but not when it comes to church reform in this moment of history. "It is best not," he concludes, "to flip an omelette step by step," and "One has to jump a stream if one wants to avoid getting wet feet."[4] Now, as I am an heir of the Reformation my natural inclination is to want the bishops and the Pope to do even more than Hans Küng asks; but it is doubtful that he is right if he thinks that would diminish the crisis.

The conservatives hold that progressive policies such as Küng advocates only make matters worse. This is the argument of James Hitchcock, in his *Decline and Fall of Radical Catholicism,*[5] and, from a rather different perspective, of Garry Wills in *Bare Ruined Choirs.*[6] Their books are often unfair and unbalanced, but they are brutally effective. They point out that many of those who claim the progressive name have misused the Council as a cloak for innovative ego-tripping. These have appealed to the Council to justify their own loss of faith, their mindless capitulation to *modernitas*, their devious and unacknowledged departures from what is essential, not only to the Roman tradition, but to Christianity itself. Even the more responsible among them, even the Council Fathers, have done great damage. In their search for contemporary relevance or for a biblical purity, they have undermined that popular, traditional, cultural Catholicism which, however oppressive and obscurantist it may seem to the upwardly mobile or the educated elite, is still the source of meaning and life to multitudes.

The Catholic ghetto provided the masses with group and individual identity, a sense of community, the dignity of belonging somewhere amidst the anonymity of post-industrial civilization. It gave them access to glimpses of transcendence, apprehensions of the sacred, awareness of ultimate significance. Perhaps their lives were bedeviled with primitive taboos and superstitions, but the terror and beauty of the primitive are vastly preferable to the flat, moralistic reasonableness of liberal religion, or the mechanical triviality, superficiality, and sensuality of commercialized American secularism. It is hard not to think of the youth of the parents in so-called Catholic ghettoes as vastly healthier than the liberated unchurched lives of their children.

From the point of view of such considerations, the actions of the bishops and Popes have at times been unwise, not only when they have been overly rigid (as in the case of birth control), but also when they have been progressive. Perhaps they were much too precipitous in liturgical reform, for example. But it is to their credit that they show respect and concern for the traditionalist masses, for the religion and culture of the ordinary Catholic. It is precisely this kind of respect and concern (so the argument goes) which are woefully lacking in back-to-the-Bible academicians like Hans Küng or let's-catch-up-with-the-world modernizers like Gregory Baum. The progressive *avant garde* is basically the Catholic wing of contemporary Western liberalism and has all the elitist defects of the liberal establishment.

In short, the process of reforming popular Catholicism started by the Council is draining it of its communal, cultural, and religious substance. Traditional Catholicism may have needed reform both for worldly reasons and from the point of view of the original Christian message, but not at the cost of administering cures worse than the disease.

This summarizes only a part, but in my view the most plausible part, of what authors like Wills and Hitchcock are getting at. The argument, it will be observed, avoids the pitfalls of non-historical orthodoxy. It makes no appeal to atemporal, eternally valid formulations of transcendent truth or empirically unchanging church structures and customs. Its antecedents can perhaps be found in nineteenth-century romanticism, in the Catholic conservatism of a Chateaubriand or a De Maistre. Yet it can provide a much more subtle and powerful critique of contemporary reformism than is available from these earlier ideologues of reaction.

Its understanding of religion has been enriched and nuanced
by the sociological traditions of Weber and Durkheim. It can
appeal at many points to the modern scientific study of
religion, to anthropology and social psychology. It sees
religions as, first of all, cultural systems in a way congruent
with many of the insights of a Clifford Geertz or a Peter
Berger. It can form alliances with the new ethnicity espoused
by a Michael Novak or an Andrew Greeley.

Anyone who takes empirical evidence seriously cannot
help but be impressed by the jaundiced view of the Catholic
efforts at renewal which emerges from these historical,
cultural, and psycho-social analyses. When looked at in this
way, furthermore, the Catholic crisis appears, not as an
isolated phenomenon, but as an acute form of a malaise
common to all the historic Christian traditions. That, indeed,
is my reason as a Protestant for being concerned about it.
The Catholic problem is also a non-Catholic problem. The
strength also of Protestant Churches rests on particular forms
of traditional cultural Christianity. They also are in need of
both updating and of a return to the sources, of greater
relevance and greater faithfulness to revelation, of *modernitas*
and *Christianitas*. Otherwise the traditions will continue to
decline, increasingly unable to serve either the human needs
of their members and of the larger society, or the imperatives
of Christian faith.

Yet the difficulties are immense. Most of the Christian
faith and vitality which persists is deeply embedded in ever
more archaic and unfaithful traditional forms. Nine-tenths of
the church members in America, whether Protestant or
Catholic, are, in Gordon Allport's terminology, "extrinsically
religious." They use their religion chiefly as a security
blanket, as a legitimation and support for the way they
already live, for the so-called values of an often reactionary
version of the American Way of Life. As a result, they are

more prejudiced against blacks and Jews than the majority of non-churchgoers. Yet there is also a minority of men and women who are intrinsically religious, consisting largely (so the sociologists surprisingly report) of those who go to church and pray and read Scripture most often. For them, substantially more frequently than for the mass of church members, faith is an often uncomfortable transforming power, freeing them in statistically reportable ways from the standard prejudices of their milieu.

There are, to be sure, innumerable exceptions. The ranks of the pious contain the worst hypocrites—viz., the self-deceived ones—as well as men and women of faith. What we need to remember is that these latter have, in most cases, personally interiorized the faith, not apart from their traditions but in and through them. They have developed their transforming loyalty to the God and Father of the Lord Jesus Christ by means of some specific traditional interpretation of the Christian story, whether Catholic or Protestant, not by unmediated leaps into transcendence or into mystical or romantic interiority, nor even by jumping directly back to the Bible. Therein lies the problem. The destruction of these traditions—whether of fundamentalist revivalism or of Marian devotion, whether by modernization or by insistence on chemically pure Christianity—is also the destruction of the seedbeds of most of the genuine Christian vitality and authentic Christian faith still living in our world. To paraphrase what Luther said about the Bible, traditional religion, though often extrinsic and perverted, is the cradle of Christ.

It is from this perspective, then, that I shall try to assess the present state of Catholicism. We must start with the people, with the religion of the masses, for that is where the strength of any Church lies. As long as they retain a strong sense of Catholic identity, institutional and theological collapse can be survived without mortal damage. History provides many examples of this.

From the external point of view, the American Catholic infrastructure looks fairly solid. The lay folk are in part disturbed, in part pleased, by the changes of recent years; but in any case they are not leaving the Church in large numbers. The growth-and-decline statistics have come since the Council to look more like those of liberal Protestant denominations than like those of the Southern Baptist Convention. In other words, Catholicism is no longer growing as it was before the Council, but this by itself is scarcely traumatic.

Still, my guess is that the erosion of traditional piety is proceeding faster in Catholic than in Protestant circles. Its sociological base in the immigrant sub-cultures is disappearing as Catholics move upward and outward in the social, economic, and educational spheres. The devotional practices that were its emotional-experiential core have swiftly disappeared or been downgraded since the Council. Younger Catholics even from devout traditional backgrounds know little or nothing of the novenas, Benediction, Rosary recitation, and the cult of the saints that were the major affective components in their parents' religion. The reformed liturgy does not seem to serve as an adequate substitute—in part, as frequently has been pointed out, because it is in its essential structure a celebration of the intimate communion of believers with Christ and with one another, and simply does not fit in large parish settings. Thus, like the old Mass, the new liturgy is for many Catholics a duty rather than an experience; and now the Counter-Reformation sense of discipline is itself weakening.

Traditional piety is threatened also by changes in catechetical method—changes which, in turn, reflect the current theological pluralism and confusion. The Baltimore Catechism may have been grossly inadequate, but at least it gave the young Catholic the sense that he knew what he believed and did not believe. Now, some reports from college campuses suggest that Catholics are even less certain on these points than liberal Protestants and much less so than conservative ones. Religiously trained Catholics, some observers think, are more susceptible than religiously trained Protestants to the new religions and diabolisms of East and West. They suffer even more acutely from lack of a viably articulated meaning system and personally significant religious experience. In short, piety and articulated conviction seem to be draining out of popular Catholicism much as they have out of liberal Protestantism; and this is rather more dangerous for Catholics because they have no remaining, coherent mass of traditionalists to recruit from as liberal Protestant denominations have recruited and may expect to continue to recruit from conservative ones.

There are, to be sure, signs of new types of popular spirituality, most notably the Catholic charismatic movement; but it is too early to say whether or when these will provide large-scale replacements for the waning traditional forms. I do not mean to underestimate the enormous reservoirs of devotion that remain, but simply to say that they seem in danger of rapid dissipation, leaving a Catholicism which, while containing pockets of privatistic piety and many social activists, is religiously as bland and conventional as most suburban Protestantism.

This is the short-term picture. If I were to risk long-range prognostications, I would be more optimistic. Given a generation or two, the liturgical reforms may well be the source of a renewed and far more biblical popular spirituality. It took that long or longer in some areas (so historians tell us) for the Reformation's changes in worship to shape a new piety among the people. Furthermore, to the extent that mass Christianity and mass Catholicism disintegrate, the new liturgy may prove admirably adapted to the small-group, intensely communal celebrations that would then be the norm. Thus my guess, for what it is worth, is that popular Catholicism here in America and elsewhere will at first be substantially weakened by the conciliar changes, but that eventually the liturgical and biblical renewals in particular will be assets in forming a new and more Christian Catholic culture. This will be the more likely to occur to the degree that the Church declines in numbers and becomes a *diaspora*, a scattered minority, in the world.

Given this outlook, one is inclined to be a bit cavalier about the more dire predictions regarding the outcome of the institutional and theological turmoil. Even total institutional collapse on the highest levels is likely to be transitory. For the foreseeable future, there will be millions and millions of people throughout the world who take pride in thinking of themselves as Roman Catholic Christians as did their fathers and fathers' fathers for scores of generations. If a great schism were to occur, as happened in the Middle Ages, they would be most unhappy. A precious part of their identity would be threatened. They would have difficulty in thinking of themselves as Catholic because there would no longer be an agreed-upon successor to the bishops of Rome with whom they could be in visible communion, along with Asians and Africans and Europeans. This would generate an enormous and lasting popular pressure on the leaders—who would be leaders of nothing without the people—to settle the disputes. Eventually, in all likelihood, there would be another council, which, like that of Constance in the fifteenth century, would heal the schism. This is simple elementary social psychology. It is also, I would suppose, elementary Catholic theology, now that the Council has made clear that the Church is, first of all, not the institution of salvation, but the people of God. The Roman Catholic Church does not endure first of all because of the Papacy; rather, the Papacy endures because its symbolization of universality and continuity exerts a powerful attraction on the imagination and emotions, will and mind, of multitudes of human beings.

Nevertheless, having granted this, one must immediately add that the present institutional crisis is extremely grave, worse than what exists in any other Church.

One way of trying to explain why this is so is to point out that current Catholic difficulties involve a special problem of legitimacy. It is true that the legitimacy of all institutions is being attacked these days, but what has happened in Roman Catholicism, I think it can be safely said, is that the church authorities have unwittingly de-legitimized themselves. This has happened in a rather precise, almost juridically precise way. What might be called a constitutional crisis has erupted. There are radical and fundamental ambiguities in the most authoritative of recent formulations, those of the Second Vatican Council. Comparable equivocity would be a recipe for disaster in any large and highly organized society. When the supreme law of the land directly authorizes rival, perhaps contradictory, positions and provides no way of settling the disputes, conflict becomes inevitable and, unless changes are made in the supreme law, irresolvable.

The ambiguities I have in mind can be easily illustrated. Principles were laid down by Vatican II which theologically justify sweeping reforms in the structures, procedures, and goals of the Church. The Church is in its essence the pilgrim Messianic people of God which should optimally be characterized by a substantial measure of participatory democracy—that is, by subsidiarity and collegiality. Its fundamental aim should be, not the salvation of individual souls in abstraction from their material and social situations, but rather the sanctification of the world and the unification of all mankind as a sign and anticipation of the coming

Kingdom. At the same time that these revolutionary principles were enunciated, the old formulations were also repeated. What the First Vatican Council said a hundred years ago about the Papacy, for example, was simply reiterated, inserted without modification or reinterpretation in what is a radically different vision of both Church and world. Similarly, individualistic otherworldliness is juxtaposed rather than joined with a cosmic and communal eschatology which makes the humanization of social and cultural structures a primary Christian duty.

Thus biblicists, modernizers, traditionalists, and papalists can all appeal quite consistently to this or that aspect of the Council's teaching, and can argue that the features they choose as primary provide the hermeneutic key for the interpretation of the whole. The Berrigans and their supporters can point to the Conciliar social and political interpretations of the commandment of Christian love as authorization for their opposition to the Vietnam War, while their opponents can argue that tradition forbids, and the Council never specifically approves, the kind of civil disobedience in which the Berrigans engage. Hans Küng can insist that the Council's emphasis on the Bible demands a thorough review of the doctrine of infallibility, while his critics reply that the biblical emphasis must be understood in the light of tradition, especially the tradition of Vatican I, rather than the other way around. There is no publicly persuasive way of showing who is the faithful Catholic, simply because the Council is equivocal on these and a whole range of other questions.

The ambiguity, it should be remembered, was for the most part deliberate. In order to get as wide a consensus as possible, the new and the old were simply placed side by side in the documents, leaving open the question of whether the new is to be interpreted in terms of the old or vice versa. At the time, most observers thought of this as a politically necessary compromise, but of no great practical moment. The ambiguities would give the Pope and bishops greater freedom in interpreting and implementing the Conciliar decrees, but the Catholic faithful would remain obedient. We could not have been more mistaken. The lower ranks remained obedient, perhaps, but not so much to the church leaders as to what they took to be even more authoritative—viz., the Council.

As a consequence, non-Catholic church leaders, oddly enough, are now less likely to be attacked than Catholic ones. Their authority is more clearly legitimated. The Eastern Orthodox, when challenged, can take refuge in tradition, and the Protestants in past or future general conventions. "If you don't like what we do," they can generally say, "then get the next assembly to vote on your side." The Roman Catholic hierarchy has no such recourse. It still has, of course, tremendous power. It controls appointments and the purse, makes and unmakes rules and determines policy. But illegitimate power is perceived as tyranny, and at point after point the bishops can't help but act tyrannically because they contradict what many in the Church sincerely believe to be the import of the Council.

The difficulty, to repeat, cannot be resolved. A Pope who agreed theologically with Hans Küng, for example, might well have every whit as difficult a time as Paul VI, except that now the opposition would shift. People like Bill Buckley make it clear that conservatives also are able to refer to Council, Church, tradition, and even the Bible against the Pope or bishops whenever it suits their purposes. Another example of this might be cited from the extreme clerical right wing in Spain. In the Fall of 1972 the leader of the reactionary Sacerdotal Fraternity, which is vehemently opposed to Pope Paul's support of the reformist anti-Franco bishops, addressed a meeting of a thousand priests by saying:

> Just as during the war a lieutenant or simple soldier is bound to
> replace his commanding officer if the latter shows cowardice, so it
> is with us priests: if the head of the Church no longer represents
> Christ, then he ceases to have any authority over us.[7]

It is not difficult to imagine what he would have said about a
Pope of the type Küng would favor. In addition, a Küng-like
Pope would have the additional handicap of being too
biblical for the modernizers also.

What then should be done? In raising this final question, it
would be absurd to try to instruct Catholics in their
obligations and opportunities. That would be pretentious.
But we who are Protestants do need to ask ourselves what we
think of the crisis, and what are our expectations and hopes.
This is an ecumenical duty. More and more, each part of
divided Christendom affects the others. Catholic lack of
enthusiasm for COCU, for example, may have had a
substantial, even if undocumented, role in its demise. In the
reverse direction, non-Catholic opinion was clearly a significant factor in the Council's deliberations. It is important,
then, that Catholics and Protestants think in the most
responsible and Christian way possible about what is happening in each other's camps, for we mutually influence each
other.

Responsibility requires enlarging our concern and sympathy to those whom we usually neglect. We must learn to
sympathize, first, with Catholics who, at this juncture in
history, are being stripped of traditional religious securities
even more rudely than are Protestants. This is happening
both to laity and to church professionals—including, it will be
recalled, bishops. As the traditional rationales weaken and as
new freedoms become conceivable, the ecclesiastical routine
becomes increasingly petty and oppressive. Some leave the

Church, but others who remain within also suffer from heightened frustration or meaninglessness. The outcome, to be sure, is not always disastrous. Some reconstruct their lives in a new cultural context with the help of humanistic principles that are not thought of as explicitly Christian. Others are freed by the collapse of the old for the development of Christian authenticity, for trust in God rather than in what Luther called "works righteousness." They learn, as we all need to learn, not to use God to justify themselves, but rather to respond to him as crucified and transforming love. But for multitudes, there is no happy ending. The loss of extrinsic (or, in some cases, intrinsic) religiousness is not replaced by anything better and leaves their precarious human identities and values without support. One evil is driven out, but seven devils each worse than the first threaten to rush in.

Second, and more difficult, Protestants need to sympathize not only with individual Catholics but also with their Church. For the Christian as for the Jew, the people of God itself suffers when members depart. The individuals who leave sometimes are the gainers, and for that God is to be praised; but the community suffers. Part of its own body has been cut off and it loses, usually through its own fault, someone entrusted to its care. It is judged thereby, and its own ability to bear witness to redeeming and reconciling love is injured.

In the third place, and most obviously of all, Protestant sympathies are immediately engaged by Catholic reformers. It is a matter for rejoicing that for the first time in hundreds of years Catholicism is again blessed with a full-fledged loyal opposition. Like the prophets of old and Jesus Christ himself, the members of this opposition are unalterably committed to that part of the visible People of God in which they find themselves. They may denounce its leadership and accuse the people of whoring after false gods, but for them it remains the betrothed of Jahweh, the bride of Christ. Theirs is the most difficult and important role in the present crisis. The Christian future of the Church—of any church—depends above all on her ecclesial majesty's loyal opposition. From this perspective, the true heroes of this period of Catholic history are people like Dorothy Day, Ivan Illich, Hans Küng, and, in a very different way, Karl Rahner.

Finally, however, there are the leaders of the Church, especially the bishops and the Pope. These usually do not arouse much sympathy in the Protestant, or, for that matter, the progressive Catholic, breast. Yet it is their plight that in some ways seems the most pitiable. They are, by and large, run-of-the-mill Christians, like most of us; and yet for a variety of reasons, sometimes not at all self-seeking, they have been vested with inhumanly weighty powers and responsibilities; and now—the cruelest blow of all—they find themselves in the midst of a constitutional crisis for which their training did not prepare them and which deprives them of legitimacy. Whatever policies they pursue, whether traditionalist or progressive, whether emphasizing the return to the sources or adaptation to the modern world, will be regarded as unjustified, unfaithful, and tyrannical by large groups of vocal Catholics. Even if all these shepherds were as wise as serpents and innocent as doves, they would still be in trouble. Inevitably, as would also be true of most of us, they are becoming increasingly paranoid. Communication is deteriorating. In most countries, so it seems, fewer and fewer bishops trust theologians and other Catholic scholars, and the sentiments are reciprocated. Even a pro-institutional Catholic sociologist like Andrew Greeley hints darkly of occasional bishops who are "quite devoid of any sense of personal integrity and will reward competent work with a knife in the back." He suggests that it has perhaps become impossible to work any longer with the American hierarchy; but then he adds that one must sympathize with them and especially with the liberal bishops whose dilemmas are often intolerable.

If this general view of what is happening has any validity, then the crisis cannot be solved—not even by a new Pope—but only lived through. Another Council will in all likelihood eventually settle the constitutional question—i.e., the question of how to interpret Vatican II, just as the Council of Constantinople quieted the storms raised by Nicaea, and Chalcedon by Ephesus. This settlement, however, cannot be rushed. It would be disastrous to try in the near future to remove the ambiguities of Vatican II. A wide consensus ranging from the people through the clergy and theologians to the bishops has not yet been forged. When it is, perhaps Catholics will have come to think that the solution of their constitutional crisis is inseparable from the question of Christian unity. They may have come to believe, for example, that the full symbolic, even if not canonical, ecumenicity of a Council requires the participation of all interested Christian bodies, not just of the Roman communion. If so, perhaps generations will pass before the basic institutional problem is finally resolved.

As we come now to the end of this analysis, I am acutely aware of a great gap in my presentation. Crisis spells, not only threat, but opportunity as well. I have said scarcely anything of the immense vitality and creativity of contemporary Catholicism. I have said not a word about what Archbishop Helder Câmara represents in Brazil, or about the exhilarating conflict in Spain, or the depressing one in Holland, or about developments in Africa—to mention just four points that may prove decisive for world Catholicism and therefore also for the United States. The major excitement these days is on the Roman Catholic, not the Protestant side. Nothing in the non-Catholic world remotely compares in tragedy and comedy, both high and low, with what is now happening in Catholicism. A half-filled Catholic seminary is, in my experience, often much more lively, as well as chaotic and frustrating, than a full Protestant one. This liveliness is both pastoral and theological, extending both to the struggle for the personal reality of faith and for its intellectual formulation and understanding. Perhaps the future of Christianity as a whole, to the degree that it has a future, is now bursting forth in a thousand often absurdly unexpected forms within the Roman Church. Most of the innovations will and should perish, but some contain the seeds of what is to come. The losses and confusion are great, but so is the hope.

NOTES

1. Malachi Martin, *Three Popes and the Cardinal* (Farrar, Straus and Giroux, 1972), p. vii.

2. George G. Higgins, "The True Story of Vatican II," *America* 126. 11 (March 18, 1972): 280.

3. John Tracy Ellis, "American Catholicism in 'an Uncertain, Anxious Time,' " *Commonweal* 98. 8 (April 27, 1973): 177.

4. Hans Küng, *Diskussion um Hans Küng "Die Kirche,"* ed. B. Häring and J. Nolte (Freiburg: Herder, 1971), pp. 302-3.

5. James Hitchcock, *The Decline and Fall of Radical Catholicism* (New York: Herder and Herder, 1971).

6. Garry Wills, *Bare Ruined Choirs* (Garden City, N.Y.: Doubleday, 1972).

7. Quoted in "Post-Conciliar Catholicism: Spain. The Candle and the stick," by Alain Woodrow, *Commonweal* 98.6 (April 13, 1973): 130.

II

APPLICATIONS
IN HISTORY

THE PATTERN OF THE PAST:
AUGUSTINE'S DEBATE WITH
EUSEBIUS AND SALLUST

Glenn F. Chesnut, Jr.

The ideas about history that were proclaimed in Augustine's *City of God*[1] did not arise in a vacuum. Augustine was reacting against other, already established views of history—views that differed from his own. To understand the full measure of Augustine's own peculiar genius, and the full significance of what he was trying to say, we must know the viewpoints he was rejecting, two of them in particular. On the one hand there were the conservative, pessimistic theories of the classical Roman historian Sallust; on the other, was the liberal, rationalistic optimism of the church historian Eusebius and other such Eastern representatives of the Constantinian settlement and the Hellenistic view of man. The issue at stake was the basic shape of history. Did it run downhill or uphill? Had Rome sunk into a decline and fall from some past era of virtue and inner strength, as Sallust claimed? Or had the history of the preceding millennium or more been a line of almost unbroken progress in civilization and morality, as Eusebius and others of that opinion claimed?

Augustine rejected both these views and came up with a new understanding of historical process, as summed up in his

---

The author is Assistant Professor of Ancient and Medieval History, Indiana University at South Bend.

doctrine of the Two Cities. History had no complete solutions in this world, either in a golden age in the past or in a perfect human society in the future. History was lived in perpetual tension, often ironic, frequently tragic; the delicate balance of the Augustinian understanding of history depended upon a sure vision of that fact.

Eusebius of Caesarea was the most important historical thinker in the Christian world prior to Augustine.[2] His *Chronology* established a coherent dating system for all of Western history. But more important, his *Church History* was the first full-length narrative history written from a Christian perspective. It thereby became one of the five or so truly seminal works in the development of Western historiography. Augustine referred by name to the *Chronology* (which had been translated into Latin by Jerome) all the way through his *City of God*. He had also definitely read Rufinus' Latin translation of the *Church History* before he finished writing the *City of God*; and there is no reason to assume that he did not read it soon after it first appeared, in A.D. 402-3, ten years before the *City of God* was begun.[3] Eusebius' theology of history had become enshrined as the official ideology of the Christian empire.[4] Its effect was so pervasive that Augustine found it coming at him indirectly from every side. Even the great church historians who came after Augustine (Socrates, Sozomen, and Theodoret in the fifth century, and Evagrius in the sixth) were so much under the sway of Eusebius' ideas that they followed unquestioningly in his tracks, and quite literally ignored Augustine's very existence. Augustine therefore did not attack Eusebius by name. He was attacking what was, by the early fifth century, no longer an individual human but rather a generally believed, unconsciously accepted set of presuppositions, widely spread among pious, intelligent Christians. But if we look back over the centuries from our present standpoint, it is clear that

Eusebius was the great founding father of the complex of
ideas that Augustine was attacking, and it is by referring to
Eusebius that we see its theological, philosophical, and
psychological underpinnings—fundamental ideas that Augustine had to modify or refute in order to establish his own,
new interpretation of history.

Eusebius' basic presuppositions were different from Augustine's in many ways. Eusebius was an Origenist,[5] and his
theology of history was an Origenistic one. The "Garden" of
Eden had been a realm outside this present space-time
continuum, and "Adam" had been the totality of mankind.
All our souls pre-existed before this earth was ever created.[6]
An act of disobedience on the part of some of those
unembodied noetic beings caused God to cast them into
human bodies and imprison them on earth for a period of
discipline.[7]

Most of those first men cast down on earth soon fell into
what Eusebius regarded as a sub-human, animal-like existence[8]—the life of desert nomads, without *polis* or *politeia*,
without *technē* or *epistēmē*, without legal system or any concept of *aretē* or philosophy.[9] The lack of real knowledge of
God condemned them to the lowest sort of existence even on
earth; and conversely, any widespread growth of civilized
human community would have to take place in company
with the appearance of some sort of renewed knowledge of
God. In Eusebius' basically humanist, rationalist perspective,
civilization and true religion went hand in hand.

Nevertheless, even in the first primitive centuries of this
earth's history the picture was not entirely black. Amidst the
mass of fallen men were some of a quite different sort—
Enosh, Enoch, Noah, Seth, Japheth, Abraham, Isaac, Jacob,
Job, and Joseph—a whole series of figures from early biblical
history.[10] Eusebius called them the *theophileis*, the "Friends
of God." Their religion was based upon knowledge of the

Logos, the Rational Structure of reality as a whole.[11] It was natural religion which they had—that is, one based on "natural concepts,"[12] a piece of (originally) Stoic phraseology that Middle Platonism had taken over by Eusebius' time. Even though the Friends of God lived centuries before the coming of Jesus, and practiced a religion based on reason alone, Eusebius believed that they were properly to be described as "Christians in fact, if not in name."[13] Eusebius was rather like an eighteenth-century Deist in that he believed that the basic truths of religion—the immortality of the soul, morality based upon natural law and right reason, and so on—were easily demonstrable to any intelligent, intellectually free, educated man. There was no Thomistic distinction, for him, between "truths of reason" and "truths of revelation": *all* truths were basically truths of reason.

But Eusebius was a Greek, and he was not so naïve as to believe that a simple, rational counterargument would stop a man hell-bent for the destruction of himself and those around him.[14] Eusebius had a Euripidean sense of the daemonic. As the old Greek tragedies showed, there were strange powers that could destroy men. When Aphrodite crept into her heart, Phaedra in blind passion killed both her stepson and herself; at the very moment when Heracles had triumphantly rescued his wife and sons, Hera sent madness into his mind, and in his insanity he turned and slaughtered those he had come to save; it was Apollo who drove Orestes to the murder of his mother Clytemnestra; the maenads tore King Pentheus into pieces with their bare hands under the inspiration of Dionysus.[15] From the time of Homer, these strange mental occurrences were ascribed to "gods" or "daemons"—external forces that sometimes brought a sudden flash of insight or recognition, but equally often brought foolish refusal to understand, or pounding emotion that blocked the clear perception of sanity and reality.[16]

In Eusebius, the daemonic was continually described as *misokalos*,[17] "hater of the good," and *philoponēros*,[18] "lover of evil." It was an attempt to deal with that same dark part of the human personality with which Augustine also tried to struggle, more than two generations later, in his account of the pear-stealing incident in the *Confessions* (ii. 4.9–9.17). Augustine searched his memory of those adolescent years to try to analyze the motives that drove him to that act of pure vandalism, and finally decided that the major component was a love of evil itself—not a selfish desire to gain any material thing that he needed or wanted, nor a thirst for revenge, nor a fear of losing anything he already had, but seemingly a desire of evil for evil's own sake. For Eusebius, this was a basic part of the character of the fallen human soul,[19] and so it can be seen that he did not make the simple-minded rationalist's equation and claim that sin is only ignorance, nothing more. Eusebius was well aware of the dark depths of the fallen soul and saw within it a frightening, uncanny, willful opting for the evil which he could only display in its full horror by calling upon the mythological concept of the daemoniacal. One of the most important aspects of Christ's saving work was his coming to defeat the daemons and free men from their grasp.[20]

The key attribute that separated the saved from the damned in Eusebius' system was also something more than simply rationality; it was *eusebeia*, "piety." It was the great fundamental criterion that served to divide the sheep from the goats, and therefore played the same role as *caritas* in Augustine's system, or "faith" in sixteenth-century Reformation thought. In what we can recognize as a foretaste of later Byzantine spirituality, Eusebius regarded *eusebeia* basically as human participation in the cosmic liturgy. All rational creatures, from the lowliest human being to the highest rank of angel, were supposed to be engaged in a continual, harmonious hymn and prayer to the God above the cosmos.[21] The only ultimate alternative to *eusebeia*, Eusebius believed, was hedonism, a captivity to the pleasure principle in its crudest sense.[22]

The *Heilsgeschichte*, the history of man's salvation, was viewed by Eusebius as a societal phenomenon, involving a gradual evolution, over long eras of history, of progressively better integrated and more humane social institutions and social mores, until humanity finally reached the high level of civilization represented in the Roman Empire of his own day. The cosmic fall that took place before this world began had given men bodies and cast them into history, but in spite of this, there were still within this historical existence authentic human possibilities well worth struggling for. Over the long centuries, early man had normally lived in savagery, without the One God or true civilization; but that did not mean that a perfected human society, built around full dedication of God, was impossible within the historical dimension in which human beings had been placed. Like many other Eastern theologians, Eusebius in his understanding of history showed no trace of that fundamentally tragic view of fallen man's irrevocable brokenness such as is found, to a certain extent, in Augustine, and carried out even farther in Luther and Calvin: that is, that brooding sense of man's utter inability to achieve his full, natural, *historical* possibilities after the Fall.

The divine Logos was the agent whereby the human race was lifted out of savagery and superstition, and was gradually, over the centuries, led to civilization and a rational religion. In both creation and revelation, this distinct Second Person of the Trinity was the necessary intermediary between the world and the unknowable Father, the supreme God. The Logos disclosed himself to selected men in the great series of theophanies recorded in the Old Testament, such as the appearance to Abraham at the Oak of Mamre (Gen. 18) and

Moses and the burning bush (Exod. 3:1-3).[23] These self-revelations of the divine structure of the universe then led indirectly to the progressive spread of high religion and the arts of civilization to the whole Mediterranean ecumene. Eusebius adopted a diffusion theory of civilization, and asserted that advanced ideas about philosophy and ethics had spread outward from a Palestinian center during the millennium following Moses by ordinary trans-cultural intellectual contacts.[24] This was an argument that had already been used in earlier Christian apologetic—i.e., the insistence that Plato had borrowed his best ideas from Moses.

A situation was thereby created in which a large part of the human race was finally prepared for the crucial act in the plan of redemption: at the end of the first century B.C. the Logos actually became incarnate, in the life of Jesus of Nazareth. Closely connected with this, in God's plan, was another event happening at roughly the same time: the creation of the Roman Empire under Augustus. An epoch of history unlike any before was introduced. The continual warfare of the Mediterranean world was replaced by the *Pax Romana*. For Eusebius, the eschatological Kingdom of Peace prophesied in passages like Isaiah 2:4 and Micah 4:1-1, when swords were to be beaten into plowshares, and spears into pruning hooks, was not the miraculous future kingdom of the millennialists, in which grapevines gave 225 gallons of wine from each grape (Irenaeus, *Adv. haer.* v.33.3), but the Roman rule he himself lived under.[25] As a typical Roman, of course, Eusebius normally tended to regard the Empire as the ultimate World State, embracing the majority of the human race (and *all* civilized men!) within its boundaries.

The course of history soon showed that God was guiding the path of the Empire in a special way. He gave success to each emperor who tolerated Christianity (success in battle, prosperity and peace for the Empire, a long reign, a happy end to his life, an honored memory, children, and a rightful heir as his successor on the throne), whereas the emperors who persecuted the Christians always came to a bad end.

The victory of Emperor Constantine at the battle of the Milvian bridge in 312 then came as the fulfillment of the divine plan of history. Constantine had been foreordained by God[26] to defeat the pagan persecutors and Christianize the Empire. He was a charismatic figure, continually guided by ecstatic experiences,[27] one who set about, with the aid of the defiant bishops of a martyr Church newly baptized in its own blood, to build the truly Final Empire. The Christian Roman imperial regime was the universal goal, at the end of time, toward which all preceding history had been directed. It would reign over all the earth, till the end of the world. There would be a Constantinian dynasty, Eusebius predicted, for some generations to come.[28] Nevertheless, at the end, the full paraphernalia of apocalyptic horrors would fall upon the earth, and bring history to its final end.

Augustine's *City of God* was written roughly a century after Eusebius' *Church History*. His theology of history differed in a number of obvious points from that of Eusebius. To begin with, Origenism[29] was rejected in the Augustinian doctrine of original sin: Adam was an individual, flesh-and-blood human being who committed an act of sin at a particular instant within the same continuum of chronological time within which we also exist today; the fallenness of Adam was then passed on to each of his biological descendants through the lust accompaning the act of sexual intercourse by which each of these human beings was fathered. This was the theory which was to become dominant in the West during the Middle Ages.

Furthermore, Augustine rejected the sort of Logos theology Eusebius had used, in favor of a quite different doctrine of the Trinity[30] based on personal analogies like the relations between the lover, the loved, and the love that binds them. This meant the rejection of the theophany sequence as the central theme of ancient history. Augustine developed his doctrine of the Two Cities as a replacement. At one point (*De civ. Dei* xvi.29) he actually mounted a head-on attack on the Logos-doctrine interpretation of an Old Testament passage that was one of the foundation stones of the Logos-theophany schematization of history. There were different understandings of grace and fallenness involved here as well.

For Eusebius and the Logos tradition in which he stood, salvation was a return from the delusions of destructive, emotional, compulsive behavior to the clear light of conscious rationality. Fallen man was a figure from Greek tragedy: blind, raging, destroying himself and those around him as he obstinately refused to listen to his fellow men who tried to bring him back to reason. The agent of salvation for these Christian heirs to Homer and Euripides was therefore fittingly said to be the Divine Logos, Holy Reason itself. For Augustine, on the contrary, salvation was not construed as a de-emotionalizing of human beings but as a re-channeling of their most primitive fears, desires, griefs, and joys onto Christian objects.[31] These were spontaneous emotions that Augustine was interested in, welling up out of the human heart—such as his own childhood love of Latin and hatred of Greek. They developed from roots far below the level of conscious rationality. Human civilization, the fruit of conscious rationality, could therefore have little or no effect on the true motives of human actions, and the factors that made them good or evil. Eusebius had held that high civilization and true religion necessarily went together, but Augustine could not agree.

A completely different schematization of history was necessary, and this Augustine provided in his concept of the

Two Cities. The Eusebian scheme had read past history in terms of a liberal doctrine of progress[32]—the light of the Gospel and of Western civilization brought progressively to more and more of mankind with each generation, and the regeneration of mankind as a whole taking place over the sweep of centuries and resulting in the creation of the perfect human society on earth. But to Augustine there had been no real progress, not at the fundamental level of the heart.[33] To Augustine, the world of history was always marked by tension: tension within the individual's own psyche, as the power of sin struggled against the desire to do good, and tension between one segment of human society and another, as the proud and selfish struggled against those who loved God. These two segments of mankind were the two "cities" of Augustine, which had co-existed in human history, side by side, from almost the very beginning. In the City of God were such men as Abel (*De civ. Dei* xv.1), Noah, and Abraham (xvi.2). In the city of man were Cain at the beginning (xv.1), and then the two great empires of Assyria and Rome (xvi.17, xviii.2). In this fallen world there would never be one city without the other.

It was a defiant act of unpatriotism to link Assyria and Rome as the two great imperialistic examples of the city of man. The Assyrians—cruel and without mercy, systematic perpetrators of atrocities on small, defenseless peoples—had taunted the God of the Hebrews and sworn to wipe out his people (2 Kings 18-19). That Rome was no better than a second Assyria was an offensive thing to say. But, as we know, the event that moved Augustine to write the *City of God* and create on paper this massive reformulation of the Christian doctrine of history, was the sack of Rome in A.D. 410 by Alaric and his warband of Visigoths. It became clear that the Empire itself was shaken and would soon fall. Augustine now knew that as bishop and proclaimer of the

Word of God he had to speak a prophetic word against his own country. Rome was not the promised Kingdom of God on earth which Eusebius and other supporters of the Constantinian settlement had claimed. Rome had conquered the world by force of arms, and now by force of arms was going to be destroyed. Augustine had to make it brutally clear to his readers that the Roman Empire that was collapsing before their eyes was not, as the imperial ideology had taught, the final embodiment of God's reign on earth.

The Two Cities of Augustine were formed by two loves—one, the love of God above everything else, the other, the love of something less than God with the ultimate devotion due the Deity alone. Eusebius on the contrary had contrasted " piety" with "hedonism" to distinguish between the saved and the unsaved—the saved worshiped God as Lord of all, while the damned were captive to the pleasure principle in its crudest physical sense, living an animal-like existence[34]—like white rats, as we would say today, running mazes so that the psychology student will reward them with a piece of cheese. Eusebius' dichotomy was vivid, but Augustine's alternative provided a more subtle awareness of sin. As Augustine knew, many things that were sinful, like spiritual pride, could not be understood as simply desire for sensual pleasure.

On these grounds as well then, Augustine rejected the Eusebian notion of progress. Eusebius had held that Western civilization and true religion went hand in hand. He had both the good points and the bad of the nineteenth-century Christian missionaries who put Mother Hubbard gowns on naked Pacific islanders. Education, law and order, and the restraints of a sophisticated urban civilization might force men to hold in check many of their more violent emotions; as Augustine knew, however, the subtler sins of pride and power that infiltrate any form of civilized life, could make such a society just as un-Christian at bottom as the most benighted, supposedly savage tribe.

Eusebius had not only explained how the Kingdom of God had been brought about on earth, he had also explained how it could be maintained: when the reigning emperor tolerated, or even better, actively supported Christianity, God rewarded both him and the Empire with success and prosperity. Now Augustine also believed, as devoutly as any church historian in the Eusebian tradition, that it was God who granted victory and empire.[35] It was God who decided how long every particular war lasted.[36] It was God who put a Nero on the throne, or brought about the defeat in battle of a Radagaisus.[37] But the Eusebian notion that the pious Christian emperor was invariably rewarded with success while the impious emperor was just as invariably punished, did not match up with the actual empirical course of history: the same God who gave power "to the Christian Constantine gave it also to the apostate Julian."[38]

But this was only part of the matter; Augustine's basic criticism of the Eusebian-Constantinian ideology of empire ran far deeper than the mere factual discrepancies in their reading of history. Their approach and attitude represented nothing less than an attempt by men to manipulate and use God for their own selfish human purposes:

> And this is the characteristic of the earthly city, that it worships God or gods who may aid it in reigning victoriously and peacefully on earth not through love of doing good, but through lust of rule. The good use the world that they may enjoy God: the wicked, on the contrary, that they may enjoy the world would fain use God.[39]

Eusebius and Augustine set up two alternative schemes for interpreting the nature of God's providence. In the Eusebian version, providence is seen as an empirically observable, objective pattern in the *external* course of events; in the

Augustinian version, the true significance of providence appears instead in the *inner* history of each human subject involved in the course of events. For Augustine, God controls the passage of external events, of course, but for him "the meaning of history lies not in the flux of outward events, but in the hidden drama of sin and redemption."[40] Sometimes the good prosper, but often they suffer misfortune; sometimes the wicked suffer misfortune, but often they prosper. But the meaning of history, Augustine asserts, is not to be sought in any simple-minded, externalized calculation of materialistic success and prosperity; instead, the meaning of history is to be sought in the inner spiritual history of each individual human soul, as God providentially arranges each external historical situation in which the soul finds itself, in order to chasten it, comfort it, reward it, warn it, divert it from future spiritual dangers—all with the goal of maintaining the perseverance of the elect until the end, when they will go to receive everlasting rewards in their heavenly home.[41] The important thing to Augustine is a man's subjective reaction to the situation in which he is put:

> For as the same fire causes gold to glow brightly, and chaff to smoke..., thus it is that in the same affliction the wicked detest God and blaspheme, while the good pray and praise. So material a difference does it make, not what ills are suffered, but what kind of man suffers them.[42]

To sum up Augustine's *City of God* in a single line, he was preaching the gospel of suffering love to human beings who were about to be engulfed by one of the worst catastrophes that human civilization has seen. In the dark time that followed, Augustine's writings were one of the greatest consolations of a world often struggling for bare survival. But Eusebius' dream did not die either. In the lines concluding his *Church History* (x. 9.6-9) he sketched out that golden vision of a Christian empire that was to continue to haunt idealists in both East and West for centuries to come—the Kingdom of Peace had brought freedom from international war to the whole *oikoumēne*, all mankind had been bound up into the united hymn to God of the cosmic liturgy, and the good emperor, the Friend of God, ruled with philanthropy and piety. Those church historians who carried on Eusebius' work—Socrates, Sozomen, Theodoret, and Evagrius—continued to be haunted by that dream, and let it dominate some of their basic historical judgments. This golden vision was the spiritual force that held the Byzantine Empire together for a thousand years. In spite of Augustine's attempt to provide a different understanding of history for the West at the time of the fifth-century collapse, as soon as Western Europe began to pull itself together again (as we all know from our reading of medieval history) there too the dream of a Holy Roman Empire captured men's imaginations once again.

The other great historian with whom Augustine was debating was Sallust.[43] This man was, to many Romans, the greatest of their historians. His life was lived in tumultuous times: in the civil war that erupted when Julius Caesar crossed the Rubicon in 49 B.C. Sallust became one of the officers of the great military leader. But then when the triumphant dictator was assassinated on the Ides of March five years later, Sallust found it prudent to retire from public life. He withdrew into dignified retirement in the magnificent mansion and gardens he had built in Rome (the *horti Sallustiani*), while writing away at several works of history dealing with selected events from the preceding seventy years. The central theme of all his historical writings was that of the decline and fall of Rome.

His theories were laid out especially clearly in the first thirteen chapters of his monograph on the conspiracy of

Catiline. Thus, in the beginning men had been free of cupidity, free of the lust of domination, moved by the virtues of self-restraint and justice. When Rome was newly founded, and the tyrannous kings had been expelled, the city was filled with men of primitive virtue—men who preferred hardship, discipline, and victory with honor over all the lures of riches, revelry, and harlotry. These men, their forefathers, had made Rome great; but now, Sallust said, he had to tell the sad tale of the way in which, "by gradual changes" over the preceding hundred years, Rome "has ceased to be the noblest and best, and has become the worst and most vicious" (*Cat.* v.9).

One of the grandest periods in ancient Roman history had been the wars with the African city of Carthage in the third and second centuries B.C. In spite of their naval power and wealth, and generals like Hannibal, the Carthaginians eventually lost. Rome, a small city-state on the western coast of Italy, had toppled a world power, and in 146 B.C. stood triumphant over the ashes. At the final defeat of mighty Carthage, Sallust says, was where Rome's decline began. When Rome was small and struggling, primitive virtue reigned; but now with her greatest enemy gone, all pressure was relaxed. "Those who had found it easy to bear hardship and dangers, anxiety and adversity, found leisure and wealth, desirable under other circumstances, a burden and a curse" (*Cat.* x.2). The purely virtuous desire for glory with honor began secretly to turn into *ambitio*, which sought the same ultimate goals but by the despicable route of "craft and deception": "one thought locked in the breast, another ready on the tongue" (*Cat.* xi. 1-2, x.5).

The next step in Rome's moral downfall took place during the reign of the dictator Sulla. Sulla's takeover had begun in 88 B.C. when he seized control of the army that was to fight the vicious attack of King Mithridates in Greece and Asia Minor. In reprisal for their massacre of Roman and Italian residents, the people of the province of Asia were forced to billet Sulla's troops in private homes for the winter of 85/84 B.C., each homeowner providing the soldiers in his house with clothes, spending money, and dinner for them and their "friends." That one long, uproariously drunken winter introduced the vice of *luxuria* into the Roman national spirit, Sallust said. "Those charming and voluptuous lands . . . easily demoralized the warlike spirit of his soldiers," as they learned too great a love of women, drink, and classical Greek *objets d'art* (*Cat.* xi.5-6). When Sulla finally gained complete control over the Roman state in 83 B.C. he subjected Rome and Italy to an incredibly bloodthirsty and avaricious reign of terror. Thousands were killed in mass executions. Since proscription meant confiscation of one's property, men were frequently put on the list of the proscribed and executed simply because their houses or formal gardens or country estates were coveted. This had a profound effect on the Roman national character, Sallust believed. The already existent vice of *ambitio* was supplemented by the even worse vice of *avaritia*, the "desire for money, which no wise man covets." Thanks to Sulla, "all men began to rob and pillage," and Rome sank into total degradation (*Cat.* xi.3-4).

This had all happened something over forty years earlier, and Sallust was now writing about the historical consequences. The moral guidelines of Roman society were permanently erased. As a result, the Rome of Sallust's own day was depicted by him in what has become the classic image of Roman decadence and debauchery, the basic scene repeated again and again in Roman literature: fat men with greasy fingers stuffing their mouths with over-rich dainties, then waddling outside to vomit so that they could gorge themselves again; wealthy women of easy virtue, sleeping with a dozen illicit lovers while they went through a series of divorces; rampant homosexuality; rich, childless old men surrounded by a host of human vultures with oily smiles, pretending kindness while they wished in their hearts for the man to include them in his will and then die at once.

Sallust was a classic example of the arch-conservative, the "self-made man" who has risen to position and wealth, condemning the present generation and preaching the primitive virtues (as he imagined them) of a century earlier. Sallust, together with other conservative Roman writers who associated themselves with the ideals and interests of the propertied class, impressed this image of classical Roman society so thoroughly in the minds of later generations that it is difficult to disengage ourselves from it even now. The vivid picture of Roman history as a "decline and fall" from primitive vigor into moral corruption and internal spiritual decay is a seductive image even today.[44] We must, however, be careful not to let twentieth-century Western biases distort our reading of Sallust. He was a pagan. It was not Christian virtue that he was contrasting with the decadence of his own time. Virtue for Sallust was built upon a naked thirst for glory. The word *gloria* runs like a thread through all his work. At the very beginning of *The War with Catiline* he announces this theme in a vigorous sermon to his readers:

> It behooves all men who wish to excel the other animals to strive with might and main not to pass through life unheralded, like the beasts. . . . Therefore I find it becoming, in seeking glory, that we should employ the resources of the intellect rather than those of brute strength, to the end that, since the span of life we enjoy is so short, we may make the memory of our lives as long as possible. For the glory which riches or beauty confer is fleeting and frail; mental excellence (*virtus*) is a splendid and lasting possession (*Cat.* i.1-4).

The "virtue" or mental excellence of which Sallust speaks here is simply the capacity for wise advance deliberation upon tactics and strategy which brings victory in battle (*Cat.*

i.5-ii.2), or the sort of practical knowledge that brings success in agriculture, navigation, and architecture (*Cat.* ii.7). But fame and glory are the goals.

In the golden era of Rome's past, it was "the thirst for glory (*cupido gloriae*) that had filled men's minds" that had made their country strong and great. The incredible discipline and bravery of the Roman troops was produced by this overriding lust for fame, praise, and renown (*Cat.* vii). The search for glory was the key to human psychology, Sallust believed; and even the fallen man's motivation could be understood as merely the perversion of that basic urge. The vice of *ambitio* was the attempt to win glory by craft and deception (*Cat.* xi.1-2). The vice of *avaritia* arose out of the mistaken idea that the possession of great riches was the necessary and correct route to undying glory (*Cat.* xii.1). The possession of this great wealth then dragged its owner down into vices like *luxuria* (*Cat.* xii.2).

The human mind was a seething mass of lusts and desires. These libidinal urges were the wellsprings of human motivation: the lust for domination of others (*lubidinem dominandi, Cat.* ii.2), the desire for money, the desire to rule (x.3), the coveting of another man's house or lands or goods (xi.4, xi.2), the lust "for lewdness, gluttony, and the other attendants of luxury" (xiii.3). But basic to these was "the lust for glory" (*cupido gloriae*, vii.3); and if this one object of desire were sought after in intelligent fashion, its intrinsic overwhelming strength would bring the other libidinal urges into line. This would lead human life to its proper goal, for if men would only seek glory with virtue, they "would attain to that height of greatness where from mortals their glory would make them immortal" (*Jug.* i.5).

This is therefore the proper goal of human life—to cheat death by winning undying fame; and to achieve this praise from the lips of other men, a human being must be willing to sacrifice riches, comfort, bodily pleasures, aggressive and coercive behavior toward those around him, and even life itself. The desire for praise and glory is the root of human motivation, and it is powerful enough, Sallust says, to suppress and dominate all these other seething desires that fill the heart of man.

The writings of Sallust were held in great respect by those to whom Augustine addressed his *City of God*. Because of his status as an ancient pagan classic, Sallust's works could be quoted against the pagans of Augustine's own century with great rhetorical effect. But more than mere rhetoric was involved; Augustine believed that Sallust's analysis of Roman greatness did in fact drive to the very heart of the imperialistic spirit. For Augustine, Rome was the outstanding example of the Earthly City, and Sallust was the one great penetrating analyst of the spirit that had created that proud but fallen commonwealth. Sallust the conservative saw the pattern of the past as a steady decline from a period of primitive virtue down to a degenerate and degraded present; and Augustine, interestingly enough, accepted half of this picture—the part dealing with the present. We must never forget that Augustine was a Roman himself, to the core. When we read Sallust and Tacitus and the other great Roman pagans of that spirit, we must mark well the characteristically Latin cynicism that sees virtue often parodied but never practiced, that sees vicious self-interest hiding everywhere under a mask of sweet words, that sees a sensual Latin sexuality and love of good food and drink leading a haughty aristocracy into elegant but idle ruin.

This pagan Latin cynicism we see mirrored almost perfectly in Augustine's conception of original sin. Original sin explained for Augustine the image of the world he had inherited from his own Roman tradition. What Augustine did to Sallust, therefore, was just to push this native Latin cynicism a bit farther: why should one accept at face value the moral pretenses of the famous men of the past any more than one accepted the moral pretenses of the politicians of one's own time? Back in the days of the founding fathers, Sallust said (as quoted by Augustine), "Equity and virtue prevailed among the Romans not more by force of laws than of nature." "I presume," Augustine replied, "it is to this inborn equity and goodness of disposition [that] we are to ascribe the rape of the Sabine women" (*De civ. Dei* ii.17, quoting *Cat.* ix.1). From the pages of Sallust himself one could show the falsity of his extravagant claims about the early days of Rome and its supposedly harmonious society of just men (*De civ. Dei* ii.18).

Again, the desire for glory was not nearly so important psychologically, Augustine said, as a far different motive. The only times in history when good order seemed to prevail in the Roman state were when men's attention was polarized by *fear,* fear of some external foe like King Tarquin or the Carthaginians (*De civ. Dei* ii.18; cf. iii.16-17). And even fear did not work all that well, since the threat of King Tarquin certainly did not stop Lucius Junius Brutus and Lucius Tarquinius Collatinus from creating strife in the city in 509 B.C., as the legends about Rome's beginnings related (*De civ. Dei* iii.16).

Furthermore, how could desire for victory in battle ever be motivated by a so-called pure desire for "virtuous" glory with no taint of the "lust for domination of others" (*lubidinem dominandi*; *Cat.* ii.2)? As early as the seventh century B.C., in the ancient period of the kings, "Rome was overcome by this vice, when she triumphed over Alba, and praising her own crime, called it glory" (*De civ. Dei* iii.14). At its best, this desire for glory could only be naked militarism, a "prayer . . . that Bellona would excite miserable nations to war, and lash them into agitation with her bloody scourge" (*De civ. Dei* v.12).

Augustine's *City of God* was a work of anti-patriotism. Traditional conservatives must have reacted with sharp hatred to his acid attacks on the founding fathers and guiding principles of their national glory.

> this . . . . For we speak no more diligently than their own authors . . . . . yet they diligently read these authors, and compel their children to learn them. But they who are angry, what would they do to me were I to say what Sallust says? (*De civ. Dei* iii.17).

This plea to put away anger was purely rhetorical on Augustine's part; he was quoting Sallust against Sallust to undermine the pious myths upon which Roman conservatives had built their lives, and he knew exactly what their reaction would be.

But let us grant, Augustine says, that Sallust's position had a fair amount of truth in it, that the growth and triumph of the Roman Empire was based upon the desire for glory. "Glory they most ardently loved: for it they wished to live, for it they did not hesitate to die. Every other desire was repressed by the strength of their passion for that one thing." It was "that which accomplished those many wonderful things, laudable, doubtless, and glorious according to human judgment." But what was this "glory" of which Sallust spoke, in its most ideal form? Here Augustine put his finger on the root of Sallust's understanding of human motivation, and spoke correctly of Sallust's position: "The glory with the desire of which the Romans burned is the judgment of men thinking well of men" (*De civ. Dei* v.12). That was the heart of it. In the words that Martin Luther was to use later on, these were people who looked for the righteousness of men rather than the righteousness of God. God, for his own purposes, had granted the Roman Empire to men who were willing even to die for it, "suppressing the desire of wealth and many other vices for this one vice, namely, the love of praise" (*De civ. Dei* v.13). "Since those Romans were in an Earthly City," with only earthly goals laid out in front of them, "what else but glory should they love, by which they wished even after death to live in the mouths of their admirers?" (*De civ. Dei* v.14).

Sallust had said that desire for praise was the true psychological root of all human motivation, and that when sought after by thoughtful self-interest it produced the virtues of the ideal human life. Augustine responded by saying that the love of human praise was not the necessary basis of human psychology but rather an unnecessary vice. Augustine was just like Sallust in regarding the human heart as a seething mass of desires, but it was the desire itself—the "love" or *caritas*—that for Augustine was basic. For him, every man had a *caritas*—an "ultimate concern," as Tillich would have said—which had to be directed toward something. For every human being there was always something more important than anything else. Love or *caritas* could be directed in one of two basic directions, Augustine said: either toward God or toward something less than God. From that idea of the Two Loves, of course, flowed his entire doctrine of the Two Cities, the central theme of *The City of God*. This raw power of spontaneous love, which served as the truly basic motive power of all human action, could be perverted into what Sallust called the "lust for glory" (*cupido gloriae*); but that was perversion, and the true Christian would have directed that basic surge of desire and concern toward a quite different object: the eternal God, who stood above human history in untouchable majesty and could never be threatened by the vicissitudes of purely human events.

So Augustine rejected both Sallust's conservatism and his theory of human motivation. The rejection of the conservatism was the more important observation, for Augustine saw clearly that the pattern of the past could not be captured by Sallust's naïve conservative theory of decline any more than it could by Eusebius' naïve liberal theory of progress. Augustine had stood back and looked at history from a far wider point of view. Thousands upon thousands of faces peered at him from the centuries, the faces of people from innumerable societies and situations, striving for countless different things in their individual lives. What mattered, ultimately, was simply whether they had put their ultimate love upon the eternal Goodness and Truth that survived the cycle of birth and decay, or whether they had put an infinite love upon something less, and been cheated finally by its destruction.

> Accordingly, two cities have been formed by two loves: the earthly by the love of self, even to the contempt of God; the heavenly by the love of God, even to the contempt of self.... For the one seeks glory from men; but the greatest glory of the other is God, the witness of conscience (*De civ. Dei* xiv.28).

Two classes of human beings emerge, present since the beginning of history, always in tension with one another: the Heavenly City, usually a minority living as sojourners in a world controlled by the City of Earth. One age is not more godly, or less godly, than another. In our own century we face the same threats and are graced by the same promises as any other century. My individual act of faith is not made easier, or harder, by any other man's act of faith. No progress has occurred to make loving God and my neighbor any easier for me than it was for my ancestors who lived in a technologically more "primitive" age; no historical decline has taken place that makes it any harder for me to recognize the name of God and direct my life toward him.

The challenges and the opportunities that bring man's

earthly life to its fulfillment are equally present in every period of history. That was an affirmation that very much needed to be made in the particular historical context in which Augustine was writing. Already in 410, when the refugees from Italy started arriving in Africa, all perceptive men in the West could see that the end had come. The Roman Empire in the West was going to fall. The surviving pagans started muttering that this was a punishment from the old gods, who were angry because they were no longer worshiped. This new religion, Christianity, was responsible: if the Empire had not been converted to Christianity it would have lasted forever and never fallen.

The City of God was an attempt to speak about all this—the rise and fall of empires, and the base upon which their power rested. World empires were monuments to human selfishness, Augustine said. They had risen and fallen throughout human history, and they always contained the seeds of destruction within themsleves. Christianity had nothing to do, one way or the other, with the destruction of this particular empire. But there was another human community that always survived, no matter what was happening to the great imperialistic war machines: the people led by Abraham and Moses and the prophets back in the centuries before Christ, the people who made up the true members of the Church in these days after the coming of Jesus. The City of God would survive, in martyrdom or starvation or whatever God's providence sent, until the end of the world.

There was no escape, in this world of history, from eventual death and destruction and defeat and injustice. But a small minority of men could resolve to acquit themselves as Christians while they suffered and died; a small minority could resolve not to let the struggle for survival drain every last drop of human decency out of their souls. On that note the Middle Ages began.

NOTES

1. *De civ. Dei* = Augustine, *De civitate Dei,*, ed. B. Dombart (Leipzig: B. G. Teubner, 1909). For quotations in English I have used or adapted the Marcus Dods trans., *The City of God* (New York: Modern Library, 1950).

2. The texts of Eusebius' works used for this study were as follows (in quotations in English I have frequently used or adapted existing translations): *H.E.* = *The Ecclesiastical History,* 2 vols., Greek text with trans. by Kirsopp Lake and J. E. L. Oulton, Loeb Classical Library (London, 1926-32). *V.C.* = *Vita Constantini,* ed. I. A. Heilel, vol. 1 of *Die griechischen christlichen Schriftsteller* edition of Eusebius' works (Leipzig: J. C. Hinrich, 1902). *De laud.* = *De laudibus Constantini,* ibid., pp. 193-259; trans. as *The Oration of Eusebius Pamphilus in Praise of the Emperor Constantine Pronounced on the Thirtieth Anniversary of His Reign* by E. C. Richardson, in *Nicene and Post-Nicene Fathers,* 2d ser., vol. 1 (Grand Rapids, Mich.: Wm. B. Eerdmans, 1961), pp. 581-610. *P.E.* = *Praeparatio Evangelica,* ed. Karl Mras, in *Die griechischen christlichen Schriftsteller* (Berlin: Akademie-Verlag, 1954-56); Greek text ed. and trans. E. H. Gifford (Oxford: E typographeo Academico, 1903). *D.E.* = *Demonstratio Evangelica,* ed. I. A. Heikel, *Die griechischen christlichen Schriftsteller* (Leipzig: J. C. Hinrich, 1913); trans. as *The Proof of the Gospel,* by W. J. Ferrar, 2 vols. (London: S.P.C.K., 1920). *Theoph.* = *On the Theophania or Divine Manifestation of Our Lord and Saviour Jesus Christ,* trans. from Syriac by Samuel Lee (Cambridge: Cambridge University Press, 1843). *Armen. Chron.* = *Die Chronik: aus dem armenischen übersetzt,* ed. and trans. Josef Karst, in *Die griechischen christlichen Schriftsteller* (Leipzig: J. C. Hinrich, 1911).

3. The position likewise held by Berthold Altaner, who gives the evidence for Augustine's knowledge of Eusebius in his article, "Augustinus und Eusebios von Kaisareia: eine quellenkritische Untersuchung," *Byzantinische Zeitschrift* 44 (1951): 1-6. Augustine explicitly referred to the *Church History* in a work he wrote in the first half of the 420s, but this does not mean that he had not read it long before that date.

4. In addition, many of Eusebius' basic ideas had been derived from commonplace sources, such as classical Greek historiography, the second-century Apologists, and Origen.

5. For the historical background to this, see Robert M. Grant, "Early Alexandrian Christianity," *Church History* 40 (1971): 133-44.

6. Eus. Armen. *Chron.*, p 36; *P.E.* vii.18.7-10 (332cd).

7. Eus. *P.E.* vii.18.7-10 (332cd); *D.E.* iv.1.4 (144d-45a).

8. Eus. *D.E.* iv.6.6-10 (155c—56a), see also viii. introd. 5-12 (363c-65b).

9. Eus. *H.E.* i.2.18-19; *D.E.* viii. introd. 5-12 (363c—65b).

10. Eus. *P.E.* vii.8.4-36 (306d—12b); *D.E.* i.2.3-7 (12—13), i.5.7 (10b).

11. Eus. *H.E.* i.4.

12. *Physikais ennoiais*, Eus. *H.E.* i.4.4; *D.E.* i.5.2-4 (9cd).

13. Eus. *H.E.* i.4.6.

14. See also Glenn F. Chesnut, Jr., "Fate, Fortune, Free Will and Nature in Eusebius of Caesareas," *Church History* 42 (1973): 165-82.

15. Euripides, *Hippolytus* 26—28; *Heracles* 815-73, *Electra* 1266-67 and 1296-97; *Bacchae* 1074-1152.

16. E.R. Dodds, *The Greeks and the Irrational* (Berkeley and Los Angeles: University of California Press, 1968), pp. 3-12.

17. Eus. *H.E.* ii.14.1; iv.7.1; v.14.1, 21.2; x.4.14, 8.2. *V.C.* iii.1, iv.41.

18. Eus. *H.E.* v.14.1; x.4.14, 4.57, 8.2.

19. Eus. *H.E.* x.4.57

20. Eus. *H.E.* x.4.13-16; *P.E.* vii.16 (328a-30b); *D.E.* vii.3.50-51 (359c).

21. Eus. *H.E.* viii.1.5; x.4.69-71; *P.E.* vii.16.11 (330ab), 17.3 (330d); *De laud.* 10.5-6; see also *Theoph.* i.39-40.

22. Eus. *P.E.* vii.8.4-7 and 11 (306d-7b and 307d).

23. Eus. *H.E.* i.2.6-16; *P.E.* vii.12.8 (321d); *D.E.* i.5.10-18 (10d-11d), v.19.4-5 (246d-47a).

24. Eus. *H.E.* i.2.23.

25. Eus. *P.E.* i.4.2-4 (10ad); *D.E.* vii.2.20-23 (344c-45a), viii.3.9-15 (406b-7b); *De laud.* 16.7-8; *Theoph.* iii.2.

26. Eus. *H.E.* viii.13.14.

27. Eus. *V.C.* i.28-29, 32,47; ii.12-13; *De laud.* 18.1-3.

28. Eus. *V.C.* i.9.

29. See *De civ. Dei* xi.23.

30. Albert C. Outler has given a detailed discussion of Augustine's use of the Logos doctrine at various points in his intellectual development.

See his "The Person and Work of Christ," in *A Companion to the Study of St. Augustine,* ed. Roy W. Battenhouse (New York: Oxford University Press, 1955), pp. 343-70.

31. *De civ. Dei* xiv.9.

32. Cf. the general views of pagan antiquity; see, e.g., E. R. Dodds, "The Ancient Concept of Progress," in *The Ancient Concept of Progress and Other Essays on Greek Literature and Belief* (Oxford: Clarendon Press, 1973), pp. 1-25.

33. See Peter Brown, "The Lost Future," *Augustine of Hippo* (London: Faber & Faber, 1967), chap. 15, pp. 146-57.

34. Eus. *P.E.* vii.8.4–7 and 1 (306d-7b and 307d).

35. *De civ. Dei* iv.17, 33; v.1, 13, 21; xviii.2.

36. *De civ. Dei* v.22.

37. *De civ. Dei* v.19, 23.

38. *De civ. Dei* v.21; cf. v.24 and 25.

39. *De civ. Dei* xv.7; cf. v.25.

40. Henry Chadwick, *The Early Church* (Baltimore: Penguin Books, 1967), pp. 226–27.

41. *The Confessiions* is the account of one human soul's inner spiritual history written along those general lines. It is often a drama of irony, as Augustine makes the right decisions for the wrong reasons, is led in the proper paths by people acting out of improper motives, and gradually makes his progress *toward* his conversion by struggling as hard as he can to *renounce* Christianity. See, for example, *Conf.* i.9.14, 10.16, 12.19; v.6.10-7.13, 8.14, 12.22-13.23; vii.9.13. The over-all effect is to deny any value to human pragmatic calculations when it comes to dealing with God's providence, a point of view that also puts Augustine at odds with Eusebius.

42. *De civ. Dei* i.8; cf. xviii.54.

43. *Cat.* = Sallust, *Bellum Catilinae; Jug.* = *Bellum Jugurthinum.* The Latin text, and the English translations I have quoted, may be found in the Loeb Classical Library edition of Sallust, trans. J. C. Rolfe (London, 1931).

44. For a short summary of the most famous modern theories of when and how Rome fell, see Bryce Lyon, *The Origins of the Middle Ages: Pirenne's Challenge to Gibbon* (New York: W. W. Norton & Co., 1972).

THOMAS AQUINAS, JOHN PUPPER
VON GOCH, AND MARTIN LUTHER:
AN ESSAY IN ECUMENICAL THEOLOGY

Harry McSorley

One of the many things I have learned from Albert Outler is that the Christian theologian, exegete, or church historian ought never to separate himself and his scholarly work from the life and concerns of the Church. Surely one of the greatest concerns of the Church today is reflected in the desire of Christians in all churches to reverse what Outler called "the centuries-old drift into division, in the prospect of overcoming the stubborn, self-righteous fragmentation of the people of God."[1] By his own description an "ardent and unembarrassed advocate of Christian unity, grown old in the service of the ecumenical cause,"[2] Outler stood before the international array of New Testament scholars gathered at the "Festival of the Gospels" in Pittsburgh in 1970 and asked them, among other things, whether "the New Testament guild [has] contributed as much as it might have" to the cause of Christian unity.[3]

In the same address Outler reminded his audience of something that might not be noticed because it is too obvious: if they are Christian scholars, then they are more

The author is Professor of Religious Studies, St. Michael's College, the University of Toronto.

than just New Testament experts, for they speak not only to one another, but also "in and to the Christian community." Using his own work as an illustration, Outler sees himself as a church historian, as a theologian, and as an ecumenist. The strong suggestion here is that the Christian scholar, be he exegete, church historian, or whatever, ought not to narrow the horizons of his inquiries to such an extent that he thinks the only real issues, questions, or concerns are those of his specialized discipline.[4]

It is with these more than simply methodological considerations in mind that I turn to the specific concern of this essay: the relations between Thomas Aquinas, John Pupper of Goch, and Martin Luther. What I have to say here about Luther will scarcely go beyond what I wrote in my earlier study.[5] But what I have to say about the relations between the two theological giants and the relatively obscure Goch[6] will involve a critique of what might be called a status-quo approach to church history in favor of an ecumenical theological approach that asks more rather than fewer questions of the historical materials than does the status-quo approach.[7] The ecumenical theological approach raises these additional historical and theological questions precisely because the one asking them sees himself not just as a church historian or a historical theologian speaking to other church historians and theologians but also as an ecumenical theologian who wants *also* to speak "in and to the Christian community" and to "the cause of Christian unity" today.

I

STATEMENT OF THE PROBLEM AND AN ECUMENICAL-THEOLOGICAL APPROACH TO IT

In my Luther book I reached the cautiously formulated conclusion that had Luther *carefully studied* Thomas' teaching on the evangelical law . . . and the necessity of grace . . . , as well as Thomas' doctrine on faith and works, grace, predestination and man's bondage to sin as set forth above all in his commentaries on the Pauline epistles, there is *every reason to suspect* that he would not only have accepted this doctrine, but would actually have cited it, along with the teaching of Paul and Augustine, against the errors he found in some of the late Scholastics concerning the unaided powers of man's fallen nature in respect to justification.[8]

Working in close contact with me, though quite independently, Otto Pesch, in his monumental study of the doctrine of justification in Luther and Thomas Aquinas—a study intended above all to be a "service to the contemporary ecumenical dialogue"[9]—did not speculate concerning Luther's possible reaction to a careful study of Thomas (which study Luther demonstrably never undertook[10]). Instead, Pesch subjected both great thinkers to a penetrating ecumenical theological analysis. His conclusion, of extraordinary importance for the cause of Christian unity, was that, despite their great differences, not only of conceptualization, but also of over-all theological structure and outlook—differences that do not allow a facile "harmonization"—Luther's "existential theology" and Thomas's "sapiential theology" do not require a mutual anathematization, since both kinds of theology can be regarded as legitimate expressions of the Christian life and both must be retained if Christianity is not to be impoverished.[11]

Alongside these recent Roman Catholic efforts toward a more positive reappraisal of Luther, one finds those of younger Protestant theologians such as Thomas Bonhoeffer,[12] Ulrich Kühn,[13] and Hans Vorster,[14] who are discovering the evangelical character of Thomas Aquinas's theology to such an extent that some want Thomas to be seen as the "common doctor" of both Protestant and Roman Catholic theology.[15]

In the light of the ecumenical concern manifested in this sector of Christian theologians in their approach to historical texts, one is somewhat astonished to read:

> Studies which show the Augustinianism of St. Thomas or the depth of agreement between Luther and Aquinas are interesting, but ultimately irrelevant. The real question is not whether *we* find sufficient Augustinian resources in Thomas, but whether *they* [i.e., Luther, Carlstadt, Staupitz and Goch] did.[16]

The above judgments are contained in a study whose author holds that Luther would have reacted no more favorably to Thomas Aquinas than did the pre-Reformation Catholic, John Pupper of Goch, who "read" Thomas and rejected his teaching on grace as Pelagian.[17]

To an ecumenical theologian the above-cited judgments about what is "ultimately irrelevant" and what "the real question is" indicate what Outler might call a "metahistorical interest"—or rather, disinterest—in the contemporary ecumenical movement. Granted that there are some issues a church historian may want to deal with strictly in terms of the historical materials before him: to determime, for example, who objected to what idea of whom. But when a church historian is dealing with materials and issues quite central to the problem of Christian division, and he sees *in the historical materials* some possible avenues to bypass or surmount Christian division, can he, without betraying a metahistorical non-interest in the cause of Christian unity, say that those possible avenues are "interesting, but ultimately irrelevant"?

The question of relevance inevitably raises the question: Relevant to whom or to what? To those church historians, theologians, and other Christians concerned with the restoration of Christian unity, it is enormously relevant for Protestants to be able to see, for example, the evangelical and

Augustinian quality of the theology of the "common doctor" of Catholic theology, and for Roman Catholics, for example, to learn that it is seriously being contended by Roman Catholics that Luther's central ideas are fundamentally compatible with the Catholic tradition.

For a church historian to say that "the real question" is whether Luther and Goch saw Thomas as sufficiently Augustinian—and to stop with the obvious or easily reached *No* to this question—is to leave the Christian Churches in the grim situation of the status quo (or worse) as far as Christian union is concerned. It may indeed be *a* "real question"—to which varying degrees of negative answers can be given—whether Luther, Goch, or Carlstadt found sufficient Augustinian resources in Thomas. But it is surely not the *only* real question. An ecumenical church historian or theologian always will see it as an equally important question: Did Luther, Goch, *et al.*, try very hard to find sufficient Augustinian resources in Thomas? We know that Luther did not. We are told that Staupitz and Carlstadt did, because "they were trained in Thomistic thought."[18] This overlooks the important fact that to have been trained in Thomistic thought, especially on the eve of the Reformation, is not necessarily the same as to have carefully studied the thought of *Thomas Aquinas*, any more than to have studied Lutheran theology means that one has carefully studied Luther's theology.[19]

As for Goch, whose attack on Thomas we shall examine later, several points should be noted. First, the fact that he refers in general to and cites but twice the *prima secundae* of Thomas's *Summa theologiae* is no evidence that he has either "read" in any degree of completeness this important part of the *Summa*[20] or, *a fortiori*, that he has "evidently read St. Thomas with care."[21] Such contentions can be verified only by the tedious method of comparing what Goch says of

Thomas with what Thomas himself says in the *prima secundae* and elsewhere on the question at issue. Moreover, in those rare instances in which Goch does cite Thomas, we never find him citing the treatise on grace, justification, and merit in the *prima secundae* (qq.109-14). It is thus quite misleading to say, as Steinmetz does, that "Goch, . . . who has read *prima secundae*. . . not only does not quote Thomas's teaching on grace as a model of Augustinianism, but even rejects it as Pelagian."[22] The evidence indicates, on the contrary, that Goch has simply not quoted—and possibly has not even read—Thomas's teaching on grace. If Goch rejects Thomas's teaching on grace, it has to be on some other basis than his having read Thomas's treatise on grace in the *prima secundae*. Another thing: in the passage cited earlier where I spoke of the possible acceptance by Luther of Thomas's teaching on the evangelical law, on the necessity of grace, and other questions, I referred to Thomas's teaching in the *Summa* (qq.106 and 109), but "above all" to his teaching in his Pauline commentaries. Goch gives no indication that he is aware, and strong indication that he is unaware, of Thomas's biblical commentaries, as we shall note below.

The preceding considerations immediately suggest a second additional question, one that could conceivably be at least as "real" to the church historian as the previous two questions, and will always be so for the ecumenical theologian and the ecumenical church historian. Thus, even granting for the sake of discussion that Goch and the other theologians who regard Thomas as "insufficiently Augustinian" had read the entire corpus of Thomas, is this sufficient evidence that they *understood* him? If, as Pesch has pointed out, contemporary authors, even in presumably careful studies of monographic proportions, can still overlook the Christian context of the *secunda pars* of the *Summa*, and if Thomas experts often disagree with other such experts in interpreting him, it is surely not unreasonable to suggest that Goch, in no sense a Thomas specialist, may have misunderstood him.[23]

Despite the fact that historians such as R. R. Post and Luise Abramowski believe Goch's charge that Thomas is Pelagian to be unfounded and based on misunderstanding, [24] David Steinmetz regards such "an appeal to misunderstanding" on Goch's part as "unsatisfying." "Whatever else Goch may be accused of," Steinmetz contends, "he may not be charged with carelessness in reporting and responding to the theological debates of his own time."[25] This high estimate of Goch's interpretative powers is supported by reference to the fact that Goch accurately quoted "from a letter of Stephen of Paris in connection with his discussion of the debate between Peter van den Beeken and Henry of Someren at the University of Louvain,"[26]

Aside from the obvious facts that accurate citation is only the first step toward sound interpretation, and that it is possible to quote someone accurately while grossly misunderstanding him or wresting the accurately cited words from context, it is surely risky business for a historian to regard a particular author as virtually immune from misunderstanding other authors simply because he has accurately *quoted* one or more of them. Goch is not exempt from the (not exclusively) medieval foible of mixing up biblical chapters,[27] nor from the more serious failing of paraphrasing Thomas quite accurately and then placing an interpretation on the text that Thomas elsewhere explicitly repudiates.[28] Worse still—and precisely at the point where Goch believes he has demonstrated that Thomas is Pelagian—he cites St. Paul in opposition to an alleged position of Thomas (it is actually a citation taken out of context) when he could have found a perfectly evangelical, anti-Pelagian statement in Thomas had he consulted Thomas's commentary on the very words from Paul he had cited against Thomas![29] This is just a sample of the many patent and serious misrepresentations of Thomas's thought that can be found in Goch's work. We shall have occasion to note more of them below.

A third "real question" arising from the kind of material we are dealing with is always raised by the ecumenical theologian, even though the church historian as such might not raise it. When there is clearly a case of real disagreement between two theologians, and not mutual or unilateral misunderstanding, does their disagreement demand that one of them be anathematized or regarded as heterodox? Or can one recognize two really different theological viewpoints as legitimate expressions of the one, holy, catholic, and apostolic faith?[30] As we look more directly at John Pupper of Goch and Thomas Aquinas we shall keep in mind all three of these additional questions—questions which, to the ecumenical theologian, are at least as real and as relevant as, What did Luther and Goch think of Thomas Aquinas?

II

GOCH AND HIS POLEMICAL CONTEXT

Separated by almost two centuries, John Pupper of Goch and Thomas Aquinas were never able to enter into dialogue with one another. Having read some of Aquinas's work, however, Goch found it necessary to attack Thomas because he thought that Thomas tended toward Pelagianism and contradicted "the manifest and patent truth" of Sacred Scripture.[31] On the face of it this seems to be, as Steinmetz calls it, an "absurd and misdirected slur on what was patently one of the most Augustinian theological systems to be developed in medieval Europe."[32] When one realizes, however, that Goch wrote in a context quite different from that of Thomas—he faced a revived Semi-Pelagianism—then one can better understand his sensitivity to questions concerning grace, merit, works, and such items.[33] But why should he attack Thomas Aquinas, whose anti-(Semi-)Pelagianism is so well established?[34]

In the light of what we have already seen and shall continue to see concerning Goch's inadequate dealing with Thomas's work, it is hardly satisfying to suppose that, after a careful study of Thomas's teaching on grace and merit, he judged Thomas to be in fundamental opposition to "canonical truth." A comparison of Goch's charges against Thomas (or, more often, "the Thomists") with the actual text *and context* of Thomas has convinced me that, in more cases than can be listed in this essay, Goch is rejecting a straw-Thomas. As was noted at the end of the previous section, there are indeed some *real* points of opposition between Goch and Thomas, as there are between virtually any two theologians. One thinks of their over-all estimate of the role of the vows (for Goch they were for the weaker Christians),[35] the way they understand the distinction between bishops and priests,[36] and their disagreement concerning which Christian lifestyle should be regarded as the "state of perfection."[37] On these and other such points there has been and still is room for diversity of opinion in both the pre- and post-Reformation Roman Catholic Church.

Why should a man like Goch fail to be a competent reporter (especially concerning contexts), not to mention interpreter of Aquinas when, in another situation, he was given high marks?[38] Perhaps the key to Goch's puzzling attack on Thomas is to be found precisely in the polemical situation that arose out of Goch's struggle with "the Thomists." We are reduced to a "perhaps" here because, while applauding Steinmetz's insistence on locating Goch "within the setting of the late 15th century,"[39] we still need more historical information about that setting in order to assess better the polemical *attitude* evidenced in Goch's treatment of Thomas.[40]

Who *were* Goch's contemporary, Semi-Pelagianizing opponents? It is clear that they were members of the mendicant
orders, mainly the Thomists, whom we may presumably
identify as the Dominicans and, to a lesser extent, the
Franciscans.[41] It also seems likely that one specific opponent
was Engelbert Cultificis (Messmaker), O.P., a teacher in
Zütphen and prior of the convent at Zwolle, who had
attacked Goch before and after publication of the *De
libertate christiana* and seems to have occasioned that and the
Epistola apologetica.[42] Locating and making available the
works of Messmaker and other opponents of Goch would
seem to be an indispensable historical task if we are to situate
Goch properly in his context. Who are the authors of his day
who advanced the kind of horrendous theses Goch rightly
attacked, such as: In the early Church the Apostles and all
the faithful lived their Christian lives under the obligation of
a vow?[43] Until such questions are resolved by historians it is
only to a partial extent that we can speak of understanding
the context of Goch's work.

In the meantime, is it implausible to work with the
hypothesis that this devout but angry Christian theologian,
fed up with the extravagant claims made for the life
according to the vows by some of the Flemish Dominicans
around him, decided that the best way to overthrow their
pretensions was to poke holes in the work of their great
theological luminary, Thomas Aquinas?[44] Until further
historical research suggests another hypothesis, this seems to
be a reasonable way to explain not only Goch's attack on
Thomas, but also its poor quality, arising as it did out of
polemical concerns and not out of a desire to achieve genuine
understanding of Thomas.

A final word about Goch's context. Granting that he was a
nominalist, is it correct to say that he found in *nominalism*
the resources to attack the revived Semi-Pelagianism of the

fifteenth century?[45] When I read Goch's works there is no question in my mind that the weapons Goch uses above all—as did the nominalist Gregory of Rimini a century before against similar opponents—are, first, the New Testament, and second, St. Augustine.[46] Goch does not reject Thomas because he is insufficiently nominalist but because he is "insufficiently Augustinian."[47] When we see specified the twofold basis of this rejection, however, we find that they are the distinctly *non*-Augustinian themes of the divine accepta- tion and the denial of man's cooperation with grace.[48] Nor does it clarify the picture when we are assured that "if nominalism is purged of inadequately Augustinian views of the fall and of the disposition for the reception of grace, it allows itself to be exploited in a radically Augustinian direction."[49] Precisely the same can be said, *mutatis mu- tandi*, of both Semi-Pelagianism and Pelagianism!

III

GOCH'S CRITIQUE OF THOMAS AQUINAS

Goch has a number of negatively critical things to say about Thomas and "the Thomists." We shall restrict ourselves to examining only that "false opinion contrary to canonical truth" which Goch attributes to Thomas and to the refutation of which he devotes the entire third part of his treatise, *De libertate christiana.*

The "False Opinion" on Merit and Its "First Error"

The false, anti-biblical opinion is "that merit is an act or a labor to which a reward is owed out of a debt of justice, according to Matt. 20: 'Call the workers and give them their pay.'"[50] This opinion, says Goch, distinguishes between *meritum digni, congrui*, and *condigni*, which distinctions he

then proceeds to explain.[51] Up to this point Goch has not
attributed the false opinion to Thomas. In fact, the threefold
distinction of merit he mentions is found in Bonaventure and
other Scholastics, but not in Thomas.[52]

Continuing, however, Goch says, "This and things like this
which are foreign to canonical truth you will find many times
in the writings of modern doctors on the *Book of Sentences*,
especially in the various writings of doctor St. Thomas
Aquinas."[53] He then lists, with no more precise reference,
Thomas's commentary on *I Sent.*, d.7, *II Sent.*, d.27, *III
Sent.*, d.18 and "the *prima secundae*, etc."[54]

Before continuing, it is useful to note that, in contradis-
tinction to Capreolus, the early fifteenth-century "prince of
the Thomists,"[55] and to such nominalists as Gerson[56] and
Biel,[57] the affirmation that merit is an act to which a reward
is due *ex debito iustitiae* is foreign to Thomas. When the
mature Thomas deals with the question of merit explicitly in
the *prima secundae*, question 114—a text Goch unpardonably
never cites even though he criticizes Thomas's doctrine of
merit—Thomas says:

> Because our action has no *ratio* of merit except on the presupposi-
> tion of the divine ordination, it does not follow that God is simply
> made a debtor to us, but to himself, inasmuch as it is *debitum* that
> he should fulfill his ordination.[58]

If Goch is opposing a view of merit in which God owes man a
heavenly reward out of a debt of justice, then he is not
opposing the teaching of Thomas. Goch would *really* be
opposing Thomas only if he were to maintain that God is not
obliged or bound *to himself* to keep the promises he has
made or if he were to hold that the divine grace of adoption
does not tend of itself to eternal life.[59]

The Pelagian heresy, says Goch, had trouble distinguishing
"the natural movements of the will from the supernatural

movements of grace,"[60] and it "totally ascribed the merit of
eternal life to the natural faculty of the will, leaving nothing
to grace."[61] This heresy, he says, still grows imperceptibly
like a cancer "in various writings of various doctors" who,
although they say the grace of God is necessary for merit,
foolishly do not attribute merit to grace alone, but say that
the human will and the grace of God together cause merit.[62]
This is an error, Goch claims, which St. Paul tried to
eliminate in nearly all of his epistles, especially in the first
eleven chapters of Romans. "Thus it is very astonishing that a
man of such holiness and excellence as doctor St. Thomas
presumed to write something against such manifest and
patent truth."[63]

Having stated and elaborated upon the false opinion, Goch
next lists four errors arising out of the false opinion. For the
sake of brevity and because the method used in our critique
of Goch in the next section is readily applicable to the other
three "errors," we shall give direct attention only to the
"first error" of this false opinion—namely, "that the natural
will of man cooperates with the grace of God in man's
justification and in meriting eternal beatitude."[64]

According to Goch, Thomas Aquinas holds this error when
he says in two different places: (1) in *II Sent.*, d.28:
"Although the free will is not a sufficient cause of merit, it is
however an efficient cause"; and (2) in the *prima secundae*,
q.21: "Although a man is moved by God as an instrument,
this does not exclude that he can still also move himself by
free will. And therefore through his act he merits or demerits
in the sight of God."[65]

In opposition to the first of the two citations from
Thomas, which I have been unable to locate, Goch cites
Rom. 3:32f.; Rom. 8:30, 33f.; Rom. 9 (concerning Esau and
Jacob), and Augustine's comments on the latter passage in his
Enchiridion. He then concludes:

Behold, you see through these testimonies of the Scriptures that
the natural will of man does not cooperate with the grace of God
for the merit by which a man is justified, but this only happens
through justifying grace with the consent of the will, lest anyone
believe a man can be justified unwillingly.[66]

Against the second statement of Thomas, which is a direct
citation from I-II, q.21, a.4, ad 2, Goch says it is true that,
by his own act, man "demerits" in God's eyes, but false to
say that man merits by his own act. He cites the Vulgate
rendering of Hos. 13:9: "Your perdition is from yourself,
Israel; your help is from me alone." This means, says Goch,
(1) that by his proper act man demerits, since God is not the
author or the cooperator of evil; and (2) virtuous good is
only from God, since God is the author of all good things,
not however without the consent of man's will, although
without the cooperation of the will, for no one is forced to
accept the gifts of God if he doesn't want to do so. "Many
more things are required for merit than for demerit," he
continues, and "man cannot move himself through free will
to an act of virtue meritorious of eternal life."[67]

A Critique of Goch's Critique

In assessing Goch's critique of Thomas Aquinas, two things
should be noted first of all from the methodological
viewpoint. First, Goch accuses Thomas of a teaching on
merit closely akin to Pelagianism and of contradicting the
New Testament by citing only the early work of Thomas[68]
and that part of the mature work preceding his anti-Pelagian
doctrine on grace in which his systematic teaching on merit is
located. He cites a question in the *prima secundae* which
simply is not dealing with the "many more things" that Goch
knows, and Thomas knows, are required for an act to be
meritorious of eternal life.[69] In short, Goch does not
undertake a careful study of Aquinas's teaching on merit, but

simply reacts to passages taken out of the context of Thomas's complete, mature teaching. Is this not a sign of the worst kind of polemical argumentation?

Second, against this abridged and distorted version of Thomas's teaching on merit, Goch invokes the testimony of Scripture, especially of St. Paul, with no apparent awareness that the holy doctor he is attacking has commented extensively on virtually all the biblical passages he cites. Again, the basic methodological, and perhaps psychological, conditions for a critique of the real Thomas are lacking.

These methodological shortcomings lead to substantive errors which, at least by implication, grossly misrepresent Thomas contradicts the clear truth contained in Rom. 1-11, commentary on Romans, for example, Goch can say that Thomas contradicts the clear truth contained in Rom. 1-11, where Paul "commends the efficacy of the grace of God and eliminates all presumption of human acts."[70] Anyone who has read Thomas's commentary on Rom. 1-11 will perceive the absurdity, if not the calumny, of Goch's accusation. In the prologue to his commentary Thomas notes that the reason Romans is listed first among Paul's epistles, despite the fact that it was not chronologically first, is that the Romans dominated the world and needed to have the malice of pride exposed as "the beginning of all sin." Moreover, Thomas regards Rom. 1:16*b* through Rom. 11 as a treatise "on the power of evangelical grace."[71] Indeed, Paul's epistles are "a complete doctrine of the grace of Christ."[72] The reader of Thomas's commentaries on Paul will soon see that Thomas has learned from Paul "to eliminate all presumption of human acts."[73]

When Goch asserts that "the modern doctors . . . do not attribute merits to the grace of God alone, but affirm that the human will and the grace of God together cause merit,"[74] it is necessary to examine the two clauses

separately. Concerning the first clause, we have already seen
evidence that Thomas—if not the other "moderns"—does
attribute all justification and merit to God.[75] Concerning the
second, it is clear that for both Goch *and* Thomas the human
will and the grace of God are *involved* in merit and
justification.

For Thomas, free will is *involved* in merit but, as Pesch
puts it after intensive research of Thomas's texts and
contexts, the free will is involved insofar as the meritorious
act is an act of man, not insofar as it is meritorious: "The
free act is the *locus* of merit, its condition, if you will—but
not its ground."[76]

When Goch comes down against "the human will and the
grace of God" as together causing merit, these words can be
misleading unless they are taken in the context of his earlier
important distinction between "the natural will" and "the
graced (*gratuita*) will."[77] "The natural will ... can do
nothing to merit eternal beatitude," says Goch, who is
completely at one here with Thomas Aquinas.[78] And it is
this *natural* will that does not cooperate with grace in
meritorious acts or in justification.[79]. But merit does
proceed from the "graced will"—that is, "the will reformed
through grace."[80] In this sense Goch accepts the statement
that "merit proceeds from grace and from the will."[81]

For Goch, grace both heals the corrupt natural will and
prepares it for doing good in two ways: (1) "by the infusion
of supernatural liberty and power it prepares the will that it
might will good through a love of justice"; and (2) "it
cooperates with the will that wills good through a love of
justice so that it might will efficaciously, that is, that it might
achieve its effect by the *cooperation* of [grace]."[82] Goch goes
so far as to say: "This [graced] *will alone* is the principle of
all those things which we supernaturally will and can do, and

therefore all merit is from it," indeed, "as from an efficient cause."[83] From the graced will "proceed works of justice with the cooperation of the Holy Spirit."[84] And, in an important nuance, Goch seems to say that even the *natural* free will, although it does not cooperate as does the graced will, from which it is readily distinguished,[85] nevertheless consents to the grace of justification.[86]

Aware that some of Augustine's statements appear to say that the "natural will cooperates with grace in justification," by appealing to Augustine's larger context Goch is able to conclude:

> When [Augustine] says nothing should be attributed to the will in regard to man's justification, but only to God and his grace, this should be understood as the natural will. But when he says man's justification takes place from grace and the will, this should be understood as the graced will.[87]

Although an actual dialogue between Goch and Thomas never took place, it is possible for an ecumenical theologian to create or at least suggest the outline of such a dialogue, especially when he sees Goch's willingness to interpret an author in context, as he does with Augustine. The theologian would point out to Goch that, if Thomas seems to be saying that the human will and the grace of God together cause merit,[88] just as in the case of Augustine this should be understood of the "graced" will, not the natural will. Nowhere will Goch find either the younger or the mature Thomas saying that "the natural will of man cooperates with the grace of God in his own justification or in meriting eternal life."[89] And if Thomas says that man, although he is moved by God, is still able to move himself by means of free will, thus making his act meritorious,[90] this is to be understood in the light of Thomas's fuller context—namely, in the sense that "the Holy Spirit causes the very movement of the free will in man, according to Phil. 2:13."[91]

When Goch cites Rom. 3:23 against those who say that man is "justified by his own acts of the natural will," let it be pointed out by the ecumenical theologian that such a thought is totally foreign to Thomas Aquinas, who says in his commentary on Rom. 3:23: "Man must not ascribe this glory [that mentioned in Rom. 3:23] to himself," for he cannot be justified of himself, but is justified "without any preceding merits of works" through the grace of God, "to whom is owed the glory."[92]

And when Goch invokes Rom. 8:30 and 8:33f. against those who say that the "natural will of man does not cooperate with God," and that "man does not cooperate in his justification except by his will consenting to God working in him," let it be noted that Thomas, in his commentary on Rom. 8:30, teaches that an internal call of God is necessary "because our heart would not turn to God unless God himself draws us to him."[93] In his treatise on grace, moreover, Thomas rejects the view that God does not work justification in us by grace alone.[94]

Goch cites Rom. 9:11-15, presumably against Thomas, to show that the "natural will of man does not cooperate with the grace of God in the merit by which a man is justified."[95] Leaving aside the fact that, for Thomas, man can in no way merit justification,[96] and turning only to Thomas's commentary on Romans, we find him saying: (1) "the will of God is the cause of every good that is in the creature"; (2) the just are promised a reward "because of merits which they do not have from themselves";[97] (3) these good merits themselves are from God and are the effect of predestination;[98] and (4) "God's will alone" and not any merits following grace is the ground (*ratio*) of God's mercy and predestination and of our liberation.[99]

Finally, when Goch invokes Hos. 13:9—"Your perdition is from yourself, Israel; your help is from me alone"—to support his attack on the second text drawn from Thomas which allegedly favored the "first error" arising from "the first false opinion," it might have interested and perhaps even pleased Goch to see how Thomas understood the same biblical verse. In his Romans commentary Thomas uses Hos. 13:9 to testify to the view that the wicked are punished because of the sins they have of themselves, not from God. The just are rewarded, however, "because of merits which they do not have from themselves."[100] In the *Summa theologiae* Thomas sees the verse as teaching "that the first cause of the loss of grace is from God."[101] Again, in man, "whatever pertains to a defect is of man, but whatever pertains to salvation and perfection is of God."[102]

Space limitations do not permit me to scrutinize as carefully as I have the first, the other three errors Goch sees as arising out of the false opinion he is attacking. To some extent at least, the second and fourth errors have already been addressed.[103] A very brief response can be made to Goch's treatment of the third error—"that merit also has some efficacy from the genus of a good work."[104] Goch argues against this error by pointing out that generically good acts do not have of themselves a remunerable goodness, but receive this from the graced will as cause and principle of merit and from a right intention toward God as the principal end.[105] Accordingly, "a vow, even though it is an act of worship, if it is without charity it is not meritorious."[106]

With this conclusion, of course, Thomas would completely agree. He says, in fact: "An act of *faith* is not meritorious unless faith works through love. . . . Likewise an act of

patience and of fortitude is not meritorious unless someone
does this out of charity."[107] Once again Goch has attacked
an unreal Thomas, by taking the real Thomas out of context.
In this case Goch isolates a text in the *secunda secundae* from
the grace context of the *prima secundae*, whereas Thomas
surely expected the careful reader of II-II, q.88, a.6, to
remember that he had already insisted earlier that there can
be *no* merit without charity.[108]

This is an essay in ecumenical theology, not the monograph that still needs to be written if one wishes to
investigate further the questions: How well did Goch understand Thomas on other matters where he is critical of him?
Were his other criticisms of Thomas theologically and
historically better founded than the ones we have examined
in this essay? To what extent is there real opposition between
the two theologians? Is it the kind of opposition that involves
legitimate theological differences of opinion, or is it of a
more serious nature? These questions are just as important,
if not more so, to the ecumenical theologian as the questions: Did John Pupper of Goch attack Thomas, and on
what grounds? In attempting to answer historical and
theological questions such as these, I hope I have demonstrated that the ecumenical theologian has to do more, not
less, historical work than the one who does not deal with
such questions.

IV

CONCLUSION

To summarize the main findings of this study and some of
their historical, theological, and ecumenical implications:

1. John Pupper of Goch, attacked by theologians from the
mendicant orders who apparently set forth extravagant
claims for their form of the Christian life, responded (a) by a

radical distinction between the helplessness of man's "natural will" and the power of man's "graced will" as far as justification and merit are concerned, and (b) by defending the superiority of the *status perfectionis* of the secular clergy.

2. Perhaps out of a desire to attack his Dominican opponents at the presumed source of their theological inspiration, Goch launched an attack on Thomas Aquinas, accusing him of a new form of Pelagianism and of contradicting biblical truth.

3. In his attack on Thomas, Goch flagrantly violates basic canons of interpretation—above all, the precept of interpreting texts within their context. Moreover, although he repeatedly accuses Thomas of contradicting the Scripture, Goch shows no awareness of Thomas's extensive biblical commentaries, a factor that is of decisive importance for understanding Goch's negative judgment of Thomas.

4. Goch's negative judgment of Thomas, however misplaced, is grounded primarily on the New Testament and on St. Augustine. One does not find him appealing to any specifically nominalist tenet in opposing what he thinks are Pelagian tendencies in his contemporaries and in Thomas.

5. By confronting Goch's critique of Thomas's teaching on merit with the actual texts and the context of Thomas, one finds no substantial disgreement between them concerning justified man's cooperation with grace in the merit of eternal life.

6. It is quite possible that the reading of Goch's anti—Thomistic treatises was an important factor in the shaping or the hardening of Luther's negative attitude toward Thomas, whose actual works he never studied.

7. Had John Pupper of Goch or Martin Luther *carefully studied* Thomas's teaching on grace and merit as set forth above all in the *Summa theologiae* and in his commentaries on the Pauline epistles, there is every reason to suspect that

they would not only have accepted this doctrine, but would actually have cited it, along with the teaching of Paul and Augustine, against the errors they found in some of the late Scholastics.

8. Characteristic of the work of ecumenical theologians, among other things, is the refusal to allow past opposition between Christian theologians or Churches to escape critical contemporary examination along lines such as were suggested in this essay.

NOTES

1. Albert C. Outler, *The Christian Tradition and the Unity We Seek* (New York: Oxford University Press, 1957), p. 3.

2. Albert C. Outler, Preface to *That the World May Believe* (New York: Board of Missions of the Methodist Church, 1966), p. xi.

3. Albert C. Outler, "The Interpretation of the Gospels Today: Some Questions About Aims and Warrants," in *Jesus and Man's Hope*, ed. D. G. Miller and D. Y. Hadidian, vol. 2 (Pittsburgh: Pittsburgh Theological Seminary, 1971), p. 53.

4. Ibid., pp. 48, 51–52.

5. *Luther: Right or Wrong?* (New York: Newman Press—Minneapolis: Augsburg Publishing House, 1969). Henceforth cited as *Luther*.

6. A priest of the dioceses of Malines (d. 1475) Goch became rector of a house of Augustinian canonesses. He published four theological works (in Antwerp in 1521/22; see n. 27 below) in which he attacked Scholastic theology. They caught Luther's attention, and in a congratulatory letter serving as a preface to a 1522 or 1523 printing, Luther praised Goch as a *"vere Germanus et gnesios Theologus"* (WA 10/II, 330, 5). Whether Luther studied Goch's works carefully or understood him correctly has been doubted by such Luther scholars as H. Boehmer; see his *Martin Luther: Road to Reformation* (New York: Meridian Books, 1957), p. 146. In any event, the context of Luther's letter makes it clear that Luther was heartened by Goch's attack on the Scholastics. The possibility thus arises—and it cannot be further pursued in this essay—that Goch's anti-Scholastic, and conspicuously

anti-Thomistic, work may have been an important factor in shaping and/or hardening Luther's negative attitude toward Scholasticism in general and Thomas Aquinas in particular. See *Luther*, pp. 139 – 41.

7. On the concept of ecumenical theology see the Preface by H. Fries to *Luther*, pp. 1-4.

8. Ibid. (emphasis added). This view, which is based on my own study of the texts and thus stresses the Paulinism and Augustinianism of Thomas on the decidedly Christian themes, *may* also have been influenced by my reading of J. Lortz, and especially by his contention (which I continue to share) that Luther was rejecting a "Catholicism that was not fully Catholic." Despite my admiration for Lortz's achievement in altering the course of Roman Catholic Luther scholarship, at an early stage in my own Luther research I abandoned his major critique of Luther's alleged "subjectivism." In any case I do not see myself as a member of the "Lortz school," having studied under neither Lortz nor his students.

9. *Die Theologie der Rechtfertigung bei Martin Luther und Thomas von Aquin* (Mainz: M. Grünewald-Verlag, 1967), p. 6.

10. *Luther*, pp. 139-41. On p. 9 Pesch does insist, however, that it is not just hypothetical game-playing to ask whether Luther would have become embroiled in so hopeless an argument with Thomas himself as he did with Eck and Cajetan.

11. Pesch, pp. 947-50. On pp. 5 and 951 Pesch refers to the increasing number of Protestant and Roman Catholic scholars who share similar conclusions about the basic compatibility between Luther and Thomas.

12. *Die Gotteslehre des Thomas von Aquin als Sprachproblem* (Tübingen: J. C. B. Mohr, 1961).

13. *Via Caritatis: Theologie des Gesetzes bei Thomas von Aquin* (Göttingen: Vandenhoeck und Ruprecht, 1965).

14. *Das Freiheitsverständnis bei Thomas von Aquin und Martin Luther* (Göttingen: Vandenhoeck und Ruprecht, 1965).

15. T. Bonhoeffer. p. 3; Kühn, pp. 13-14.

16. David C. Steinmetz, "*Libertas Christiana*: Studies in the Theology of John Pupper of Goch (d. 1475)," *Harvard Theological Review*, 65.2 (April, 1972): 209. Henceforth cited as HTR.

17. HTR, p. 207, n. 6. We shall examine below the extent to which Goch has "read" Thomas.

18. HTR, pp. 207-9.

19. Cf. Pesch, pp. 9 and 952, and *Luther*, p. xi. In the Preface to the 1933 edition (Paris: Lethielleux) of Book III of Thomas's *Scriptum super Sententiis M. P. Lombardi* (henceforth *In III Sent.*), the editor, M. F. Moos, laments that too many people still know Thomas from afar and not from the sources. I personally know of a Dominican house of studies where, at least until recently, the students learned at least some of their "Thomism" from neo-Thomistic manuals, not from the writings of Thomas himself. To equate opinions that Goch ascribes to "the Thomists" with "the idea of Thomas" himself, as is done in HTR, pp. 225-26, is something like equating the anathematizations of the Council of Trent with the teachings of Luther and Calvin.

20. HTR, p. 207, n. 6.

21. HTR, p. 205.

22. HTR, p. 207, n. 6. For Goch's use of the two texts cited from the *Prima secundae* see nn. 28 and 29.

23. Pesch, p. 405 and his n. 24.

24. HTR, p. 206.

25. HTR, p. 207.

26. Ibid., n. 5. Leo X likewise cites Luther many times, word for word, in *Exsurge Domine*, but few would contend that this evidenced a careful study of Luther by Leo or his advisors. Cf. *Luther*, pp. 251-53.

27. For example, John 15 instead of John 13 in *De libertate christiana*, IV, 10, 247[= *Lib.*] , ed. F. Pijper, *Bibliotheca Reformatoria Neerlandica*, 6 (Hague, 1910): 1-236. Other works of Goch, along with their abbreviations, are: *De quatuor erroribus circa legem evangelicam exortis et de votis et religionibus facticiis dialogus* [*Dial.*] , ed. C. G. F. Walch, *Monumenta medii aevi*, 1.4 (G 1760): 74-239; *De scholasticorum scriptis et religiosorum votis epistola apologetica* [*Epist.*] , ed. C. G. F. Walch, *Monumenta . . .* , 2.1 (Göttingen, 1767): 1-24; *Fragmenta* [*Frag*] , ed. F. Pijper, *Bibliotheca Reformatoria Neerlandica*, 11 (Hague, 1910): 267-347; partially reproduced in G. A. Benrath, ed., *Reformtheologen des 15. Jahrhunderts* (Gütersloh: G. Mohn, 1968), "Texte zur Kirchen- und Theologiegeschichte," pt. 7, pp. 9-38.

28. See Goch's handling of *Summa theologiae* [= ST], I-II, q. 108,

a.4, in *Lib*. IV, 9-10, 245-50, where he attributes to Thomas, with no basis in the text cited, the view that there is a "two-fold perfection of the evangelical law, one consisting in the precepts, for the generality of Chrisitans, the other in the counsels, for prelates and religious," *Lib*. IV, 10, 247. As Pesch, p. 446, n. 22, has pointed out: It is decisive "that the doctrine concerning commandment and counsel does *not* involve a two-fold perfection." Curiously, just a few pages later, *Lib*. IV, 11, 253, Goch correctly cites Thomas's teaching in ST II-II, q. 184, a.3, that perfection consists in the precepts, not in the counsels, to support his earlier incorrect charge *against* Thomas's alleged teaching that there is a twofold perfection.

29. The margin of *Lib*. III, 3, 190, like that of the text just cited, IV, 10, 247, has been equipped by the 1910 editor with a small hand, the index finger of which points to the lines where Goch makes the reader choose between St. Paul and St. Thomas. Goch contrasts Titus 3:4-5—we are saved not by our works of justice but by God's mercy—with a sentence from ST I-II, not from the questions dealing with grace, justification, and merit (qq. 109—14), but from q.21, a.4, ad 2, where Thomas is examining the basic structure of any meritorious act and is abstracting *for the moment* from the requirement of grace that is stressed in I-II, q. 114. See Pesch, p. 773, n. 75.

Goch has Thomas saying more than he does in I-II, q.21, a.4—where eternal life is not mentioned—and less than he does in I-II, q.114, where the grace of God *is* mentioned. In neither place does Thomas speak of a "*praemium ex debito iustitiae*." Goch also neglects the simplest way in which his reader can "compare the words of Paul and of Thomas"—namely, by consulting Thomas's commentary on Titus 3:5:

When he says "Not by works, etc." he posits the basis of salvation: and he first excludes the presumed basis and secondly he shows the true basis. The presumed basis is that we are saved on account of our merits, which he excludes. . . . But the true basis is the mercy of God alone. . . . *S. Thomas Aquinatis Super Epistolas S. Pauli Lectura*, 2 (Rome: Marietti, 1953), *In Titum*, 3:5, n. 89.

30. One thinks, for example, of Goch's view, which contrasts with

that of Thomas, that the priesthood, not the life according to the vows, is the *status perfectionis* (cf. *Dial*. 20, 199ff., and ST II–II, q.184, a.5), and the related opinion, also in conflict with Thomas, that it is only according to the *consuetudo ecclesiae*, not according to the original *ordinatio divina*, that priests cannot administer all the sacraments (*Dial*. 20, 207ff.). The Council of Trent was aware of both sets of views and it rejected neither of them, in keeping with the over-all intention of Trent not to settle questions disputed among the Scholastics which were not directly involved in the crisis of the Reformation. Goch's view (not his alone, to be sure) of the relation of the *sacerdos* to the *episcopus* is in fact gaining ground in contemporary Roman Catholic thinking about the ministry. For the ecumenical implications of Goch's view, which reaches back at least to St. Jerome, see my "Recognition of a Presbyterial Succession?" *Concilium*, 4 (1972): 23-32.

31. *Lib*. III, 1, 184.

32. HTR, p. 205.

33. Cf. *Luther*, pp. 193-215.

34. Cf. ibid., pp 167ff.

35. *Dial*. 15, 163-71.

36. *Dial*. 20, 206-10.

37. See n. 30 above. HTR, p. 208, n. 8, and 210, n. 13, exaggerates the extent of the disagreement between Goch and Thomas by asserting, with no reference to Thomas's teaching, that the two theologians disagree on (1) the simplicity of God (but cf. *Lib*. II, 40, 165, and ST I, q.3, a.7); (2) the goodness of God (cf. *Lib*. III, 7, 200, and ST I, q.21, a.3; I-II, q.114, a. 3, ad 2); (3) predestination first to glory, then to grace (cf. *Lib*. II, 29, 140, and ST I, q.23, a.4); (4) the dialectic of the *potentia dei absoluta* and *ordinata* (cf. *Lib*. I, 14, 65, and ST I, q.25, a.5, ad 1); (5) the notion that Mary did not merit being the *theotokos* by her *own*, *natural* powers (cf. *Lib*. I, 23, 86, and ST III, q.82, a.11, ad 3); (6) the doctrine of acceptation (df. *Frag* 306-7 and n. 78 below).

38. See the text above at n. 26.

39. HTR, pp. 205 and 207.

40. Goch is able to read Augustine with great care and sensitivity, benignly interpreting texts that could otherwise be given an unevangelical meaning. Cf. *Lib* II, 29, 141-44, and I, 25, 90. Yet, in dealing with Thomas, when confronted with a clarification from the *Summa contra*

Gentiles, III, 138, that would nullify the tendentious interpretation he has just given to ST II-II, q.88, a.4, Goch, instead of concluding that he ought to study Thomas more, simply says Thomas "doesn't understand himself" (*Dial.* 8, 119; 9, 130).

41. HTR, p. 224, n. 38, and p. 230.

42. Cf. Pijper, *Bibl. Ref. Neerl.*, VI, 19, 275-76, and *Lib.* I, 1, 42-45.

43. Cf. *Lib.* I, 7, 54, and *Dial.* 1, 75-76.

44. E.G., *Dial* 7, 108-13.

45. HTR, pp. 207 and 217.

46. In *Lib.* III, 1, 184, for example, Goch states that Thomas errs because he opposes "such manifest and patent truth" as is found in Paul's epistles. Cf. *Dial.* 1, 77-78.

47. HTR, p. 211.

48. Ibid.

49. HTR, p. 216. Is it really fair to say that Goch, through nominalism or otherwise, "was able to defend the Augustinian *sola gratia* against Ockham and Biel in a far more emphatic way than was possible for Aquinas" (ibid.) and to buttress this judgment with two Gochian misinterpretations of Thomas's thought (on *Lib.* III, 3, 190, see n. 29 above; on III, 1, 184, see section 3 below), instead of searching out the texts in which Thomas defends the *sola gratia* by *affirming* it, along with the *sola fide* and the *sola misericordia Dei*? Cf. n. 29 above and Thomas, *Super Epistolas S. Pauli Lectura*, 1, *In Rom.* 3:28, n. 317; 4:5, n. 330; 7:25, n. 592; 9:15, nn. 773 and 775; and 2, *In I Tim..* 1:8, nn. 22 and 23.

50. *Lib.* III, 1, 182: "Quod meritum est actus vel labor cui ex debito iustitiae debetur premium, iuxta illud Matth. xx. Voca operarios. . . . "

51. *Lib.* III, 1, 182-83.

52. See J. Auer, *Die Entwicklung der Gnadenlehre in der Hochscholastik*, pt. 2 (Freiburg: Herder, 1951), pp. 77-80, and J. Rivière, art. "Mérite," *Dictionnaire de théologie catholique*, vol. 10, col. 688. In HTR, p. 211, n. 19, on the contrary, we are told that "Goch is familiar with" this threefold "Thomist distinction" and that if he disagrees with Thomas "it is not because of his ignorace of Thomas' position in the *Summa theologiae*." Goch does differ from the real Thomas by defending Peter Lombard's thesis that charity is *only* to be understood

as the indwelling Holy Spirit, the *gratia increata*. On this question and the related question of grace as a *quaedam habitus* see Pesch, pp. 628-59. For the role of the *acceptatio divina* and the *gratia increata* in Thomas see Pesch, p. 632.

53. *Lib.* III, 1, 183.

54. Ibid. *In I Sent.*, d.7, the subject matter concerns the generation of the Son by the Father, not the doctrine of merit. *In II Sent.*, d.27, q.1, a.3, ad 4, Thomas explicitly states that God is not made a debtor to us, except perhaps because of his promise, since he has promised a reward to those doing good. He says distributive justice is involved in Christian merit, not strict or commutative justice; and in distributive justice the notion of debt is not required on the part of the one distributing, since he can distribute *ex liberalitate*. In ST I, q.21, a.1, ad 3, Thomas elaborates on the notion of God as *debitor sui*. *In III Sent.*, d.18, a. 2, he also speaks of a reward *secundum iustitiam*, but explains again that he is speaking of distributive justice, not the justice involved in buying and selling. Cf. ST I-II, q.112, a.3, ad 1. Theologically one might find Thomas's use of "justice" even in this derived sense misleading, and prefer not to use it. But to say that in doing so Thomas is totally unsupported by, or contradicts, the Scriptures is quite another matter. Cf. his commentary on Hebr. 6:10, but also the greater reserve he shows in ST I-II, q.111, a.1, ad 2, where he refused to admit that God is in any way obligated to creatures. Cf. also *In Rom.* 9:15, n. 773.

55. *Defensiones theologiae D. Thomae Aquinatis*, ed. C. Pabant and T. Pègues (Turin, 1900), p. 88. As in Thomas, however, this is a debt owed not to man but to God himself.

56. See Rivière, *art. cit.*, col. 689.

57. See H. Oberman, *The Harvest of Medieval Theology*, rev. ed. (Grand Rapids, Mich.: Wm. B. Eerdmans, 1967). pp. 170 and 467. In opposing such a thesis as is held by Biel but not by Thomas, Goch relies here as elsewhere primarily on "the manifest testimonies of Scripture" (*Lib.* III, 1, 183).

58. I-II, q. 114, a.1, ad 3.

59. In I-II, q.114, a.3, Thomas, invoking Rom. 8:17, speaks of the inheritance owed to us as adopted sons of God under the *ius adoptionis*. Cf. n. 54 and Pesch, pp. 771-92.

60. *Lib.* III, 1, 184.

61. Ibid.

62. Ibid.: "Doctores vero moderni et si gratiam dei ad meritum necessariam asserunt, in hoc tamen desipiunt, quod soli gratiae dei simul meritum causare affirmant."

63. Ibid.

64. *Lib*. III, 2, 184.

65. *Lib*. III, 2, 184-85.

66. *Lib*. III, 2, 184-87.

67. Ibid., 187.

68. I have been unable to find in Thomas's commentary on *II Sent.*, d.28, the language Goch attributes to him. One has to agree with Pesch, p. 665, however, that we find in this early work a sometimes "shocking teaching." Pesch does not agree that this can rightly be called Semi-Pelagian teaching. It is better, he thinks, to see there the "latent principles" of the more mature teaching.

69. Pesch, p. 771, n. 70, points out that "Only the *Sentences Commentary* and the *Summa theol*. (2, d.27: 1, 3-6; 3, d.18: 1, 2-6; I-II, q.114) contain systematic treatises on merit. Particular questions of the doctrine on merit occur elsewhere. E.G., esp. I-II, 21, 3, 4; *S. contra Gentiles* III, 149; *In Rom*. 2:7." So far as ST I-II, q. 21, a.4, is concerned (a particular question that Goch accurately cites), Pesch notes, p. 774, n. 75, that Thomas is dealing with merit here "from a general perspective, that of providence." He is by no means dealing here with the questions: Does the free will suffice for merit? or: Does the free will cooperate with the grace of God in the merit of eternal life? When he does take up such questions it is perfectly clear that the *natural* free will of man cannot merit anything salvific, only the free will *iam per gratiam informata*, which is what Goch calls the *voluntas gratuita*. Cf. I-II, q.112, a.3, ad 1, and *Lib*. II, 22, 126; 26, 134f.; III, 7, 200; also n. 78 below.

70. *Lib*. III, 1, 184.

71. *In Rom*., prol. n. 12. Cf. Sir. 10:14 (Vulgate).

72. Ibid., n. 11: "Est enim haec doctria tota de gratia Christi. ... "

73. *In Rom* 3:12, n. 277: " ... nullus est iustus in se ex seipso, sed ex se quilibet est peccator, ex solo autem Deo habet iustitiam." *In I Cor.* 1:31, n. 72: "Si salus hominis non provenit ex aliqua excellentia humana, sed ex sola virtute divina, non debetur homini gloria, sed Deo. ... " Ibid., 4:7, n. 202: "Et ad hoc pertinet prima species superbiae, qua scilicet aliquis superbiendo, quod habet, dicit a seipso

habere... Ille autem gloriatur quasi accipiens, qui omnia Deo ad-scribens, gloriatur de ipso...."; *In II Cor.* 4:7, n. 132: "Nunc vero, quia pauperes et contemptibiles sumus, huiusmodi sublimitas Deo, et non nobis, attribuitur."

74. *Lib.* III, 1, 184.

75. See n. 73. Also: *In II Sent.*, d.27, q.1, a.6, ad 2: "... meritum Christi est sicut radix omnium meritorum, a quo omnium merita efficaciam trahunt." *In III Sent.*, d.18, a.2, ad 4, where charity is the *radix merendi.*

76. Pesch, pp. 776–77 and 792. This interpretation contrasts with that of HTR, p. 211, which sees "two bases" of merit: the divine ordination and the free will. The movement of the free will in justification is not the cause but the effect of grace: ST I–II, q.111, a.2, ad 2. Ibid. and in I-II, q.113, a.7, ad 1, Thomas speaks of this movement of the free will as *consensus* and *consentire*, as does Goch, *Lib.* III, 2, 185. R. R. Post, "Johann Pupper van Goch," *Nederlandisch Archief voor Kergeschiedenis*, n.s. 47 (1965/66):89, followed by HTR, p. 213, n. 34, needs correction, not only for stating that the *acceptatio divina* is not seen as a condition for merit by Thomas, but also for suggesting that Goch, in contrast to Thomas, is somewhat of a reductionist in holding that the role of the free will in merit is that of a "mere *consentire*." For reference to the activity of the "graced will" see n. 77. On the decisiveness of the *ordinatio (acceptatio) divina* for *Thomas's concept of merit and justification see I-II, q.114, a.1 corp. and ad 3; q.111, a.1, ad 2; De veritate*, q.27, a.5 corp. For the interchangeable usage of *acceptatio* and *ordinatio divina* by Thomas, Biel, and Eck, see *Luther*, pp. 170, 203, n. 102, 248f., n. 153, and Biel's *Canonis Misse Expositio*, ed. H. Oberman and W. Courtenay, pt. 2 (Wiesbaden: Franz Steiner, 1965), lectio 59, p. 441, Cf. Pesch, pp. 774-75 and n. 78.

77. *Lib.* II, 5, 101-32, 147.

78. Cf. *Lib* II, 29, 140, and Thomas *In II Sent.*, d.27, q.1, a.4, ad 5. Also ibid., a.3, sol.: eternal life "praemium est quod omnem facultatem humanae naturae excedit," and I-II, q.114, a.3 corp. See also *In Rom.* 6:23, n. 517.

79. *Lib.* II, 28, 140; cf. 29, 142; 31, 147; III, 2, 185.

80. *Lib.* II, 26, 134.

81. *Lib.* II, 29, 141.

82. Emphasis added. *Lib*. II, 29, 141. See *Lib* II, 29, 143, for a reaffirmation of the cooperation of the graced will.

83. *Lib*. II, 29, 142, *Lib*. III, 4, 192 (emphasis added). These texts must also be noted, along with those where Goch says "grace alone is the cause of all merit" (*Lib*. II, 29, 142), if we are not to interpret his doctrine in an extreme way. Failure to take note of the entire section in *Lib*. II dealing with the crucial distinction between the two wills leads HTR, pp. 209, n. 8, and 211-13, to misinterpret some of Goch's other remarks concerning cooperation and merit. To state, e.g., that Goch denies "any significance to human cooperation with grace" or denies "the doctrine of human cooperation with grace" (HTR, 215 and 211) clearly overlooks Goch's teaching about the "graced will" and makes him out to be not only anti-Thomistic but anti-Augustinian and anti-Lutheran as well. And it is surely to fabricate opposition between Thomas and Goch by implying that Goch *replaces* the Thomist "basis for merit"—i.e., the *ordinatio divina* and the human will—by positing the *gratia increata* and the *acceptatio Dei*; HTR, pp. 211-12.

Both these elements are operative in Thomas, just as the will is operative for Goch. The necessary requirements for a meritorious act are stated diversely by Goch: sometimes it is grace and the will (*Lib*. II, 29, 141); sometimes solely the interior movement of the will (*Dial*. 17, 180: "in quo consistit omnis merita causa et principium"); sometimes four elements are necessary (*Lib*. III, 7, 200); sometimes there are "many things required" (*Lib*. III, 2, 187). This diversity of formulation must be kept in mind when reading other statements of Goch such as are reported in HTR, 211, n. 20, 212, n. 22, and 214, n. 37, lest Goch be interpreted extremely.

84. *Lib*. II, 31, 147.

85. *Lib*. II, 29, 140-41. Such a radical distinction of two wills is found in neither Thomas nor Augustine.

86. *Lib*. II, 31, 147: In the justification and glorification of man "nec in minimo cooperatur naturalis facultas liberi arbitrii, nisi quod deo in operante voluntate consentit. . . . Et sic intelligi vult Augustinum omnia dicta sua, ubi loquitur de gratia iustificante, non tamen sine libero arbitrio, id est non sine libero arbitrio consentiente, sèd non sine libero arbitrio cooperante." In the light of Goch's comments on these same words of Augustine in *Frag*. 302: "non iustificabit te sine te volente, non autem cooperante" (cf. *Lib*. III, 2, 187), there is good reason to

suspect that the final "non" in the above citation from *Lib*. II, 31, 147, is a misprint. This notwithstanding, Goch's own rules for interpreting Augustine indicate that he intends to exclude only the cooperation of the *natural* will.

87. *Lib*. II, 29, 143-44.

88. *Lib*. III, 1, 184.

89. Ibid.

90. Cf. *Lib*. III, 2, 185, and ST I-II, q.21, a.4, ad 2.

91. *In Rom*. 8, 14, n. 635.

92. Cf. *Lib*. III, 2, 185, and Thomas, *In Rom*. 3:23, nn. 305—6.

93. Cf. *Lib*. III, 2, 185, and Thomas, *In Rom*. 8:30, n. 707.

94. Cf. *Lib*. III, 2, 185, and ST I-II, a.2, art.2 and ad 2: "Unde tota operatio pertinet ad gratiam."

95. *Lib*. III, 2, 186-87.

96. ST I-II, q.114, a.5. Thomas is so insistent on this that in the ad 1 of this article he suggests that Augustine was deceived when he said, "Faith merits justification."

97. *In Rom*. 9:13, nn. 763-64: " . . . merita quae a seipsis non habent." Hos. 13:9 is cited.

98. *In Rom*. 9:15, nn. 771-72.

99. Ibid., nn. 773-74.

100. See n. 97 above.

101. I-II, q.112, a.3, ad 2.

102. II-II, q.161, a.3 corp.

103. *Lib*. III, 3, 187: the second error says, "Merit is an act to which a reward is due *ex debito iustitiae*." See n. 29 above. *Lib*. III, 6, 196: the fourth error is "that an act informed by charity is an act proportionate to eternal beatitude *secundum debitum iustitiae*." Goch cites Thomas *In III Sent*., d.18, as fomenting this error. See n. 54 above.

104. *Lib*. III, 4, 190. Thomas, ST II-II, q. 88, a.6, is cited as a source of this error with his thesis that it is more meritorious to do something good with a vow than without a vow. Goch calls this view "completely false and erroneous" but he does not explicitly denounce it as contrary to Scripture, as he does with other theses. This may be because it is a question of an error in ethical theory rather than a matter of direct biblical interpretation.

105. *Lib*. III, 4, 191-92.
106. *Lib*. III, 4, 195.
107. ST I-II, q.114, a.4, ad 3.
108. ST I-II, q.114, a.4.

J. S. BACH AND J. A. ERNESTI:
A CASE STUDY IN EXEGETICAL
AND THEOLOGICAL CONFLICT

Paul S. Minear

Two and one-half centuries ago a struggle emerged within the faculty of St. Thomas School in Leipzig, a struggle that has never been fully resolved but still marks a schism in the soul of the modern Christian. It was the struggle between the now famous cantor, Johann Sebastian Bach, and the once famous rector, Johann August Ernesti—the one a musical genius and the other a pioneer in the historical criticism of the Bible. Both were gifted interpreters of the New Testament, although the media of interpretation they utilized were very different.[1] A case study of this struggle may, I trust, be an appropriate way of honoring Albert Outler, who is an illustrious heir of both Ernesti's historical convictions and Bach's liturgical insights.

As an ecumenical theologian Outler has grounded his comprehension of the Gospel upon those biblical and liturgical realities that found such magnificent expression in the *St. Matthew Passion*. As a protagonist of the Christian faith in its address to secularized culture, he has utilized the

---

The author is Winkley Professor of Biblical Theology (Emeritus), Divinity School, Yale University.

freedom from dogmatic fixations for which Ernesti fought. As a historian he is equally at home in the early eighteenth and the late twentieth century. He will therefore not be surprised at my discovery that many cultural and religious forces in the intellectual ferment of our day were latent within the faculty of a single secondary school in Germany during the 1730s. Let us, then, examine the source and shape of those antagonisms.

THE CONFLICT

When we uncover the source of enmity between rector and cantor it may appear at first that the struggle arose out of nothing more than personal allergies and professional jealousies—factors not unknown in other faculties. In this case, however, that is hardly an adequate explanation, as we shall see. In 1723, at the age of thirty-eight, Bach was appointed musical director of two churches in Leipzig and cantor of St. Thomas School. Each Sunday he directed the choirs, alternating between St. Thomas and St. Nicholas churches. Each year he composed some sixty cantatas to be performed by choirs and orchestras in either church. Members of the choirs and orchestras were drawn from students in St. Thomas School, where Bach was instructor in music, Latin grammar, and the Latin catechism. In addition, he spent one week out of each month as an inspector and supervisor at the school. In this role he roused the boys in the morning (5 A.M. in summer, 6 A.M. in winter), said grace before meals, checked attendance, supervised Bible readings during the meals, taught his courses, conducted evening prayers, and checked the dormitories at "lights-out."[2]

It is evident from this roster of duties that Bach needed help. He secured it as his predecessors had done, from several prefects, who were appointed as the cantor's assistants. These were "senior pupils who took over much of the cantor's duties and whose satisfactory work was of vital importance to a smoothly running musical organization."[3] They directed the choirs in the churches, in the streets during public festivals, and at the weddings and funerals of prominent families. For some years the system worked satisfactorily. Such troubles as disturbed the relations between Bach and the town council or the church consistory (and the troubles were many) stemmed from other causes.

In 1734 the Leipzig Council chose as new rector of the school a young philologist, Johann August Ernesti. He began his new post at the age of twenty-seven, and hence was more than two decades Bach's junior. He wanted to make St. Thomas an outstanding center of humanistic studies, and in his judgment this required a definite break with tradition. The school had been designed to combine scholastic and musical purposes, and admission had been restricted to boys with both scholastic and musical capacities. At his appointment, approximately one-fifth of the students' time was occupied with theology and one-fifth with music.[4] Ernesti believed that higher scholastic excellence could be attained only by reducing the time and status given to music. He "hated to see his charges waste so much time by singing in the streets, attending funerals or weddings and rehearsing for performances."[5] In his judgment, students were there to study and not to sing. Accordingly, a basic objective of the school was abandoned: "to guide the students through the euphony of music to the contemplation of the divine."[6]

It was inevitable, then, that rector and cantor should differ strongly. The occasion for overt conflict arose in 1736 over the question, who should have authority to appoint, and therefore to discipline, the student prefects? On one occasion, in singing at a wedding, the boy choristers had been guilty of unseemly behavior, provoking some stern disciplin-

ary action on the part of the first prefect, one Gottlieb
Theodor Krause. The rector had defended the choristers and
had punished the prefect by ordering a public flogging for
him. Because of this disgrace, this prefect and surrogate of
Bach's had withdrawn from school.[7] Thereupon the rector
had appointed a new prefect, Johann Gottlob Krause, an act
by which he openly challenged Bach's authority. In retalia-
tion Bach demoted the new appointee to the rank of third
prefect and replaced him with another student whose musical
gifts he claimed to be superior. The rector demanded the
higher post for his man. The cantor refused. The rector
instructed choristers not to obey any Bach appointee. The
cantor refused to allow the Ernesti appointee to participate
in any service.

For two years the battle raged, with both men appealing
for support to church consistory and town council. Month
after month those bodies showed their expertness in post-
poning and avoiding decision. The morale of the choirs was
destroyed, the quality of their work suffered, Bach's prolific
output of new compositions was halted.[8] Finally Bach
appealed to the Saxon king, who intervened and ordered the
dispute settled in Bach's favor. But the King's decree failed to
quell the emotional bitterness. Consistory and council remained angry with Bach, the rector and teachers continued
to harass his work, the student choristers remained partisans
of one or the other leader.[9]

At issue in the conflict between cantor and rector were
other and far more important matters. As one interpreter
says, we may see here "the tragic conflict between the last
and most mighty musical representative of the age of faith
and one of the younger protagonists of the age of reason and
science."[10] Two epochs, two cultures, two philosophies of
education were at stake. Should secondary education continue to be grounded in Christian theology? If so, should
music be given a central place in such training in theology?

Also at issue were two differing approaches to the Bible, both of which have since demonstrated their efficacy. It is with such issues that the rest of this essay deals. Bach was a devout, zealous Lutheran who continued the spirit, ethos, and biblical understandings of the seventeenth century. Ernesti was a child of eighteenth-century rationalism, with its antipathy toward aesthetic, allegorical, and analogical interpretations of the Bible. He wished to ground exegesis on philological evidence, literal meanings and rational deductions. Consideration of this issue, which alienated the rector from the cantor, may thus prove instructive for readers responsible for biblical interpretation and theological synthesis today.[11]

TWO APPROACHES TO THE BIBLE

For knowledge of Ernesti's exegetical work we rely here upon a single, slight volume published by him in 1761: *Institutio Interpretis*. In those days it often took a theological book a century to leap the Atlantic. In this case the translation from Latin into English first appeared in 1822. The translator was Moses Stuart, a pioneer exegete who is still revered at both Andover and Yale.[12] Both in Germany and in America the appearance of Ernesti's book constituted a landmark in biblical studies. The following quotations, taken from the fourth English edition of *Elementary Principles* (1842), indicate the author's emphasis:

> [Interpretation is] the skill which enables us to attach to another's language the same meaning that the author himself attached to it. (p. 14)

> The interpreter must beware lest he seek for diversity of meaning where none really exists. (p. 38)

> Nothing can be more pernicious in exegesis than uncertainty. (p. 20)

> There can be no certainty unless a kind of necessity compels us to

affix a particular sense to a word, which sense must be one. (p. 22)
The literal meaning is not to be deserted without evident reason or
necessity. (p. 82)
Language can be properly understood only in a philological way.
(p. 27)
Greater weight in exegesis should be attributed to grammatical
considerations than to doctrinal ones. (p. 31)
The design of the Holy Spirit can be understood only so far as he
himself has explained it, and afforded obvious grounds for
explanation. (p. 24)

I need not spell out here either the novelty of these
attitudes in the eighteenth century or their profound impact
upon later biblical studies. Stuart rightly called this book
"one of the first respectable efforts to reduce the principles
of interpretation *to a science*" (my italics). It was not,
however, so much the scientific goal that motivated Ernesti
as it was the desire to conform biblical studies to the
standards of classical studies. Perhaps his most decisive and
influential axiom was this: "The Scriptures are to be
investigated by the same rules as other books" (p. 27). The
immediate reactions to his teaching were, as one might
expect, diverse, and not unlike those encountered in the
contemporary seminary classroom. One student said, "He
laid within me the immovable foundation of unbelief." Most
students were more appreciative. "Ernesti's approach of
cold, probing inquiry, of gimlet-eyed scrutiny of Scripture,
gained him an enormous following."[13] Ernesti's student
Joseph Semler was an effective channel by which his
influence reached later exegetes, encouraging the tendency
"to view the Bible on its human external and historical side;
to consider it in its diversity rather than in its unity, in its
fragmentary divisions and various methods rather than as an
organic whole."[14]
    It would be wrong to picture Bach's position as wholly
antithetical to Ernesti's.[15] For example, the cantor had no

less respect for the primacy of the biblical text than did Ernesti. "Nothing obsesses Bach," wrote Rudolf Smend, "but the word of Scripture."[16] For instance, in the *St. Matthew Passion* the text of the Gospel provides the structure of the oratorio without abbreviation or amendment. Moreover, the goal of his music is determined by the verbal text. His musical phrase, Schweitzer insists, is simply "the verbal phrase recast in tone." "The relation of Bach's music to its text is the most intimate that can be imagined."[17]

Nor should we picture Bach as an ultraconservative Lutheran traditionalist. As a composer he developed many new patterns of interpretation. Although they belonged to a distinct genre and were performed in a conventional Good Friday service, his *Passions* were genuinely innovative; his conception of the successive scenes was far from traditional.[18] In fact, as Smend contends, "nothing Bach adopted remained unchanged."[19] He was as vigorous an exponent of "liberation" as was his rector, though each sought to be freed from different enslavements.[20]

But at one point there is a decisive contrast between cantor and rector. The cantor believed that the biblical text was designed to release within the reader an intense kind of spiritual activity. The interpreter must therefore help the text produce in his own audience an emotional action appropriate to the text at hand. He should give priority not to the axis between the Gospel and other ancient books, nor between each successive sentence and the biblical author's conscious and literal intent, but to that between the events narrated and the contemporary audience whose members are called on to respond to those events in unqualified immediacy and with their whole being. Music should function in such a way as to bring the "stories told in the Gospel"

out of remoteness into a highly actual relation to the audience, comparable to Nathan's address to David, "Thou art the man" (2 Sam. 12:7). . . . The decisive task of the cantatas consists not in

narration or dramatic presentation of the events, but in an always
new relation of this event to the men of the present.[21]

The Bible is unlike other books in that through it God speaks
to men. And since God's purpose is sovereign and invasive,
the Bible becomes the most purposive book. It aroused in
Bach "the most purposive music, which invades the mind and
being in such a way that the listener has no rest."[22] This
conception of the literary uniqueness of the Gospels has been
cogently described by Erich Auerbach.[23] As a literary critic
Auerbach insists that the exegete must do full justice to this
feature of the Gospels. Bach does this, but many modern
exegetes, following Ernesti's lead, fail to do so.

Other contrasts between cantor and rector are related to
this basic one. Concentration on the human authors' literal
meaning leads to the philological accent; concentration on
the human responses to God's presence leads to artistic,
poetic, dramatic, and musical modes of communication. The
rector feared admitting to the text "a diversity of meaning
where none really exists"; the cantor was inclined to discover
in the events narrated an unlimited plurality of meanings,
some of which are quite irreducible to abstract concept or to
brutal prose. The rector gave primacy to grammatical analysis
and rational decuction; the cantor, who took for granted the
intelligibility of the text and the historicity of the events,
used his imagination and musical language to disclose or to
produce the free involvement of worshipers in the events
narrated. In his hands the text becomes "the elemental and
supreme expression of human endeavor."[24] Ernesti's approach stresses the full involvement of each text in the world;
Bach captures in sound the paradoxical fusion of the
temporal and eternal in the events narrated. "Complete
involvement in the world joined with utter transcendence
over it, this is at the same time the essence and the paradox
of the art of Bach."[25]

I believe that this conflict between these two modes of interpreting the Bible is central to hermeneutical debates today. If we focus attention upon the work of professional exegetes, there can be little doubt that most of them are sons of Ernesti rather than of Bach. Ernesti's emphasis upon rational philological and historical concerns is so dominant that not many exegetes consider any other alternative. But there can be heard voices of dissatisfaction, though they seldom come from card-bearing members of the biblical guild. As two sons of Bach, Joseph Sittler and Paul Ricoeur should be cited. First, Sittler:

> How, in the Bible, men grasped by the reality of God beheld and understood and dealt with themselves, their fellowmen, and their world is a fact that must be stated "beyond" the biblical mode if God and grace and contemporary men and their world are to be served.[26]

Bach's *Passion* is a superb example of Sittlerian exegesis that is faithful to the biblical reality by moving beyond the biblical mode of speech.

Paul Ricoeur gives a more extended explication of the point:

> To understand a text is to follow its movement from sense to reference, from what it says to what it talks about. . . . The text speaks of a possible world and of a possible way of orienting oneself within it. The dimensions of this world are properly opened up by, disclosed by, the text. . . . It is not the initial discourse situation which has to be understood, but that which . . . points toward a world which bursts the reader's situation as well as that of the author. . . . Beyond my situation as reader, beyond the author's situation, I offer myself to the possible modes of being-in-the-world which the text opens up. . . .[27]

Here again I propose Bach as an exegete of Matthew who followed the movement of the biblical text as it opened up for his listeners a possible world and a possible way of orienting themselves within it.

TWO AVENUES TOWARD CATHOLICITY

Having contrasted the two approaches to the Bible which, in somewhat latent and undeveloped form, emerged in the work of this cantor and this rector, we now move on to appraise their relative contributions to that twentieth-century phenomenon known as the ecumenical movement. We begin by observing that the work of each of these men resulted in making the Bible accessible to a much wider constituency, thus stimulating a movement toward universality. Developments during succeeding centuries enable us to observe the extent and limitation of each kind of universality.

Before Ernesti began his work, the study of the Bible had been severely restricted by dogmatic controls in which doctrinal considerations and allegorical distortions were allowed to displace the original intent of the text. The number of exegetes was more or less limited to those who would play the game according to rules set by dogmatic definitions of inspiration within traditional creedal boundaries. Ernesti's principles of interpretation immediately swelled the ranks of exegetes and freed them to place their interpretations within the context of ancient classical literature. The application to the Bible of the rules used for all other ancient documents gave to all humanistic scholars the full right to deal with the biblical books. The primacy given to philological and grammatical data likewise had the effect of excluding none and including all, since every literary document embodies the use of a lexicon and a language common to a community larger than those who share the author's stance. In principle, the Christian canon was thus opened for study by non-Christian scholars, as their literature was in turn open to Christians.

Similarly, the preference given to the use of objective

reason rather than subjective emotion encouraged universality to the extent that all men are capable of rational
thought. Solidarity with other students who operate on the
same basis of rational treatment of ancient books tends to
supersede any earlier solidarity with other believers, whether
with the authors of the New Testament, with their initial
audiences, or with modern Christians. By reason of this
"later" solidarity (which has expanded since Bach and
Ernesti) the modern scholar finds that he can travel to other
countries and visit men of other religions without leaving
home—i.e., without being subject to severe culture shock, so
long as he stays on a university campus where Western
patterns of historical study prevail. Far beyond his expectations and even beyond his approval, Ernesti's "elementary
principles of interpretation" have been accorded virtually
universal recognition. They helped Christians win the battle
against various obscurantisms of the eighteenth century and
they have initiated a far-ranging and open-ended investigation
of all religious literature.

No less influential, however, has been the work of Ernesti's
rival, albeit Bach's universality possesses very different traits,
relying as it does upon musical rather than verbal philology.
Bach has spoken with tremendous power to men of many
religions and cultures through his own mode of communicating biblical events and their meanings. Writing usually for a
single audience, often a Christian congregation, he has
succeeded in establishing a solidarity in emotional response
between the modern audience, the Leipzig congregation, and
the biblical author—e.g., Matthew—and his audience. It is
impossible to categorize the vast multitudes of people to
whom Bach has spoken with power. Consider a sampling of
testimonies from various sorts of listeners:

Zelter to Goethe: "If you could hear one of Sebastian Bach's
motets, you would feel yourself at the center of the world."[28]

Richard Benz: "There is no work of art which so unites in experience all men, without distinction."[29]

Charles Widor: "Bach is on the whole the most universal of artists. What speaks through his work is pure religious emotion; and this is one and the same in all men, in spite of the national and religious partitions. . . . His cantatas and Passions turn the soul to a state in which we can grasp the truth and oneness of things, and rise above . . . everything that divides us."[30]

Fanny Mendelssohn, on the occasion of the revival of the *St. Matthew Passion* in 1829: "The crowded hall looked like a church. . . . Everyone was filled with the most solemn devotion. One heard only an occasional involuntary ejaculation that sprang from deep emotion."[31]

Of that same evening, Edward Devrient, the bass soloist who sang the words of Jesus, said: "Never have I felt a holier solemnity vested in a congregation than in the performers and audience that evening."[32]

Leonard Bernstein, writing of the same *Passion*: [Bach's music] "pierces through the worldly pain with the icy-clear truth of redemption."[33]

To be sure, this sort of testimony is less than unanimous. Nietzsche, for example, found in Bach "too much crude Christianity, or Germanism, or crude scholasticism." Nietzsche continues, "He stands at the threshold of modern European music, but he is always looking back toward the Middle Ages."[34]

We have already observed Bach's concern to declaim the word of Scripture and to protect the autonomy of the verbal text. Now we see how that concern did not inhibit, but rather enhanced, the movement toward universality. His use of musical language was placed at the service of the biblical authors in the effort to help those authors address contemporary audiences. Just as modern biblical scholars find in every free university in the world a context in which their objective research can be presented to a heterogeneous and polyglot audience, so conductors of choirs and orchestras discover in every concert hall in the world a welcome for the explicitly Christian compositions of J. S. Bach.

Granted their parallel ability to speak to a universal audience, the contrasts between the methods by which Bach and Ernesti achieved a wider hearing become all the more obvious: one used an artistic mode, the other used a rationalistic perspective; one used a musical, the other a non-musical, mode of expression; one was concerned to do justice to the multiple meanings of the text, the other sought out the single meaning; one stressed the uniqueness of the Bible, the other exploited its kinship to other books; one wanted above all to comprehend the mind of the ancient author, the other sought to share the responses to the event on the part of the ancient audience.

To sum up: Ernesti gave priority to recovering the ancient language, Bach sought to communicate the whole mode of being-in-the-world toward which that language pointed. Both assumed, of course, the unity of that world as God's creation, as witnessed by the Bible; they differed with regard to perceptions of how man exists within that world. Neither would have challenged seriously the dictum of Albert Outler:

> If there is one constant and relatively consistent theme throughout the Bible and the whole of patristic Christianity, it is that God's business with creation embraces it all—the world at every level, existence in every form.[35]

Yet, although both were convinced monotheists, Bach, I think, more than his rival, was alive to the many levels and forms of existence within the created order.

However that may be, with the benefit of hindsight we may discern the contributions of both men to the ecumenical phenomenon of our own day. Consider two areas central to recent discussion. First, the attitudes toward divine revelation in Scripture and tradition. Apart from the application of those historical methods bearing the signature of Ernesti, Protestants would not have been liberated from their captivity to ossified dogmas, nor Catholics from their obscurantist absolutisms. Because of the extent to which men have respected philological and linguistic canons, we have been able together to move toward greater catholicity by discerning the role of traditions within the Bible, the role of Scripture within later traditions, and our own role as conservers and interpreters of both.

The second area in which these men have contributed to ecumenism is the impulse to Christian unity provided by shared liturgical activity. Common worship has demonstrated to Christians of varying backgrounds the fact that they already "exist" in the same world, that their Lord has already made them one and has given them the task of manifesting that oneness. Music has proved to be a major ministry of reconciliation, and no music has been more efficacious in this ministry than that of Bach. His music mediates a mode of being-in-the-world that is inherently and contagiously catholic.

Both rector and cantor, then, have made major contributions to the emergence of ecumenism. In that process, however, both have had to pay a certain price in that their work has been subjected to the sweeping, and in some senses devastating, triumphs of secularization. These triumphs have affected the rich legacy in different ways, through changes we cannot trace in great detail here. In brief, the hermeneutical convictions of Ernesti have been radically altered, I believe, by the development of secularized universities in which the prevailing ethos and worldview are implicitly, if not explicitly, a-theistic, in contrast to the Christian orientation of German scholarship in the eighteenth century. Likewise, I believe that the meaning of Bach's music has been radically altered by the fact that it is now produced in concert halls by heterogeneous artists for heterogeneous audiences. Let us explore further the effects of these changes.

TWO TYPES OF SECULARIZATION

The seemingly innocent and obvious statement that the Bible should be treated like other books meant something quite different in Ernesti's Christendom from what it does in the secularized world today. Then, as we have seen, it was a form of rebellion against the monopoly held by formal dogmas that had inhibited study. To gain recognition, exegetes needed to present orthodox credentials and to produce results in accord with tradition. In that context Ernesti's little book was a new weapon in "the battle with stark orthodoxy," a battle that had to be won before other advances could be made.[36] This weapon effectively liberated scholars, widened the areas open to research, and produced vast alterations in the reconception of biblical history.

Today, however, that rebellion has become a new "establishment," with its own restrictive axioms.* A "union card" is now virtually limited to scholars who have been professionally trained to apply objective methods and to restrict their conclusions to data which can be verified by those methods. All scholars are allowed equal access to the text, but believing scholars must take extra care not to pollute their findings by their faith.

Now, a historical methodology that finds in the Gospels nothing distinguishing them significantly from Seneca, Epicurus, and Herodotus is not a methodology equipped to deal

---

*In using this term "establishment" of the present company of biblical teachers I do not wish to condemn all individuals equally. Practitioners in this field, as in others, exemplify a vast diversity of perspectives and tendencies. I have, however, selected what seems to be the dominant and growing tendency in this field of study.

with the active presence of God in human affairs. It casts presumptive doubt upon the authenticity or accuracy of every verse in the Gospel and especially on every verse in which the theological component, God's action, is central. It encourages readers to covet solidarity with contemporary historians at the cost of solidarity with Matthew or Matthew's intended audience. It appears often to limit the ground of faith either to a diminishing residue of authentic facts which remain in the historian's sieve or to a growing body of legends and myths which can be readily disjoined from historical reality. Matthew's own point of view, although allowed as a valid object of study, can no longer be accepted by the student as providing an essential basis for comprehension. Study can no longer be oriented or shaped by the features that distinguished the Bible from other books. Such matters as the presence of a book in the canon or the one-time claim to inspiration exert no noticeable influence on its interpreters. Thus the parochialism of orthodox dogma has been replaced by the parochialism of historical relativism, the inevitable result of a methodology that presupposes an a-theistic view of historical process.

Surely Ernesti did not contemplate such consequences from his original protest. He took seriously the role played by the Holy Spirit in the Bible. He recognized that, in speaking of God, biblical authors used a figurative language to which later interpreters must be sensitive.[37] A secularized worldview embodied in the secularized methods of secularized schools has betrayed his intention and meaning. The price paid for achieving this kind of universality has been very high indeed, notwithstanding the fact that many scholars have been happy to pay it. The vulnerability of the method depends, of course, not on the price but on its claim as an adequate means to the fullness of understanding.

Bach's interpretation of Matthew has also lost much as a

result of the expansion of his audience. Originally he composed the *Passion* for a Good Friday service of worship in St. Thomas Church, to accompany the sermon for the day. Thus at least a modicum of kinship between his audience and Matthew's was assured. Schrade stresses the degree to which a lifetime goal of Bach's was the creation of a new liturgical service in which music would provide the organizing principle, the very structure of the congregation's praise and prayer.[38] Although for a time, while he was serving as court musician in Anhalt-Köthen, he surrendered this goal for a more secular one,[39] at Leipzig Bach returned to his first aim, "a well-regulated church music" as a divine vocation. In this he succeeded, although success brought him "complete loneliness as an artist." His accomplishment as a servant of the Church "echoed in a vacuum,"[40] in St. Thomas School, in the Leipzig churches and in churches elsewhere. The spirit of the Enlightenment, as represented by Ernesti, made it impossible for others to understand his task.

It is therefore one of the strange ironies of history that when the *St. Matthew Passion* was revived after a century of oblivion it was performed in a Berlin concert hall, free of any association with sermon or church. Ever since then its use in churches has diminished in contrast to its use in concert halls, in part because of the demands of production and the standards of musical excellence. No longer do audiences join in singing the chorales as familiar confessions of their own distinctively Christian convictions. No longer does the sung text of the Gospel take the place of "the reading of God's Holy Word." No longer does an evangelical sermon intervene between the two parts, nor does the evening close with a congregational hymn and the benediction. Probably many who hear Bach's music have never participated in a Christian worship service. The secularization of the *Passion*, therefore, in spite of furnishing a larger audience for Bach since 1729, marks the reversal rather than the consummation of Bach's conscious intentions. The latest example is the first American dramatization of the *Passion* by the Spring Opera Theater of San Francisco. According to a press report,

> The work opened with the four solo singers surrounding the dead body of Jesus in a tableau. . . . The chorus was dressed in gold turbans and vestments clearly inspired by Rembrandt. . . . Judas did a dance with a rope before hanging himself.[41]

When the devout Christian becomes aware of the irony of this situation and when he listens again to the *Passion* as fruit of Bach's heroic effort to develop a fitting liturgical celebration of Good Friday, he may be pardoned for finding in this secularization an institutionalized form of blasphemy no less shocking than other perversions of the Cross. We should not dismiss too hastily the slogan that appeared as early as 1904 in the *Bachjahrbuch* (p. 25): "The church works of Bach for the Church."[42] Moreover, when we recall how tenaciously Bach held to his liturgical goals, we hesitate to agree with Schweitzer's glib rationalization, "Any room becomes a church in which his sacred works are performed and listened to with devotion."[43] Bach's ecclesiology was more discriminating than that. Contemporary Jewish citizens of Israel who in 1971 protested vigorously against performances of Bach in Jerusalem were not without substantial theological grounds for that protest, grounds that may relate them more closely to Bach than to Israeli musicians.

Even so, something else must be said. Although the price of a universal hearing has been a secularization which runs counter to Bach's intention and although the separation of this art from the Church has done damage to both,[44] we must in the end rejoice over the process of secularization from which Bach's music has gained more than it has lost. Why so? For one thing, the boundary between the sacred and the secular has become increasingly difficult to locate. The two realms have changed their character since the days of Ernesti and Bach, changed in ways that defy definition either by Lutheran dogmatists or by atheistic sociologists. In producing this erosion of the boundaries, music has been one of the most effective agents. As David and Mendel have well said, "The fact is that we, though we live in an irreligious age, have come back to the realization that there is no essential difference between religious and secular music."[45] Bach himself seems to have viewed all his work as integral to his vocation under God. He used different texts and different surroundings for his secular compositions, but he did not hesitate to adapt secular music to sacred occasions or sacred music to secular occasions. As Ulrich Simon has insisted:

> The sacred and the secular cannot be divided any more than a Bach cantata can be divided from a Bach concerto; the same inspiration covers both. Thus a moving away from religious subjects by no means lessens the revelation of music.[46]

Second, the secularization may be seen as an illustration of the intercessory character and vocation of the Church, which exists "not as a society of those who alone are saved, but as the sign of salvation of those who, as far as its historical and social structure is concerned, do not belong to it."[47] From this standpoint, the concert in Symphony Hall may be seen as binding together believers and unbelievers under the sign of Christ's atoning death, quite irrespective of the conscious thoughts of conductor, choristers, instrumentalists, or audience. The power of the music to accomplish this miracle derives not alone from the composer but from the Evangelist and the Messiah, neither of whom wished to erect high walls around a sacred precinct.

Third, we may see in the secularization and universalization of the *Passion* music a process implicit in the Matthean

Passion Story itself. Better than performance in churches, the performance in concert halls may dramatize the secularity of what happened in Gethsemane and on Golgotha. Although it was written for the Church, Bach's music correctly interprets the unlimited range of Christ's atonement "for the sins of the whole world." Like Matthew before him, Bach testifies to his faith in "the Providence of God as the ultimate environment of human existence."[48] This is why these two accounts of Jesus' death declare the final obsolescence of all boundaries between the sacred and the secular. In Outler's words,

> The Passion of Christ did not end at Golgotha; it goes on and on to the end of the world, wherever the passions of men go unredeemed. The sacrifice of Calvary is endlessly efficacious, not as a substitute for the sacrifices to which love calls us, but as a purgation of our sacrificial love from self-pity and bitterness.[49]

I permit myself to raise one last question, as an epilogue somewhat unrelated to the foregoing case study. What are the implications of our study for the modern exegete? The fact that I am an exegete and not a musician permits me to raise this question. The question becomes all the more pertinent if Bach actually was a better exegete than Ernesti, as I think he was, and if in the *St. Matthew Passion* he has taken us closer to the world of Matthew than have recent New Testament commentators.

Such assertions must, of course, be supported by an explicit definition of exegesis. For this purpose an old definition of F. W. Farrar is adequate: "The one aim of the interpreter should be to ascertain the specific meaning of the inspired teacher, and to clothe it *in the forms which will best convey* that meaning *to the minds of his contemporaries.*"[50] That statement of aim fits Bach in his composition of the *St. Matthew Passion*. Judged by the same statement, Bach's work still conveys to audiences today the meaning of the narrative in Matthew's Gospel more effectively than any recent scholarly commentary with which I am familiar.

If such an assertion is justified, it should constitute a more or less explicit appeal to my exegetical colleagues. First, we should recognize that we have been wholly wrong in excluding Bach from histories of modern hermeneutics. In the volume just cited, for example, Farrar makes no mention of Bach, but he gives adequate recognition to Ernesti.[51] Moreover, Schweitzer, whose work on Bach is as famous as his *Quest of the Historical Jesus* (1910), makes no mention of Bach in the latter work, and in the former, in only a few paragraphs do we find scattered indications that Bach makes any independent contribution to biblical interpretation.[52]

Second, if with Ernesti we acknowledge our obligation to treat the Gospels as we treat other literature, with Bach we should acknowledge our obligation to recognize the *distinctive* features of the Gospels to which his music has done greater justice than have even the best practitioners of our craft. We have too long denied the right of the Gospels as literary documents to determine the kinds of interpretation most apt and most adequate.

We should also covet more eagerly the potential contributions to biblical interpretation of other artistic forms of communication, incuding poetry, drama, fiction, the visual arts, liturgical celebration. There is absolutely no justification for our virtual exclusion of these from the processes of interpretation in the name of historical objectivity. We must seek liberation from the monopoly that discursive and analytic prose has established over our discipline. The various theological sciences suffered a disaster when, as a result of the work of Ernesti and his successors, they were disjoined from music.

Finally, let me observe that there is one point at which the processes of secularization meet. If it is impossible to reverse the trend toward the secularization of biblical exegesis in the context of the university curriculum, then, by the same token, it has become possible to use the secularized music of Bach and of other composers as a legitimate form of biblical exegesis within that context (e.g., Penderecki, *Passion According to St. Luke*, and Bernstein, *Mass*). On these terms it would be entirely legitimate for any graduate seminar studying the Passion Story to listen intently to Bach's *St. Matthew Passion* as one mode of penetrating its original and continuing message. For although Bach may not fully merit the title of the Fifth Evangelist, he can present excellent qualifications as an interpreter of all four Evangelists, first because he so frequently penetrated to the inner dynamics of the biblical narrative, and second, because he chose forms of expression that communicate those dynamics to a universal audience. Like the voice of those Evangelists, his is a "voice of spiritual reality that speaks from strata of thought deeper and more immutable than any intellectual forms of communication"[53]

NOTES

1. My attention was first called to this conflict by Jaroslav Pelikan, *Fools for Christ* (Philadelphia: Muhlenberg Press, 1955), pp. 145f.

2. See Imogen Holst, *Bach* (New York: Crowell, 1965), p. 62.

3. Karl Geiringer, *Bach* (New York: Oxford University Press, 1966), p. 83.

4. Jan Chiapusso, *Bach's World* (Bloomington: University of Indiana Press, 1968), p. 13. Chapter 4 gives a detailed survey of the musical training provided in a cloister school such as St. Thomas.

5. Geiringer, *Bach*, p. 83.

6. Leo Schrade, *Bach: The Conflict Between the Sacred and the Secular* (New York: Merlin Press, 1946), p. 114.

7. The most conveniently arranged collection of documents on this

affair is to be found in H. T. David and A. Mendel, eds., *The Bach Reader* (New York: W. W. Norton, 1945), pp. 137-49, 152-58.

8. Robert Stevenson, "Bach's Quarrel with the Rector of St. Thomas' School," *Anglican Theological Review* 35 (1951): 219-30.

9. Bach cultivated every opportunity for political support. A decade later he was a guest at the court of Frederick the Great, the flutist. This fact suggests a wholly irrelevant genealogical note. Among the mercenary soldiers in Frederick's armies were some Cornishmen, including one John Minear, later the first of my ancestors to migrate to America; this migration took place during Bach's period at Leipzig.

10. Chiapusso, *Bach's World*, pp. 266f.

11. Because of Professor Outler's devotion to John Wesley, I wish I could point to some contact between these two Lutherans and that Anglican Methodist. Unfortunately, no such contact has been discovered, although John Wesley (1703-91) was a younger contemporary of the St. Thomas cantor (1685-1750). Among John's musical descendants, Samuel Wesley was the first to discover and enthusiastically champion the music of Bach during the early years of the nineteenth century; see E. Routley, *The Musical Wesleys*, 1703-1876 (New York: Oxford University Press, 1968), pp. 90f.

12. See J. H. Giltner, "Moses Stuart, 1778-1852," (Ph.D. diss., Yale University, 1956).

13. Stevenson, "Bach's Quarrel," p. 229.

14. F. W. Farrar, *History of Interpretation* (London: Macmillan Co., 1886), p. 403.

15. I have analyzed in detail Bach's interpretation of Matthew's Passion narrative in an essay in *Theology Today* 30 (1973): 243-55.

16. In *Bach und Luther* (Berlin: Verlag Haus and Schule), 1947, p. 15.

17. Albert Schweitzer, *J. S. Bach*, trans. E. Newman, 2 vols. (London: A. & C. Black, 1911), 2: 26.

18. See Schweitzer, p. 35.

19. Smend, *Bach and Luther*, p. 15.

20. The degree to which Bach shared in pietism's rebellion against orthodox formalism is vigorously debated. See Schrade, *Bach*, pp. 47-58.

21. Helene Werthemann, *Die Bedeutung der alttestamentlichen*

Historien in Johann Sebastian Bach's Kantaten (Tübingen: Mohr, 1959), p. 31.

22. W. H. Scheide, *J. S. Bach as a Biblical Interpreter*, Princeton Theological Seminary Pamphlet 8 (Princeton, N.J. 1952), pp. 9f.

23. See his *Mimesis* (Princeton, N.J.: Princeton University Press, 1953), pp. 14-23, 40-49.

24. Scheide, *op. cit.*, p. 35.

25. Ibid., p. 18.

26. *Essays on Nature and Grace* (Philadelphia: Fortress Press, 1972), p. 81.

27. Quoted in Sittler, pp. 127f.

28. Quoted in Scheide, *op. cit.*, p. 12.

29. Quoted in Martin Dibelius, *Botschaft und Geschichte* (Tübingen: Mohr [Paul Siebeck]. 1953), 1:380.

30. Quoted in Schweitzer, *J. S. Bach,* 1:x.

31. Ibid., 243.

32. Quoted in David and Mendel, eds. *The Bach Reader*, p. 385.

33. Quoted in Leonard Bernstein, *Joy of Music* (New York: Simon & Schuster, 1959), p. 246.

34. David and Mendel, *op. cit.*, pp. 373f. For another negative judgment, see Karl Barth, *Church Dogmatics*, trans. G. T. Thomson (Edinburgh: T. & T. Clark, 1958), 4.2: 262f.

35. Albert C. Outler, *Who Trusts in God* (New York: Oxford University Press, 1968), p. 32.

36. See Karl Barth, *Word of God and Word of Man*, trans. Douglas Horton (Grand Rapids: Zondervan, 1935), p. 60.

37. J. A. Ernesti, *Elementary Principles*, trans. M. Stuart, 4th ed. (Andover, Mass.: Allen, Morill, and Wardwell, 1842), pp. 55f., 83f.

38. Schrade, *Bach.*, pp. 9ff., 35f.

39. Ibid., pp. 79-102.

40. Ibid., p. 111.

41. *New York Times*, February 16, 1973, p. 24.

42. See Schweitzer, *J. S. Bach*, 1: 263.

43. Ibid., p. 264.

44. *Contra* Schweitzer, *J. S. Bach* 1: 263f.

45. David and Mendel, eds. *J. S. Bach*, p. 35.

46. In *The Ascent to Heaven* (London: Barrie Books, 1961), pp. 73f.

47. Karl Rahner, as quoted in *The Christian Century*, 89 (1972): 241.
48. Outler, *Who Trusts in God*, p. 6.
49. Ibid., p. 106.
50. Farrar, *History of Interpretation*, p. 4 (italics mine).
51. Ibid., pp. 401f.
52. Schweitzer, *J. S. Bach* 2: 25-45.
53. Chiapusso, *Bach's World*, p. 1.

PHILOSOPHY AND FAITH:
A STUDY IN HEGEL AND WHITEHEAD

Daniel D. Williams

The question of what philosphy can do in giving credibility
and intelligibility to Christian faith is one with which Albert
Outler has concerned himself throughout his lifework of
interpreting the history of Christian thought. His own work
has shown that the relation of faith and reason must be
re-examined in every era, for the modes of reasoning change
in the light of science and new experience. The self-understanding of the Christian faith confronts new issues within
the believing community and in relating faith to the changing
and often explosive cultural scene.

  This paper proposes to examine one strand of the classic
and contemporary discussion of faith and philosophic reason
by analyzing the way in which Hegel and Whitehead give
philosophical accounts of Christianity. Alongside Hegel's
claim to show the truth of Christianity as the absolute
religion in the form of absolute knowledge achieved by
philosophy, we shall set Whitehead's more modest but
similarly rationalistic faith that the essential truth of Chris-

The author, who died in December of 1973, was Roosevelt Professor of Systematic Theology, Union Theological Seminary.

tianity can be exhibited in its universality through a philosophic critique of the theological tradition and the elaboration of a theistic cosmology. In so doing, we may be able to identify certain critical issues concerning the limits of reason in interpreting Christian faith, and we shall try to see what it is that Christian theology must consider in the work of philosophers who give their own account of the intelligibility of faith. Finally, we shall identify one important issue that emerges between the Hegelian and Whiteheadian accounts of reconciliation as the overcoming of tragic history. In dealing with the meaning and overcoming of evil Hegel and Whitehead stand very close together, yet there is a critical difference between them.

Since they think within the same philosophic tradition, the issues between Hegel and Whitehead offer an especially illuminating study of the limits and possibilities of reason. Whitehead disavowed ever having read much of Hegel, partly, he says, because he once found Hegel talking some "complete nonsense" about mathematics. But Whitehead acknowledges that his philosophy is of the Hegelian type, and the historic route of Hegel's idealism runs through Bradley and McTaggart to Whitehead.[1] When Whitehead says he is transposing some of the main doctrines of idealism onto a realistic base, his statement is supported and clarified by comparison of his doctrine with Hegel's.[2]

Hegel claims that religion, which is the knowledge Spirit has of itself as Spirit, finds fulfillment in the Christian religion; but the truth is expressed in Christianity in pictures and images that need to be given scientific rational form before Spirit can achieve its goal of absolute Truth.

Out of the richness and complexity of Hegel's philosophy of religion, from his early theological writings to the last lectures on the philosophy of religion, I shall concentrate on just two aspects of Hegel's view of religion and Christianity:

first, his view that reason can objectify the truth of religion as universal knowledge; and second, his view of what it is in the nature of reason that lends it this supreme power.

Hegel sees the work of Spirit (*Geist*) in history as the search for the coming to full consciousness of absolute truth. "The truth is the whole," he says in the preface to the *Phenomenology of Mind*[3] Therefore, religion is the human search for the reality that constitutes the absolute and all-inclusive truth. That reality for Hegel must be found in the coming of self-knowledge of Spirit itself. Thus religion seeks what philosophy gives:

> The aim of philosophy is to know the truth, to know God, for He is the absolute truth, inasmuch as nothing else is worth troubling about save God and the unfolding of God's nature. . . . Philosophy has been reproached with setting itself above religion; this however is false . . . it sets itself merely above the form of faith, the content is the same in both cases.[4]

The universal reality of Spirit which religion seeks and philosophy knows is not the abstract universality of concepts or ideals. It is the one concrete and absolute truth embracing the whole of the cosmos, history, and eternity. It is God knowing himself in the history of the world.

Hegel sees in Christianity the religion that has fully grasped the relation of God to the world. It is the Christological affirmation: God has become man. The Christian faith declares that "Spirit is accordingly the living process by which the implicit unity of the divine and human natures becomes actual and comes to have definite existence."[5]

The unity expressed in the incarnation is not, however, given as a bare idea or principle. It has to be won through the process of Spirit's self-alienation, which gives rise to the story of finitude and history. The full power and profundity of Hegel's view of reason is exhibited in his account of world history as the life of Spirit returning to itself, that is becoming conscious of itself as Spirit. It is the process of alienation and return that constitutes the truth of the whole, and within this perspective Hegel works out the meaning of the biblical drama of Creation, Fall, Incarnation, Atonement, Crucifixion, and Resurrection, the rise of the new community of Spirit and its participation in eternal life.

The Crucifixion can be spoken about as the death of God, for it is the point at which Spirit achieves its self-disclosure as the absolute limit of the experience of finitude. "This is the deepest depth." Here Spirit comes to self-recognition, grasping and overcoming the meaning of its own alienation:

> This death is thus at once finitude in its most extreme form, and at the same time the abolition and absorption of natural finitude, of immediate existence and estrangement, the cancelling of limits.[6]

The theme of the universality of Spirit is repeatedly affirmed in Hegel's account:

> When the fullness of time was come, God sent his Son, *i.e.*, when Spirit had entered so deeply into itself as to know its infinitude, and to comprehend the Substantial in the subjectivity of immediate self-consciousness, in a subjectivity however which is at the same time infinite negativity, and is just, in consequence of this, absolutely universal.[7]

The real internal history of Christianity therefore is the history of the Spiritual Community brought into being through the Crucifixion and the Resurrection. It is the community that bears the authentic universal within its faith, since the history of Christ by which the community lives is absolutely adequate to the Idea.[8] God is eternal love, and this absolute truth that God is not an abstraction but absolutely concrete is unfolded by philosophy; and it is only modern philosophy that has reached the profound thought thus contained in the Notion (*der Begriff*).

For Hegel, then, it becomes possible to speak of Christian faith as a justification of the ways of God to man. The story of Spirit is packed with tragedy, illusion, suffering, and death. To live as finite person struggling for understanding means to experience infinite sorrow, for we live in contradiction. The "I," the natural will, seeks particular fulfillment, It loses the concern for universality. But Spirit coming to itself in Christianity knows that this evil of self-isolation is overcome:

> Spirit can make what has happened as if it had not happened; the action certainly remains in the memory but Spirit puts it away. . . . For the true consciousness of Spirit the finitude of man is slain in the death of Christ. . . . The death of the natural gets in this way a universal signification, the finite, evil, in fact, is destroyed. The world is thus reconciled, and through this death the world is implicitly freed from its evil.[9]

Hegel thus assigns to reason the highest possible function. It is nothing other than the divine and human spirit together attaining a self-conscious grasp of the saving truth. Reason understands and fulfills what every creature and every life really needs. Reason's service to religion is to give permanent form to the message of reconciliation. Christianity therefore is rational belief. Faith attains understanding. God is known, for He is Spirit itself, the absolute source and principle of intelligibility.

These magisterial claims for reason are the hallmark of the Hegelian philsophy. They sound somewhat strange a century and a half later, even perhaps vulgar or naïve. We cannot assess his claim until we understand what he meant by reason and his view of how its work gets done. For Hegel, reasoning is not abstract reflection, nor is it the application of an analytic method seeking to achieve clarity of logical form. Reason is the progress of the total self-reflection of Spirit moving through the whole of time and history, and probing for the pattern of being as this unfolds in the total history of nature, life, and culture.

Hegel did indeed believe that there is a logical structure in existence, and his logic is a brave and obscure attempt to set forth that structure in itself. But it is no simple formula of dialectical progression, nor does it yield a simple logical pattern that can be applied forthwith to the description of every experience. The logic is the interweaving of all basic concepts with one another so that the incompleteness of every abstract concept taken by itself is exhibited, and its meaning as involved in the interlocking web of meanings is articulated. Hippolyte has called Hegel's logic a "poetic of being," and the phrase is apt.[10] Reasoning, for Hegel, is the process of bringing every partial concept and structure into relation to its history, its context, and its participation in the final truth that is the whole. Until the fundamental pattern of Spirit seeking its own self-consciousness is grasped, we do not really understand anything in particular. Hegel's ultimate assumption is that to be human is to want to know who we are, why we are what we are, and what it is that makes us what we are. It is truth that "makes us free." Every Hegelian philosopher can quote the Fourth Gospel assertion as the New Testament charter of the vocation of truth-seeking. And again, the Apostle Paul puts knowledge at the center of the Christian hope, even if he does not make it the sole content of that hope: "Now I know in part; then I shall understand fully, even as I have been fully understood" (1 Cor. 13:12).

Knowledge comes through the concrete experience that conscious beings have of the world process, and philosophy is the final expression of that knowledge. History must be lived through for Spirit to know itself, for it has no knowledge apart from that history. Here is the key thesis in the Hegelian perspective. "It is the very nature of understanding to be a process, and being a process it is Rationality." Note particularly, then, this conclusion: "This alone is what is rational, the rhythm of the organic whole. It is as much knowledge of content as that content is notion and essential nature."[11] We see that Hegel's claims for reason, whatever their exaggerations, are meaningless apart from his conviction that truth is given in the life process itself. Truth is at work shaping all things, and at work in the life of subjects who are coming to reflect on their own being. It is here that Hegel stands in the Aristotelian tradition as one of those who sees both scientific and philosophic inquiry as the search for the forms embedded in things; but for Hegel the final principle of intelligibility is not an Unmoved Mover, but the total history of Spirit's self-movement, its self-emptying, and return.

The life of reason, then, is the pilgrimage of the human spirit toward the light. Hegel's description of the pilgrimage in the *Phenomenology of Mind* reflects the ladder of mystical ascent, beginning with sense experience and its subjection to critical reflection, opening the way to the dialectical penetration of all forms of being, and moving toward the ultimate structure that they all exemplify.

> Consciousness first finds in self-consciousness—the notion of mind—its turning point, where it leaves the parti-coloured show of the sensuous immediate, passes from the dark void of the transcendent and remote supersensuous and steps into the spiritual daylight of the present.[12]

The century elapsing between Hegel's last lectures on the philosophy of religion and the period of Whitehead's metaphysical reflection is filled with revolutions of monumental significance in human thought. There is the collapse of the idealist philosophies of nature and the conquering progress of scientific empiricism in Darwin, the revolution in modern physics, the transposition of the Hegelian dialectic of Spirit into the revolutionary dialectical materialism of Marxism, the inauguration of a new era for logic and mathematics exemplified by Whitehead and Russell's *Principia Mathematica*, and the new "age of analysis," as Morton White has called it.

Christian theology has participated in this revolution and the new modes of thought, and has found in Karl Barth what appears to be the most decisive rejection of philosophic reason as having any place in the articulation of Christian faith. Yet the question of the relation of faith to reason does not go away, and we shall see in Whitehead the continuation of that mode of philosophical interpretation of Christianity which continues to pose the issue of the place of reason.

In spite of the radical new perspectives in the twentieth century, Whitehead's doctrine bears very strong resemblances to Hegel's rational vision of the meaning of Christianity. It must be said at the outset that Whitehead rejects the imperious and absolute claims that Hegel makes for speculative reason. For Whitehead philosophic reason, including its speculative search for metaphysics, is indispensable to civilization; but philosophy must live in a critical give-and-take with all other inquiries, including science and theology. "There is no short cut to truth." It follows that Whitehead rejects every claim for finality for any philosophy, including his own:

> Systems, scientific and philosophic, come and go. Each method of limited understanding is at length exhausted. In its prime each system is a triumphant success: in its decay it is an obstructive nuisance.[13]

Yet Whitehead has a high place for reason that seeks the "essence" or the essential structure of reality, and his metaphysical vision is very close to that of Hegel, as is his view of the necessity of metaphysics for religion.

To begin with, Whitehead, like Hegel, is concerned with

the two major questions of permanence in the face of flux and the relation of universality to individuality. With this emphasis on the necessity of overcoming the evil in death and passage, Hegel and Whitehead may be said to stand closer to the Eastern Orthodox tradition of Christianity than to the Western, with its central emphasis on guilt. For Whitehead it is temporality that constitutes the deepest threat to the meaning of life. He says: "Religion is the art and the theory of the internal life of man, so far as it depends on the man himself and on what is permanent in the nature of things."[14] Again, he asks theology

> to express that element in perishing lives which is undying by reason of its expression of perfections proper to our finite natures. In this way we shall understand how life includes a mode of satisfaction deeper than joy or sorrow.[15]

Process and Reality closes with the declaration that the vision of God there expounded aims to show how zest for existence can be refreshed "by the ever-present unfading importance of our immediate actions, which perish and yet live forever more."[16]

Whitehead associates the religious spirit closely with the search for "universality"—that is, the reach for a universal truth, and participation in reality which fulfills the meaning of life by binding all things to one another. It is instructive to read Whitehead's *Religion in the Making* and *Adventures of Ideas* together as a twentieth-century *Phenomenology of Mind*. As in Hegel's great work the philosopher here traces the history of culture as the search for participation in the universal and enduring values. The statements that "religion is world loyalty" and that "generality is the salt of religion" put succinctly the significance of universality, which Whitehead elaborates in many ways.[17] The decisive formal statement of the relation of the religious quest to universality of meaning is found in the following passage from *Process and Reality:*

> Religion should connect the rational generality of philosophy with the emotions and purposes springing out of existence in a particular society, in a particular epoch, and conditioned by particular antecedents. Religion is the translation of general ideas into particular thoughts, particular emotions, and particular purposes; it is directed to the end of stretching individual interest beyond its self-defeating particularity. . . . Religion is the ultimate craving to infuse into the insistent particularity of emotion that non-temporal generality which primarily belongs to conceptual thought alone.[18]

It scarcely needs remarking how closely this doctrine stands to Hegel's view of religion as Spirit seeking its own self-conscious grasp of the truth. But again, as with Hegel, we must recognize that for Whitehead the work of reason discerning the universal structure is never in abstraction from experience. Surely as clearly as does Hegel, Whitehead remains an empiricist so far as the test of truth is concerned. Reason attempts to find the general concepts that pertain to all the details of practice. Whitehead allows, of course, for logical coherence as an important aspect of the test of truth; but the final test is "wide-spread recurrent experience."[19]

It is clear why religion and theology need philosophy and science. The truth is found only in the interaction of experience with all the modes of rational, aesthetic, and symbolic expression. The same internal drive in religion and morality toward universality of outlook is present in philosophy. "All general truths condition each other."[20] "Reason is the safeguard of the objectivity of religion: it secures for it the general coherence denied to hysteria."[21]

The question of what does secure objectivity for human thinking and how far reason can be relied upon for this is a topic of much importance. It is our purpose here not to defend Whitehead's confidence in reason but to recognize that when philosophers make the claim that universality of meaning can be attained only through the exercise of philosophic reason, theologians must take account of this claim. If it be true, it says something decisive about the task of understanding religion and faith. In our time, when there is such fragmentation of experience and such despair about communication between different perspectives, both secular and religious, it is certainly worth asking whether there is a function of reason that can aid common understanding.

We turn now to Whitehead's interpretation of the place of Christianity in the history of religion. He never uses the term "absolute" for Christianity. He was clearly interested in the possibility that aspects of his own cosmological outlook might be close to some elements of Buddhism, which he describes as a metaphysic generating a religion in contrast to Christianity as a religion seeking a metaphysic.[22] But Whitehead does find in Christianity the decisive insight that became his basis for judging all traditional doctrines. Whitehead's two theses about the significance of Christianity are, first, that Christianity as expressed in the initial testimony of the Gospels understands that the salvation of the world lies in the triumph of persuasion over force; and second, that this insight was lost when Christian dogma degraded its vision of the divine persuasion by combining the concepts derived from Semitic religion of God as omnipotent will with the Unmoved Mover of Aristotle and the Neo-Platonic conception of God as the eminently real, thus producing a conception of God as world ruler which contradicts the ethical sensitivity affirmed by the Gospel itself.[23]

Here Whitehead the philosopher appeals in the name of reason and ethical sensitivity against the theological tradition to what he finds deepest in the Christian experience. He appeals to our direct intuition of the meaning of the Gospel story:

The essence of Christianity is the appeal to the life of Christ as a revelation of the nature of God and of his agency in the world ... there can be doubt as to what elements in the record have evoked a response from all that is best in human nature. The Mother, the Child, and the bare manager: the lowly man, homeless and self-forgetful, with his message of peace, love and sympathy: the suffering, the agony, the tender words as life ebbed, the final despair: and the whole with the authority of supreme victory. ... Can there be any doubt that the power of Christianity lies in its revelation in act of that which Plato divined in theory?[24]

A certain contrast with Hegel appears here. Hegel sees the end of Spirit's work as freedom; but he draws no absolute opposition between freedom and coercion. Hegel sees the whole process of Spirit as having its self-regulating necessity, and his picture of the world spirit tramping, and sometimes trampling, through history does involve an acceptance of God's agency as manifest in many apparently ruthless forms, and not stopping for the niceties of moral sensitivities.[25] Whitehead on the other hand represents what was in the early part of the twentieth century called "ethical theism." He believed that the concept of God's mode of dealing with the world must be brought into harmony with an ethical view of what freedom entails. Hence God for Whitehead does not drive the world; he lures it through the power of the vision he inspires. It is a Christological perspective compatible with the Gospel word: "I, if I be lifted up from the earth, will draw all men unto me" (John 12:32).

The critical issue for Whitehead, then, is the meaning and possibility of the "supreme victory." For Hegel it is guaranteed; but is it so for Whitehead? What is the status of evil? These are pressing questions, and Whitehead was fully aware of them. In trying to trace out his answer we find where he remains very close to Hegel; yet there is a difference about good and evil and their destiny, and it may make all the difference in two different religious understandings.

The question is, what kind of hope does Christianity hold. Both Whitehead and Hegel see history as tragic viewed from one side. Yet both come out with a positive affirmation of hope, so that Hegel can state that Christianity really belongs to Comedy rather than Tragedy, and Whitehead affirms the reality of Peace in the religious Spirit. Here some careful analysis is needed.

Whitehead clearly believes that evil is real. The Hegelian side of Whitehead is found in the way in which he sees present evil woven into ultimate good:

> The Kingdom of heaven is not the isolation of good from evil. It is the overcoming of evil by good. This transmutation of evil into good enters into the actual world by reason of the inclusion of the nature of God, which includes the ideal vision of each actual evil so met with a novel consequent as to issue in the restoration of goodness.[26]

It would require a study of a great many passages in Whitehead to get a full textual basis on which to judge what he really believed about the destiny of evil. It is clear that the "greatest evil," temporality, is overcome through participation in the everlasting life of God.[27] But do the real evils of actual events lose their quality of evil in God's assessment of them? That is the critical issue, and it is because Whitehead says some things about it which seem to suggest a complete transfiguration of all evil, that Stephen Ely could interpret Whitehead's God as the divine aesthete enjoying the world spectacle with undiminished intensity no matter what takes place in history.[28]

There is an alternative interpretation of Whitehead's view of evil which makes a much sharper difference with Hegel's doctrine that evil is always taken up into the absolute good of Spirit. I am not sure that all the Whiteheadian texts are in agreement with one another here. What saves Whitehead from the view that all evil becomes transformed into good in God is his doctrine that God and the world are together in process toward as yet unresolved issues and unachieved goods. God guides the world with an ideal vision. He imparts to the creatures the harmony and lure of the new good, including the transformation of the world that comes through God's perfect understanding and care. But for Whitehead there is no completion of this process in the sense of a static resolution. There are continuous resolutions of particular issues which enter permanently into God's experience of the world. But that experience includes the world's becoming, its limitations, and the losses attending every decision. Whitehead insists that wherever there is a choice between possibilities, something is lost as well as gained; and this is as true for God as for the creatures. Hence the world story is not the achievement of all possible good. It has its tragic side.

> There remain the final opposites, joy and sorrow, good and evil, disjunction and conjunction—that is to say, the many in one—flux and permanence, greatness and triviality, freedom and necessity, God and the World.[29]

Another way of putting the decisive point is that in the divine wisdom evil is judged. Whitehead affirms the importance of each individual occasion. It is one of his clearest differences with a purely organic idealism in which nothing is really real except the whole. For Whitehead there is an absolute importance for every individual occasion of experience, but this importance is not understood apart from the achievement and the failure of each act in experience to realize at least some of the possibility lying before it. "Every act," Whitehead says, "leaves the world with a deeper or a fainter impress of God."[30] If one takes this text as the real key to his view, then it is clear that there is loss and tragedy in all existence, but that God brings all such loss within the orbit of his understanding, his wisdom and his unflagging vision of the good. He is "the fellow sufferer who understands."[31]

> The consequent nature of God is his judgment on the world. He saves the world as it passes into the immediacy of his own life. It is the judgment of a tenderness which loses nothing that can be saved. It is also the judgment of a wisdom which uses what in the world is mere wreckage.[32]

"Nothing lost that can be saved." This is the vision of God as absorbing the world's effort into his ongoing experience. It holds with Hegel that no event is defined in its value solely by its immediacy of achievement or failure. God brings new good out of evil, and there is worth in every experience, no matter what the loss. It is the intuition of this final importance and worth of individual action which gives the sense of Peace. "Peace is the understanding of tragedy, and at the same time its preservation."[33]

In this way Whitehead's search for a rational vision does embody in its estimate of evil an alternative religious position to that of Hegel. They both hold that reason can penetrate to a supreme victory affirmed in Christian faith, but Whitehead believes that reason must acknowledge an element of incompleteness and divine suffering in the ultimate outcome.

Our point of departure was the question concerning the significance of philosophic reason for Christian faith. Both Whitehead and Hegel claim that reason can penetrate the metaphysical order on which all good and salvation depend, and give an account of alienation, estrangement, despair, and renewal of hope. Whitehead, as did Hegel, assigns to philosophy a special role in the advancement of civilization.

> ... in unthinking Nature "natural selection" is a synonym for waste! Philosophy should now perform its final service. It should seek the insight, dim though it be, to escape the wide wreckage of a

race of beings sensitive to values beyond those of mere animal enjoyment.[34]

This assigns a high vocation to philosophy. Like Hegel, Whitehead believes that in carrying out this task philosophy can draw upon insight derived form Christianity. They both see in the Incarnation the key to Christianity's distinctive place in world religions. For Hegel it is the unity of God and man. For Whitehead it is the victory of persuasion over force.

My aim has not been to judge between these two systems; but to show that Christian theology cannot ignore these philosophical interpretations of faith. The case can be stated in two points. First, the philosophers claim to set forth the universal meaning of human experience and therefore of the religious quest. The claim to universality cannot be bypassed by theology, for theology makes it also.

All great religious faiths claim to have hold on the universal meaning of life. The God of Christian faith loves the world, not just a portion of it. The Christ is the Way, the Truth, and the Life. Karl Barth has disavowed the help of philosophy in stating Christian theology, but when he says that "the truth of Jesus Christ . . . is *the* truth, the universal truth that creates all truth" we are driven to ask how this universal truth is to be given such form that its universality can be an intelligible hypothesis.[35]

Of course, it can be said that both Hegel and Whitehead work within Christian culture and consciously set out to reason about Christianity, so that we are dealing here with a "Christianized reason," not a universal reason. There is indeed no absolutely universal standpoint for reason. And there is no way of knowing what modern philosophy would have been without the history of cultures—Eastern, Western, and Judeo-Christian—in which it has participated. But the claim still remains that the human power of reasoning has a place in the critical interpretation of all traditional religious doctrines.

The second argument for the involvement of theology with the philosophic task is closely related to the first. Is Christian faith to be understood within the history of religions, or, as some modern theologians have held, is it a perspective that transcends religion?

It is the tendency of philosophers of religion to see all religions and faith in some kind of interrelationship. This may be dangerous to the individuality of particular faiths, but it is hard to see how Christianity can understand itself internally unless it takes up the biblical theme of the witness the one God has given of himself in every land. The notion that the search for communication and understanding among religions is an exercise in human good will and the desire to live in some kind of community of understanding is true but inadequate. The question is whether any religion can understand itself apart from the structure of human existence and the search for meaning in the face of alienation and despair. The search for the universal element in religion may or may not succeed, but it is essential to the religious spirit itself to find within the experience of the holy that which illumines every experience.

There is finally to be noted a difference between the way in which Hegel and Whitehead view the work of reason. While Whitehead has great confidence in reason, he does not share Hegel's belief that the whole can be brought into a completely self-conscious structure of knowledge. For Hegel the world exists to be known; for Whitehead it exists to be felt. Thus, in the response of the human spirit to God, Whitehead leaves the final word to Vision and Insight, which run beyond adequate rational articulation. Reason is an instrument of the divine Eros in achieving the higher purposes, but it is not the only instrument, since concrete reality is feeling, adventure becoming. Whitehead says that the doctrine of God in *Process and Reality* is only an attempt to add another speaker to Hume's *Dialogues Concerning Natural Religion.* The dialogue continues.

Theologians may see here the philosopher acknowledging the reality of faith as necessary to the life of reason itself, if faith is the living personal response to that reality which draws us, with our reason, out of self-preoccupation into self-transcendence.

NOTES

Note: I have given references to the paperback edition of Hegel's *Phenomenology of Mind* (trans. J. B. Baillie), and all of Whitehead's books. Most Whitehead works are out of print in the original editions.

1. Alfred North Whitehead, *Process and Reality* (New York: The Free Press, 1969), p. 194 (hereafter *PR*). The reference to Hegel on mathematics is quoted in a memoir by William Ernest Hocking in George L. Kline, ed., *Alfred North Whitehead: Essays on His Philosophy* (Englewood Cliffs, N.J.: Prentice-Hall, 1963), p. 11. On Hegel's influence on Whitehead see Gregory Vlastos, "Organic Categories in Whitehead" in the Kline volume, and Victor Lowe, *Understanding Whitehead* (Baltimore, The Johns Hopkins Press, 1962), pp. 254-56.

2. *PR*, Preface, p. 7.

3. G. W. F. Hegel, *The Phenomenology of Mind*, trans. J. B. Baillie (New York: Harper Torchbooks, 1967), p. 81 (hereafter *Phenomenology*).

4. G. W. F. Hegel, *Lectures on the Philosophy of Religion*, trans. from 2d German edition by E. B. Speirs and J. B. Sanderson. 3 vols. (London: Kegan Paul, Trench, Trubner & Co., 1895, 1968), 3:148 (hereafter *Lec. Ph. Rel*).

5. Hegel, *Lec. Ph. Rel.*, 2:349.

6. Ibid., 3:60, 93.

7. Ibid., 3:112.

8. Ibid., 3:111–13.

9. Ibid., 3:96; cf. 3:130.

10. Jean Hippolyte, *Studies in Marx and Hegel* (New York: Basic Books, 1969), p. 169.

11. Hegel, *Phenomenology*, p. 115.

12. Ibid., p. 227.

13. Alfred North Whitehead, *Adventures of Ideas* (New York: The Free Press, 1967), p. 159 (hereafter *AI*).

14. Alfred North Whitehead, *Religion in the Making* (New York: World Publishing Co., Meridian Books, 1960), p. 16 (hereafter *RM*).

15. *AI*, p. 172.

16. *PR*, p. 413.

17. *RM*, pp. 59, 42.

18. *PR*, pp19.

19. *PR*, p. 21.

20. *PR*, p. 13.

21. *RM*, p. 63.

22. *RM*, p. 50.

23. *PR*, pp. 403-4.

24. *AI*, p. 167.

25. See Preface to Hegel's *Philosophy of History*.

26. *RM*, pp. 148-49.

27. *PR*, p.410.

28. Stephen Lee Ely, *The Religious Availability of Whitehead's God* (Madison: University of Wisconsin Press, 1942).

29. *PR*, p. 402.

30. *RM*, p. 152.

31. *PR*, p. 413.

32. *PR*, p. 408.

33. *AI*, p. 286.

34. *AI*, p. 159.

35. Karl Barth, *Dogmatics in Outline*, trans. G. T. Thompson (New York: Philosophical Library, 1949), p. 26.

III

CONSIDERATIONS
THEOLOGICAL

BIBLICAL ELECTION AS SACRED HISTORY:
A STUDY IN THE ANCIENT HISTORY OF ECUMENISM

Robert E. Cushman

I

THE PARADOX OF ELECTION

As we occupy the vantage point of the New Testament it becomes evident that a "sacred history" of the Bible is inseparably connected with a pervasive paradox that is the substance of the Old Testament itself: the apparent contradiction between Israel's election as the chosen People and the implied universality of God's sovereignty and purpose in world history. The paradox was acknowledged by the late Chief Rabbi of Sweden, Kurt Wilhelm:

> Universalism and particularism are . . . inextricably interwoven in Judaism, and it is in the perpetual interpretation of national and religious elements that Judaism itself both consists, and asserts, its own specific God-idea, *viz.* that the God of Israel is the God of all humanity.[1]

It is noteworthy and significant that no book of the Old Testament surpasses Deuteronomy both in clear acknowledgment and in explicit enforcement of the paradox. As Deuteronomy affirms Israel's election under the Covenant and

The author is Research Professor of Systematic Theology, Duke University Divinity School.

predicates Israel's life upon obedience to the "ordinances and statutes," it nevertheless propounds openly the paradox throughout its pages, and emphatically, in 4:32-40: Since God's creation of man upon the earth, who has heard or when has it happened that the Creator approached and addressed man and he lived? Or took a nation from among the nations for his own—even the Lord God, beside whom there is no other?[2]

This, *in nuce*, is both the core and chief problematic of biblical history. The dynamic inherent in this apparent antithesis has created the mystery of the Hebrew inheritance and the Jewish people to this day. Likewise, however, and perhaps as the resolving fruition of a powerful resident dynamism, it issued in the emergence of the New Testament faith in Jesus Christ that was hailed by St. Paul as "the revelation of the mystery." It is our intention in this paper to review the unfolding of this historic dynamism as it at length manifests itself in the preaching witness of the earliest Christian Church. We are proposing to probe, as may be fitting for this *Festschrift* in honor of Albert Outler, the ancient history of what in the twentieth century has been called "ecumenism"—its primordial thrust in the biblical story of man's summons to faithfulness under sovereign Grace.

The question about the *Oikoumēne*, as it relates to the Old Testament and to the New, centers on the import of Israel's election as a particular people somehow charged with God's eternal purpose for all mankind. Here if anywhere is the connecting link between Judaism and Christianity. Thus, the Jewish scholar Samuel H. Bergman may be correct:

> If what is meant by *Oikoumēne* is the Church of Christ united within itself, then Israel has nothing whatever to say on the subject. If, however, it is to mean "the realm in which the expectation of God obtains" . . . the conception of the *Oikoumēne* becomes a central one for Jewish religious thinking.[3]

II

THE OLD TESTAMENT: ECUMENISM UNFOLDING

Whether, as Bernhard Anderson and Gerhard von Rad have affirmed, the Exodus under Moses definitively marks the election of Israel as Yahweh's own people, or whether it is first signalized, as Martin Buber contends, in the call of Abraham (Gen. 12:1-2),[4] it is with the declaration at Sinai, according to Gerhard von Rad, that Israel remembered corporately Yahweh's choice of her as his "own possession among all peoples" (Exod. 19:3-6).[5] The text singles out Israel as Yahweh's particular possession, while, at the same time, it is the Divine universality that accents the singularity—"for all the earth is mine!" Thus, the paradox is illuminated by the implication that the choice of Israel is set within the context of God's sovereignty over all history, with the powerful innuendo that Israel is elect for a role that perhaps a Priestly redactor later defined in the words: "And you shall be to me a kingdom of priests and a holy nation" (Exod. 19:6). The immemorial question remains: Election for what?

No less a scholar of the Old Testament than H. H. Rowley took the view that "God's choice is never to be understood save in relation to its purpose."[6] But what, according to the Old Testament, is God's purpose? Is it particular or universal? Does it comport with his acknowledged sovereignty over all of history, or is it confined within his special relation to Israel? It is Rowley's view that, even though Israel's election does not exclude privilege, it is fundamentally "election for service."[7] Apparently Von Rad concurs in Rowley's happy phrase that the service in question is "bridging the cleft between God and all mankind."[8]

If this is so, then the apparent contradiction between Israel's election as the chosen people and the implicit

universality of God's sovereign purpose is illuminated. Biblical history might then qualify as "sacred history." If election
is a divine vocation, then election of a particualr people is
instrumental to ulterior Divine purpose, namely, the sovereignty of God over world history. If, as Bultmann once said
of the creation story in Genesis 1, it is "but the first chapter
in *history*,"[9] then we may be better prepared to comprehend
Paul's teaching about the renovation of the creation in Christ
(2 Cor. 5:17) as not discontinuous with the old history, but
its long-delayed fulfillment (Rom. 8:22-23).

But, we may ask, does the Old Testament, in its preponder-
ant emphasis, provide for the implementation of God's
purpose for the redemption of world history? Repeatedly it
is acknowledged that Yahweh is Lord over the nations and
may invoke them to discipline his people Israel. Isaiah or a
later figure speaks of "the latter days" when "the mountain
of the house of the Lord shall be established as the highest of
the mountains . . . and all the nations shall flow to it." Zion
will be the supreme sacred center of the earth. Moreover,
"out of Zion shall go forth the Law, and the word of the
Lord from Jerusalem" (Isa. 2:2, 3). But Jerusalem is a
terminus ad quem, and salvation seems to be by association
along a "one-way street." Even with Third Isaiah, it is the
prophetic word "that nations shall come to your light, and
kings to the brightness of your rising" (Isa. 60:3). From
Midian, Sheba, and Lebanon shall treasure be carried: "you
shall eat the wealth of nations" (61:3).[10]

Jeremiah's travail over his people, according to John
Skinner, had led him to abandon even Isaiah's hope of the
"remnant" of Israel, bringing him to the view that "the time
had come for State and State-religion to be done away."[11]
Hence he looked for a "new covenant" between God and
men written on the heart of the individual, although with
corporate expression (Jer. 31:31-32). Yet Skinner allows

that, in the midst of the desolation of Jerusalem, Jeremiah was yet filled "with a passionate longing and hope for the return of the disinherited." Skinner's subsequent statement in explanation of Jeremiah's residual nationalism is as fair as any I know and has application also to narrowing trends in post-exilic Judaism to which we shall turn.

> This concentration of interest on the new Israel is due to a limitation in the Old Testament point of view which even Jeremiah was unable to transcend. The limitation springs from a fundamental truth of religion, that religion has a social aspect, and cannot unfold its full powers except in a community; and nationality was the only form of religious community known to men of the Old Testament. The idea of a new community created by the spirit of religion itself and founded on a relation to God common to all its members, was beyond their grasp, because conditions for the formation of such a community did not yet exist. They therefore clung to the traditional idea of Israel as the people in whose history the true God had revealed Himself, and within whose fellowship their personal communion with God was realized. This we must hold true of Jeremiah. . . . Thus while to Jeremiah the nation is no longer the *unit* of religion, it is still the *sphere* of religion. . . . [12]

If we attend to Skinner's discriminating assessment, as I believe we must, it appears that election for service encounters a social introversion that obstructs mission and encourages the chosen people to cherish their given self-identity. Election tends to accent consciousness of claim rather than of vocation and responsibility. So Israel of the Second Temple and of post-exilic times seems, indeed, decreasingly aware of a missionary role as the chosen people of God by comparison with the insights of such eighth-century prophets as Micah or Isaiah.[13] Yet it is true that II Isaiah, the prophet of the Exile, with unsurpassed vision proclaimed Israel as Servant of Yahweh: "Behold my servant, whom I uphold, my chosen, in whom my soul delights. I will put my spirit upon him, he will bring forth justice to the nations" (Isa. 42:1).

Yahweh formed Israel "from the womb to be his Servant" (49:5), to mediate his salvation: "I will give you as a light to the nations, that my salvation shall reach to the end of the earth" (49:6).

Yet when Israel returned from the Exile it seems to have been under the aegis of the cultic and theocratic exclusivism of Ezekiel (Ezek. 44:9-14). It is sobering to have the careful assessment of Oesterley and Robinson that "the universalistic teaching of Deutero-Isaiah did not bear fruit,"[14] The influence of the Servant teaching was, they think, "negligible." It is their judgment that

> From now on belief and practice narrowed down, in the main, into nationalistic grooves, and the religion which the greater prophets, and especially Deutero-Isaiah, would have made a world religion, assumed of set purpose a form which excluded non-Jews.[15]

With learning and fairness, W. D. Davies concurs respecting the post-exilic drift of Judaism toward "narrow nationalism." The spirit of Ezekiel prevailed "and the post-exilic history of Judaism became the history of a 'fenced' community . . . . The Torah, which differentiated the Jews from others, also separated him from them."[16] Thus, Davies continues, " . . . by the first century B.C. there is almost a complete absence of any expression of universalism."[17] Yet, while the "particularist spirit" prevailed without abatement, Davies perceives an emergent "uneasy conscience" regarding the Gentiles without the law, a mood expressing itself by way of proselytic endeavor as the means of salvation through "naturalization" into the Jewish people.[18]

Joachim Jeremias has interpreted this proselytic activity as intensive in the first century B.C., especially in Hellenistic Judaism of the Diaspora. He says that "Jesus thus came upon the scene in the midst of what was *par excellence* the missionary age of Jewish history."[19] The extension of the mission ranged throughout the Roman Empire, yet there remains a question as to the platform of this missionary zeal.

Jeremias concedes that the sources are scanty, and his appeal to the school of Hillel (*c.* A.D. 20) for its rationale is unconvincing. For Rabbi Hillel to justify proselytism against the School of Shammai on the supposedly liberal mandate, "Love mankind and bring them to the Law," hardly qualifies as mission in the post-Pauline sense.[20] On the contrary, it is exchange, apparently, of the posture of passivity for intensive activity along the "one-way street." Jeremias seems severely to delimit the mission to the Gentiles by his observation that "Conversion to the Jewish religion meant nothing less than naturalization, becoming a Jew."[21] Surely, "mission" had to be something more to qualify for the name; at the same time, one is not unmindful of ambiguity attaching to any historically conditioned vehicle of the universal grace of God.

In view, then, of the apparent near-absence in post-exilic Judaism of effectual awareness of a missionary role of the chosen people, may we not wonder at the basis upon which H. H. Rowley supported his assessment of Israel's election as "election for service"? Isaiah had, indeed, rejoiced in the prospect of the day when the earth should be "full of the knowledge of the Lord as waters cover the sea" (Isa. 11:9). But this spirit of universal praise hardly prevailed in the ages following the return of the exiles and the building of the second Temple. The centripetal forces of nationalism seemingly became more powerful than the centrifugal forces of universal mission.[22] The individualization of worship envisioned by Jeremiah evidently failed to leave its mark. The spirit of Ezekiel and the Priestly tradition dominated the interpretation of the Mosaic Law and the Covenant to the end of securing a separate nation, holy to the Lord, and qualified to inherit the promises fitting to God's chosen people. The deliberate particularism of Deuteronomy tended to prevail, implemented by the ordinances and the statutes of the Law under the surveillance of the Levitical priesthood. Accordingly, perhaps, the Temple cultus and the Law of ordinances, with the Synagogue, became the dominating foci of post-exilic Jewish piety.

While the main currents of post-exilic Judaism seem to move toward heightened national self-consciousness, important eddies of universalistic teaching do find expression in the Wisdom writings and such books as Jonah and Ruth. In general, however, the Servant role of Israel seems to have acquired a muted status in pre-Christian Jewish piety. Nor was it, according to the weighty judgment of Sigmund Mowinckel, in later Judaism associated with the Messiah until post-New Testament times.[23] From Mowinckel's view that the "Messiah is not the central and dominating figure in the future hope of later Judaism,"[24] we derive scanty basis for the otherwise feasible inference that in some manner the election of Israel for service was, as it were, transferred to the Messiah and conserved. So we are the more prepared for Mowinckel's eventual finding that "no one in Judaism connected the Servant with the Messiah, the mediator of the kingdom of God, and of the new relation between God and men."[25] And when we add to this his generalization, deriving from the same context, to the effect that "this national and this-worldly element remains the heart of the future hope throughout the entire Old Testament period: God's kingly rule on earth through the world-hegemony of Israel and her Davidic ruler," we may wonder about the grounds of the view that Israel's election was election for service.[26]

Adverting, therefore, to our earlier question, we may be prompted to inquire whether H. H. Rowley's attractive generalization is not largely a reading of the Old Testament in the light of the New. Does he suppose, from the New Testament standpoint, that Judaism of later post-exilic times had lost a grasp upon its authentic meaning or drew back from its manifest destiny? And is it perhaps possible that he believes, as it were, with Oesterley and Robinson that "in a very real sense the Cross was the liberation of the eternal truth of Judaism from the casing which protected it but limited its range"?[27] This indeed seems to be the bearing of the final chapter of his important study of election in the Old Testament. In the Cross he finds that Jesus espoused the missionary role of the Suffering Servant and made the Church heir of Israel's election. Through Christ the Church accepts "the obligation of Israel's mission."[28] In Rowley's understanding the leaders of the first-generation Church were Jews who regarded themselves as the Remnant of Israel and who had inherited the election.[29]

III

THE NEW TESTAMENT BACKGROUND

However many-sided may be the Old Testament meaning of election as it reflects the self-understanding of Israel and later Judaism, Rowley has doubtless enforced our realization that, with the acceptance by the early Church of "election for service," a decisive transition is made from the Old to the New Testament. In the remainder of this study the intention is to inquire how and in what measure the transition to what we venture to call an "ecumenical"—that is, an inclusive gospel of salvation to the whole inhabited world—was comprehended by the early Church as the import of Jesus' message, ministry, death, and resurrection.[30]

The understanding of election for service is, manifestly, correlative with a certain view of the range and reach of the saving purpose of God. Thus, respecting the early Church, there is question as to what degree universality of grace was in fact consented to by the Church or in what part there was both incomprehension and hesitancy surviving from the Jewish past.[31] For the New Testament, the question is not idle. For the latter recapitulates the Old in large measure even though the *dramatis personae* have changed and the historical variables have been altered. Yet the triumph of the contested Gentile mission in the third quarter of the first century A.D. early obscured for posterity the crisis through which first-generation Christianity passed.[32] During that period it was by no means obvious that an "ecumenical" *outreach* of the new faith would prevail. The measure to which the Lucan author of Acts both obscures and minimizes the dissension within the first-generation Church becomes conspicuous when the work is scrutinized from the standpoint of election for mission.[33]

Until perhaps the fall of Jerusalem in A.D. 70, there are strong suggestions that vital elements of Jewish Christianity were largely content to understand the new Way as essentially Judaism if with a momentous difference: namely, that Israel's Messiah had appeared in God's servant, Jesus of Nazareth, who had been crucified, but who had been raised up and exalted to the right hand of God, and "whom the heaven must receive until the time for the establishing of all that God spoke by the mouth of his holy prophets" (Acts 3:21). Repentance and forgiveness are in his name (Acts 3:38).

A powerful segment of Jerusalem Christianity, in the tradition of the Old Testament (cf. Acts 3:17-22), still looked to the age of fulfillment with the chosen people at the center; for was it not written: "I will put salvation in Zion, for Israel my glory" (Isa. 46:13)? Moreover, in that day shall it not still prevail as Isaiah had foretold, that "out of Zion shall go forth the law, and the word of the Lord from Jerusalem" (Isa. 2:3)? This theme is central in Acts. For this fulfillment, and the turning of the Gentiles, early Jerusalem

Christianity seems to have awaited the return of the Son of Man and, therewith, perhaps also the proclamation of a new Law of the messianic age to the nations.[34]

Surely, the pressing problem and consequent crisis of the primitive Church was that of an adequate understanding of what had taken place both *in* and *through* the ministry of Jesus together with his crucifixion and resurrection, and first of all in the given Old Testament context of "the hope of Israel" (Acts 28:20). The inherited context was limiting, however, for over it presided the ancient paradox of the people of God's own possession. The universality of grace was implied, but through what thematic structure could the universalizing import of the messianic age be applied to the *oikoumēne?*

We get nowhere in understanding the mind of the early Church, or the New Testament as a whole, unless we recognize as the first premise that what had happened in their midst could be comprehended by them only in the tradition of the history of election as disclosed in the saga of the covenanted people of God. To say, in the formula of the Schools, that this entails an eschatological view of history simply encapsules three fundamental standpoints inherited by the earliest Christian believers. The first is the basic Old Testament unanimity about God: "I am the first and I am the last, besides me there is no God" (Isa. 44:6). The second is that Israel's history lies between the beginning and the end of God's gracious purpose of salvation. And third, this history, for the eyes of faith, is more or less transparent to the Divine Purpose and, thus, the datum of any given understanding of God's ways with man in history—which always lies between the beginning and the end.

The early Church, accordingly, somehow must understand the event of Jesus as Messiah within the continuum of God's redemptive purpose, as the paramount moment somewhere

between the beginning and the end. It was not until
Christianity won a place within the late Hellenistic world that
sacred history as the medium of the divine self-manifestation
was confronted with the Greek, and specifically the Stoic,
alternative of the *Apeiron*—the cosmic Infinite—that challenged the Hebraic view of the beginning *ex nihilo* and
proffered in its stead a fate of the world as eternal
recurrence. In comprehending the New Testament we do not
confront this contrasting worldview. On the contrary, the
event of Jesus the Messiah adumbrates the mystery of the
divine fulfillment, the perfecting of God's grace in creation.
Moreover, as the beginning is *ex nihilo*—that is, of sheer
grace—so also is the ending, which has begun in Jesus as the
Christ.

IV

THE HOPE OF THE GENTILES IN THE MINISTRY OF JESUS

The ecumenical question was, is, and ever shall be: To
what extent and on what grounds is God's grace of salvation
open to all mankind? The presupposition of the ecumenical
question is the primordial paradox that the Lord of all the
world pursues his will through a people of his own
"possession" (Gen. 19:5). It is this that makes Israel's history
revelatory to the prophetic vision, and all history meaningful
or end-directed.

To the ecumenical question St. Paul's answer was that
through Jesus Christ there is no limit to the range of God's
salvation and that the death and resurrection of Christ have
redefined the conditions. He has done so by his deed of the
Cross, has become thereby the way of salvation for all who
will receive him. This is the Gospel of which Paul is not

ashamed: "it is the power of God for salvation to everyone who has faith, to the Jew first and also to the Greek" (Rom. 1:16). With Paul "ecumenism" is grounded in the revelation of God in Jesus Christ and conditional solely upon faith in him who, according to Paul, was "designated Son of God in power according to the Spirit of holiness by his resurrection from the dead" (Rom. 1:4).

The language is loaded and will bear unpacking; for the moment we note two points. The first is that Paul's consciousness of mandate "to bring," as he says, "obedience to faith . . . among all the Gentiles" (Rom. 1:5), is warranted primarily by the deed of the Cross and the deed of God in raising up the Crucified One. The second point is that Christ, "the power of God and the wisdom of God," is good news "to the Jew *first* and also to the Greek."[35] The question occurs as to whether, on this last point, Paul is in touch with the message and ministry of Jesus as it appears in the primitive tradition of the Gospels. Does Paul's stress in Romans upon a certain seemly priority of the Jew as candidate for God's new way of salvation through Christ resound to a note in Jesus' own message and ministry as reported in the Synoptics—namely, his apparent disposition to confine his message to Israel? Matthew verbalizes this into policy, first in Jesus' sending forth the Twelve with the injunction: "Go nowhere among the Gentiles, and enter no town of the Samaritans, but go rather to the lost sheep of the house of Israel" (Matt. 10:5-6). Second, there is the rather shocking rebuff of Jesus to the appeal of the Canaanite woman for healing mercies as reported by Matt. 15:24: "I was sent only to the lost sheep of the house of Israel."

In his essay *Jesus' Promise to the Nations*, Joachim Jeremias has confronted the issues of these passages with candor and discernment. He provides support for the view that Jesus expected the incorporation of the Gentiles into the

Kingdom of God with its establishment. This, however, Jesus viewed "as God's eschatological act of power, as the great final manifestation of God's free grace."[36] In this way, God raises up children unto Abraham of the very stones. So, for Jesus, the inclusion of the Gentiles awaits the decisive act of God. Meanwhile, the proclamation of the coming Kingdom to Israel is viewed by Jeremias as the prior responsibility of Jesus' message and work. In support of this view, moreover, he appeals to the rationale provided in Romans 15:7-9 where Paul declares:

> For I tell you that Christ became a servant for the circumcised to show God's truthfulness, in order to confirm the promises given to the patriarchs, and in order that the Gentiles might glorify God for his mercy.

It is possible that in this statement, which is also a summation of a portion of his concerns in Romans 9-11, Paul does address himself to the tradition preserved in Matthew 15:24. The phrase "Christ became a servant for the circumcised" may be an oblique acknowledgment of a still widely current word of Jesus, confining his ministry to Israel. It is awkward for Paul, not because his Gospel cannot answer it but because its literal espousal by a segment of contemporary Jewish Christianity constituted resilient opposition to the Gentile mission of the Pauline manner as late as the end of his work at Ephesus.[37] Meanwhile, it is axiomatic with Paul that it is indeed *through* Abraham and his seed, Israel, that the promise derives to all men.[38] But that "seed" comes to mean Jesus Christ, according to Romans and Galatians (Gal. 3:15-16), and for a complex of reasons that must be explored in the remainder of this paper. The heart of it is that, for Paul, in Jesus Christ the election of Israel for service is fulfilled.

For Paul, Jesus' ministry, *katā sarkā,* was a call for Israel to accept in the person of God's Messiah, as incognito in the flesh, the meaning of its own election. It was the ultimate sorrow and perplexity of the Apostle that both prior to the death and resurrection of Jesus the Christ and subsequently thereto, his fellow Jews could not recognize "the glory of God in the face of Jesus Christ" on account of to the "veil" of the Law of Moses that was passing away (2 Cor. 3:12-14). And much of Romans is Paul's labored effort, a generation after the fact, to explain the tragedy, but with clinging hope of "life from the dead" (Rom. 11:15-17). Thus, examination of Romans, chapters 9-11 and 15, shows Paul facing the "mystery" of the "hardening" that has overtaken a "part of Israel" (11:25).

To recur to our original question: it may then be that the Apostle's formula in Romans 1:16, "to the Jew *first* and also to the Greek," is actually an explicit reference to a sharply controverted issue of the early Church and one to which Romans as a whole addresses itself in comprehensive answer. Yet Paul's studied *apologia* in Romans is, at the same time and inevitably, an address to adamant Israel as a whole. Eloquently he testifies to his anguish over his own people (Rom. 9:1-3). In the Pauline hermeneutic there was, for those who would receive it, a luminous understanding of Jesus' words "I was sent only to the lost sheep of the house of Israel." In the strength of the plaintive irony of II Isaiah, it went beyond the understanding of late Judaism.[39] Paul championed, though not exclusively, the servant principle in II Isaiah's understanding of Israel's vocation. Rejected by most of Israel, it had for him been fulfilled in Christ and vindicated by God. He could roundly agree that, "according to the flesh," Jesus Christ is of Israel, to which belongs also the sonship, the glory, the covenants, the giving of the law, and the promises (Rom. 9:4, 5); but he could no longer concede that Abraham's children include only those according to the flesh (Rom. 9:7). A half-century later, John the Evangelist could say virtually without fear of contradiction, and by way of intended contrast, "The law was given by Moses; grace and truth came through Jesus Christ" (1:17); but he stood on the shoulders of Paul and the embattled missioners of the first age of the Church, and we for the most part have forgotten it.

And so we come face to face with the question: Was St. Paul's interpretation of Jesus Christ, and not just the crucified and risen Lord, closer to the truth than that of contemporary Jewish Christianity? Was this latter not "Christian," too, and proclamation of the faith? Whose *kerygma*, then, is to be credited and honored? The faith of which Church are we to regard as authorized, and by what?[40] We mean only to raise the epistemological question here, neither to argue it nor, much less, settle it, since it has been with us for centuries. Reference to it is, however, implied and becomes critical in face of the virtual certainty that in the first-generation Church there was profound division in respect of *kerygma* and that some historical accidents figured prominently in the eventual victory of the Pauline Gospel. All the more important, therefore, is the question of the norms of adjudication as among the competing early claimants to the truth of the Gospel respecting the message and deed of Jesus.

St. Paul's gospel is undoubtedly an interpretation of a certain history; and, while it presupposes more, it does not presuppose less than the deed of Jesus according to the flesh. So the question presses: in what measure the ministry and message of Jesus comport with the construction placed upon it by the Apostle from his given vantage point of Jesus' death and resurrection. It is, perhaps, precisely against the history of Israel's election as afforded in the Old Testament background that we may hope to avail ourselves of either the problematic or the privileged schema of interpretation essential to comprehension of either Jesus or Paul. On this matter, the stress of Martin Kähler upon the indispensability of the Old Testament background was long ago a permanent gain.[41]

What, then, can be said of the deed of Jesus in the light, not simply of Paul but of the Old Testament background and in reciprocity with the Gospel tradition? We saw earlier that the presiding meaning of election in Exodus, underscored everywhere in Deuteronomy, was the paradox of God's sovereign choice of Israel as his "own possession." Surely, the inherent logic of the paradox calls for some breakthrough, some answer to the question, *For what*? And, to this, weighty Old Testament scholarship answers: *election for service*. And what else is to square the astonishment, noted by the Deuteronomic author, of the unconditional grace of the Creator God allied with the destiny of a particular people? At length the prophet of the Exile proclaims the message of Israel as Servant of Yahweh, but the Word is mostly unheeded in later Judaism; and Sigmund Mowinckel, along with H. H. Rowley and others, agrees that "Jesus was the first to take this prophecy seriously and apply it to himself."[42]

The question is, *Did he*? and what is the New Testament evidence? Plainly the evidence, if available, would not be just a journalist's chronicle of the life of Jesus. As the matter stands, evidence is by way of attention to a variety of episodes and logia (often remembered better than they were understood, as William Manson once discerningly said) with which the Gospels are replete and with a view to sorting and sifting according to modal themes and recurrent motifs, but always against the background of the entire biblical tradition. The end product is not likely to be any sort of demonstration. Rather, it will be interpretation, answerable

to the *given* and based upon emergent patterns, which
commends itself by shedding maximum illumination over the
widest reach of the entire spectrum, and renders some
coherence. The criterion of truth in historical judgment, I
suggest, is never adequation to brute fact but is rather the
measure of light a hypothesis sheds upon the range of our
apprehension of the subject matter.

It is perhaps, then, impossible to comprehend the vocation
of Jesus save in the light of the ancient election of the chosen
people. In fact, the relation between the two is, as it were,
isomorphic. As Deuteronomy conceives Israel's calling, it is
always either acceptance or evasion of election, with atten-
dant curse or blessing (Deut. 11:26-27). Indeed, Israel is, so
to speak, man with options under the constraint of the
Divine calling; and, in the recurrent prophetic evaluation,
Israel's record was often a story of unresolved ambiguity or
even faithlessness (Deut. 9:24). Upon this judgment "the
beginning of the gospel of Jesus Christ" is surely premised.
John's call to repentance is just suited to Israel's existence as
faith-in-unfaith, a kind of *infidelis perennis*, somehow pain-
fully inherent in the paradox of election itself (Mark 1:1, 4).

For Jesus, then, to begin his ministry with a proclamation
of the imminent advent of the Kingdom of God was indeed
to require *metanoia* of his own people as a radical Divine
imperative (Mark 1:14). The unfolding of the meaning of
that *metanoia* runs through the occasional utterances of
Jesus, is embodied in his word and work, and is consum-
mated on the Cross. The corollary is rather clear: the primary
mission of Jesus was to challenge Israel to comprehend its
given vocation and to accept it in view of the imminence of
the Kingdom. The Kingdom had been imminent, however
delayed for centuries, in the paradoxical dynamism of the
singular election. For Jesus to proclaim the Kingdom as
imminent was, in the language of eschatology, to say that it

was everlastingly implicated as the future of man under God impounded in the paradox of the chosen people. In the light of this hypothesis, it is understandable that Jesus should view his mission as necessarily, and primarily, an urgent challenge to Israel. In view of the election, salvation is, indeed, "*from the Jews*" if God's declared way with the covenanted people was to be heeded—and for Jesus it could hardly be otherwise. So the Johannine Evangelist attributes this view expressly to Jesus, with intent to answer the Matthean tradition respecting the limitation of Jesus' message to Israel.[43]

If we look directly to the Matthean injunction that limits the disciples' mission "to the lost sheep of the house of Israel" (Matt. 10:6), we note that it is unique in Matthew and without parallel in the Synoptic Gospels. On the other hand, the incident involving the Canaanite woman in the region of Tyre and Sidon is found in Mark 7:24-30, but with the absence of the Matthean declaration, "I was sent only to the lost sheep of the house of Israel." Yet it is more important to note that in the Markan version, the *injustice* of throwing the "bread of the children" to the dogs is conspicuously modified by the qualification, namely, *until* the "children are first fed." Thus, Mark construes the incident not as restrictive but permissive: it is the *faith* of the Canaanite woman that triumphs for her petition. "For this saying you may go your way," says Jesus (7:29). Mark thus notes the passing of salvation to the Gentiles as part of the mission of Jesus himself.

The Markan account antedates that of Matthew; it is obviously under the influence of Paul's gospel and in notable contrast with the Matthean version.[44] The difference between the two may easily be overlooked and thereby obscure to us markedly contrasting views within the earliest Church respecting the relation of the Gentiles to salvation through the Messiah. It seems evident that the tradition respecting

Jesus' apparent limitation of his message to Israel, retained prominently by Matthew, contributed to a crisis of under-standing on the part of the first-generation Church.

In addition to the ecumenical import of his announcement of the Kingdom of God, as enforced by the Old Testament Canon, there are other motifs and themes in the Gospel narratives which are revealing, conspicuously in Jesus' para-bles. Special attention needs to be given, likewise, to the Q source, which, as T. W. Manson cogently remarked, "more than any of the synoptic sources, shows a friendly attitude to the Gentiles."[45] In this connection, the meaning of the baptism and the temptation of Jesus requires deeper probing. Both are, I believe, parabolic of the history of the election of Israel for service, as they are, likewise, most revelatory of Jesus' own self-understanding and of his identification with Israel in its historical servant-vocation and divine destiny. While Jesus' baptism by John in the Jordan is a fixed point in interpretation of his ministry, it is also, as both Mark and Luke are aware, the paradigm of a continuing trail through which, in identification with Israel, Jesus moves onward toward the fulfillment of the universal divine calling. That trail becomes the more incumbent upon him in the measure that he encounters both incomprehension on the part of his intimate disciples and hostile resistance on the part of scribes, Pharisees, and leaders of the nation.

On this view, hardly any line of the Gospels comes closer to authentic self-disclosure than the isolated saying of Luke: "I have a baptism to be baptized with; and how am I constrained until it is accomplished" (Luke 12:50). His baptism is entire submission to the divine will and purpose in immovable faith and assurance of the sufficiency of God to which Moses called Israel *to stand* in the crossing of the Reed Sea (Exod. 14:13-14). To grasp this is to perceive also that Jesus' whole existence, like the existence of Israel itself, was existence in temptation. To be the elect of God is to be under continuing temptation. It signifies the manhood of Man, of Israel, under a divine mandate to be a vehicle of God's eternal purpose. To be tempted is to yield to any contrariety opposed to that mandate. It is to fail to pass beyond the ambiguity of faith-in-unfaith to unambiguous affirmation of the summons of God to body forth His purpose in man's own history. The temptation accounts of the Q source in both Luke and Matthew are eloquent of this meaning (Matt. 4:1-11; Luke 4:1-12).

The inability of the disciples to comprehend the fundamental vocation of the Son of Man is unmistakably evident in the request of the sons of Zebedee as Jesus makes his way to Jerusalem (Mark 10:35f.). Their private intervention for preferential treatment in the Kingdom to come is, in its opprobrium, matched only by the indignation of the other disciples, who exhibit their own pride of place. So denigrative is this indubitably early tradition to the standing of the leading apostles, James and John, that Matthew makes their "mother" petitioner for their special preferment (Matt. 20:20). As for the first of the Apostles, Peter confirms his unknowing in Mark 10:28 by voicing concern for compensations for his fidelity and thereby confirms the substance of his earlier remonstrance at Jesus' announcement of his own forthcoming passion. The severity of Jesus' rebuke is in the measure of his clear recognition in Peter of a veritable Satanic temptation: "Get behind me, Satan! For you are not on the side of God but of Men" (Mark 8:33). The historical authenticity of these traditions is in good part their manifest congruence with the history of election in the Old Testament as we have re-searched its meaning.

Along these lines we are within reach of comprehending the authentic (if aphoristic) sayings of Jesus respecting both his indissoluble relation to Israel and the urgent priority of

conveying the message of the Kingdom, first, to "the lost
sheep of the house of Israel" (Matt. 15:23). In this light, if
on somewhat different grounds, it is possible to see the
partial truth of Jeremias' view that "the incorporation of the
Gentiles" was consequent to "God's eschatological act of
power."[46] My demurrer would be, however, that the act of
God was, in Jesus' view, inseparable from Israel's fidelity to
its divine election as the instrument of God's grace. Jesus
partly historicized apocalyptic and moralized eschatology by
recognizing that God's grace of salvation is also *mediated*
through the elect people. As this mediatorship *is* the paradox
of election, it was inevitably the implication for Jesus'
ministry in its outworking, namely, his passion. Insofar,
however, as the chosen people decline their role in sacred
history, they are as salt which has lost its savor, no longer
good for anything except to be thrown out (Matt. 5:13). Or
they are a light, a city set on a hill that cannot be hid, which,
nevertheless, perversity may hide rather than put on a stand
that it may give light "to all in the house" (Matt. 5:14).

Against this background may we not come closer to
comprehension of the devastating strictures of Jesus in
reference to the scribes and Pharisees in the Matthean exposé
of exclusivistic legalism in religion: "Woe to you scribes and
Pharisees . . . because you shut the kingdom of heaven against
men; for you neither enter yourselves, nor allow those who
would enter to go in?" (Matt. 23:13). And where salt has lost
its savor, why should not Jesus be impatient with those who
"traverse sea and land to make a single proselyte?" (Matt.
23:15). What is accomplished in naturalizing outsiders into a
Judaism that has lost hold upon its reason for being? The call
of God to Israel is to embody its servanthood, to be a light in
darkness. What else then but for Jesus to espouse the election
of Israel and undergo the final baptism, the final exodus and
crossing of the everlasting sea? Eschatology is historicized

because the election of Israel is *enpersonalized*. The Cross becomes liberation from bondage and, at the same time, emancipation of the gracious purpose of God for all of history. How this was more fully understood requires that we look again to the mind of Paul.

V

THE PARADOX FULFILLED AND TRANSCENDED

At bottom, Paul's gospel is proclamation of the revelation of the mystery of election of all men finally unveiled in Jesus Christ.[47] Its truth value is indemonstrable and is luminous only against the continuity of the history of election. This leaves the revelation as Paul left it, a matter of faith. Historical "knowledge" is, in the first instance, always hypothetical and, in the last, decisional. We cannot, however, disdain the first because, in the end, we must resort to the last. To do so is either to settle for some species of *fideism* or some *philosophy*, the prevaling expedients of the past half-century in Christian origins and Christology.

In a recent symposium the late Kurt Wilhelm, testifying for current Jewish theological opinion, has said:

> Eschatological speculation is unanimous to the effect that at the onset of the messianic kingdom God will bring about a visible miracle analogous to the miracles associated with the creation and revelation.[48]

If due regard is given to the qualification "analogous," then it is evidently such an event to which St. Paul testifies respecting the ministry, crucifixion, and resurrection of Jesus of Nazareth. Scandalous as was the claim, it authorized Paul's gospel and impelled his singular mission to the Gentiles. That this is so rests upon grounds as secure as any datum of the

New Testament—namely, his own testimony, with time sequences, in Gal. 1-2. There, on occasion of vigorous defense of his gospel against Judaizing detractors who had disturbed a community of his own founding, Paul set forth the credentials of his claim that "in Christ there is neither Jew nor Greek, there is neither slave nor free, there is neither male nor female; for you are all one in Christ Jesus" (Gal. 3:28).

This epoch-making affirmation is, of course, grounded in what, according to Rom. 16:25-27, Paul, near the end of his Gentile mission, still speaks of as "my gospel and the preaching of Jesus Christ." There, he speaks of it as "the revelation of the mystery which was kept secret for long ages but is now disclosed." Moreover, it is integral to the mystery and its unveiling that it "is made to all nations." In this summation we are told by Paul that his *kerygma* is directed to the *oikoumēne* and that it transcends geographical and national demarcations.

The explicit use of the phrase "my gospel" refers us at once to the autobiographical chapters of Galatians 1-2, where Paul stresses, and under oath, that his gospel was not received from men, that he was not taught it, presumably by other Apostles or by the mother Church of Jerusalem, but that it came to him "by a revelation of Jesus Christ." As is well known, he proceeds in Galatians to make plain that it entailed these outcomes: (1) that God justifies the Gentiles by faith (3:8); (2) that "no man is justified before God by the law" (2:16); and (3) that, therefore, Jew and Gentile are alike "justified by faith in Christ" (2:16-18; 1 Cor. 1:24).

Forthwith, this not only rendered ambiguous historical Israel as the chosen people and instated children by "adoption" on an equality with native sons (Gal. 4:5), but also denationalized and de-ethnicized election to salvation and, in the end, dislocated the place of worship from the Temple in

Jerusalem to the temple of the human spirit.[49] In short, it emancipated the Christian faith of particularistic associations by engendering a perspective as unrestricted as the Spirit of the living God. The *oikoumēne* was included within the sovereignty of grace; the centrifugal dynamic prevailed over the centripetal inertia. It was the dethronement of Israel "according to the flesh" (Rom. 10:12), incurring the hostility of contemporary Judaism and the consternation of Jewish Christians and, indubitably, made Paul the most embattled figure of the early Church, by a portion of whom he was, in all probability, done in on his final visit to Jerusalem while bearing alms in the interest of Christian unity.[50]

The revolution in Paul's life must be associated with the completely shattering *apocalypsis* by which he had been discovered an enemy of God in the process of prosecuting what he took to be the righteousness prescribed of God—"the traditions of my fathers" (Gal. 1:14). The mystery unveiled was many-faceted, but, in both Galatians and Romans, it is described as "the righteousness, that has' been manifested apart from the law, although the law and the prophets bear witness to it." It is, says Paul, "the righteousness of God through faith for all who believe" (Rom. 3:21-22).

When, however, Paul speaks of a new righteousness through faith, he speaks of the human side of the equation of which Jesus Christ is the correlate. Thus, in the autobiographical account of Galatians, he speaks of his gospel as "a revelation of Jesus Christ" (Gal. 1:12). And by this he means that Jesus Christ is really both its source and its substance. Its substance includes the new righteousness of God. This, again, on the one side is justification by faith; on its other side, however, it is the revelation of the incredible, because absolutely unconditional, mercy of God—namely, his grace through Jesus Christ. So Jesus Christ is both the source and the substance of the revelation which then is likewise the content of Paul's gospel. As such, it is also "the revelation of the mystery," which in Romans and Colossians, as also in 1 Corinthians, has been hidden but now is revealed.

The picture is familiar, but clarification of the import of the revelation for Paul's ecumenical mission is in order. First, it is quite evident that it was the confrontation of Paul with the risen Jesus which compelled him to subjoin to the name "Jesus" the majesty of the title "Messiah." But to leave the matter there would be simplistic, for it neglects the spiritual revolution which was entailed for Paul and of which the appearance of the risen Jesus was catalyst.

The *apocalypsis* can be understood, however, against the historic election of Israel and its inherent paradoxical dynamic, the traditions of the fathers. Fundamental to the revelation was the shattering refutation which echoes through the letters of Paul and, in the Romans passage, is explicative of the new righteousness of God through faith. Paul testifies:

> For there is no distinction; since all have sinned and fall short of the glory of God, they are justified by God's grace as a gift, through the redemption which is in Christ Jesus. (Rom. 3:22-24)

Likewise to the Galatians Paul says, if "a law had been given which could make alive, then righteousness would indeed be by the law" (Gal. 3:21). But, he adds, in explanation of the new righteousness by faith, "the scriptures consigned all things in sin, that what was promised to faith in Jesus Christ might be *given* to those who believe" (Gal. 3:22).

Adequate exegesis is impossible here; it may suffice to say that Paul is not simply citing Scripture to vindicate his views, such as Hab. 2:4—"He who through faith is righteous shall live" (Gal. 3:11). To be sure, for Paul the word of God is given in Scripture, but the decisive word to Paul now is the *apocalypsis* of Jesus Christ. And it is the Word that, in his zeal to heed Scripture by persecuting "the church" of Christ, he has become guilty of mortal sin. He has, as he saw in a flash, come under the "curse of the law" while persecuting "the church of God violently" in behalf of the law, and while he "tried to destroy it" (Gal. 1:13; 3:12).

The inaugural *apocalypsis*, then, enforced upon Paul the annihilating realization that he himself, a Pharisee of the Pharisees and a zealot for the traditions of his fathers, had come under the condemnation of God. For he, along with his own people "according to the flesh" but in company with the Gentiles also, had, together and alike, been party to the adamant rejection and death of God's own Son. This risen Jesus, in appearance to Paul, confronts him as God's elect Servant but now manifest as God's vindicated and declared Messiah.

The forgiving grace of God veiled in the scandal of the Cross had annihilated Paul the zealot for the law and the traditions of the elders. The annihilation was total. This is what Paul means everywhere as when he explains to the Galatians, "I have been crucified with Christ" (Gal. 2:20); and in Romans 6:4 it is how, after analogy with Jesus' baptismal trial, Paul understands Christian baptism: "We were buried therefore with him by baptism into death." This is first of all a personal testimony. It testifies to Paul's experience of the death of the old man.[51] In this Paul found Scripture fulfilled that "none shall see God and live." Only the mercy of God in Christ had qualified the word to mean *and live as he is!* Paul knew life from the dead, a "new creation" (Gal. 6:15). It was death to sin and new life in Christ, our righteousness (1 Cor. 1:30). This was also the revelation of the mystery; it is new "life from the dead" for all who will receive it. The revelation of the mystery included this also "that as sin reigned in death, grace might abound through righteousness to eternal life through Jesus Christ our

Lord" (Rom. 5:21). Paul gave God the glory as a recipient of incomprehensible grace that freed him from "the curse of the law" (Gal. 3:13). "There is therefore now no condemnation for those who are in Christ Jesus" (Rom. 8:1). And Paul saw that, as all had been included under sin, both Jew and Greek, so also all are included under grace (Rom. 3:23). Thus, the *apocalypsis* included also a righteousness of God, not of the law of ordinances which Deuteronomy explicitly makes conditional of grace, but "the righteousness of God through faith in Jesus Christ for all who believe" (Rom. 3:22) and to "the Jew first but also to the Greek" (Rom. 1:16).

Whereas Deuteronomy finds the explanation for unmerited grace by looking backward to God's love of the patriarchs (Deut. 4:37), Paul has lost all confidence in mere continuity of fleshly inheritance as a sufficient reason for God's goodness in perpetuity. Rather than looking to the past or hoping in Torah, Paul lives as a new creature of a new creation (1 Cor. 5:17). He has come to distinguish between the "law of ordinances" and the essence of the Law.[52] The latter is the first commandment heeded by Abraham before Sinai. Abraham "believed God, and it was reckoned to him for righteousness" (Gal. 3:6). For Paul the death of the Cross was the ultimate affirmation of God; it was believing God in perfect obedience (Phil. 2:8). So it was "the end of the Law" in the sense of the perfection of the Law (Rom. 10:4). They therefore are sons of Abraham who are united to Christ in the likeness of his death, or his perfect obedience, whether Jew of Gentile (Gal. 3:7-9).

In Christ the ecumenical breakthrough has come to pass. In Colossians it is "the mystery hidden for ages but now manifest," to wit, "how great among the Gentiles are the riches of the glory of this mystery, which is Christ in you the hope of glory" (Col. 1:26-27). The author of Ephesians is a reliable Pauline interpreter if he is not an editor of Paul. He knows that the *mysterion* of the Pauline *kerygma* issues in the view that "the Gentiles are fellow heirs, members of the same body, and partakers of the promise in Jesus Christ through the gospel" (Eph. 3:6).

The revelation of the mystery contains the consequence that, through Jesus Christ, God's grace in redemption becomes commensurate with his sovereignty in creation. It marks a new creation *ex nihilo.*[53] To the Romans Paul had driven home the logic of commensurability. Salvation cannot be by the works of the law: "Or is God the God of the Jews only? Is he not the God of the Gentiles also?" Paul's answer is the manifesto of the *oikoumēne*, "yes of the Gentiles also, *since God is one*" (Rom. 3:29-30). And to the Colossians the consequence is eloquently summarized in the famous lines:

> For he is our peace, who has made us both one, and has broken down the wall of hostility, by abolishing in his flesh the law of ordinances and commandments, that he might create in himself one new man in place of the two. (Col. 3:14-15)

VI

THE PERENNIAL PARADOX

The assumption that the eternal God reveals himself in the history of his elect people is no more at issue in the New Testament than in the Old. For Paul's gospel it is axiomatic, although the precise identity of the elect people becomes permanently ambiguous. This is because election is desecularized, and the vocation of the elect people radically revised. On this matter there was in the early Church far greater diversity of understanding than the Lucan author of Acts has allowed to appear. Paul preached a gospel disturbing to his Christian contemporaries. One must agree, I believe, with Sandmel that it was "revolutionary"; but is not equally clear that it was so simply because, with it, "the inherited Jewish Law was null and void."[54] Such a view strikes one as simplistic. The oft used expression, Paul's "universalism," comes closer to the matter; yet it is probable that this Latin word has rather more obscured than illuminated Paul's gospel beamed to the *oikoumēne.*

There is little question that Paul consistently distinguished between the Law of God eternal and laws plural—namely, the "ordinances and statutes" of the covenant of Sinai along with what Paul speaks of as "the traditions of my fathers" (Gal. 1:14). Unlike the Law eternal, the laws plural had from their inception a "fading splendor." The superseding and "permanent" splendor in Christ is the embodiment of the Law eternal—that of "a new covenant, not a written code but in the spirit' (2 Cor. 3:4-11).

Herein, again, is "the revelation of the mystery" in Christ Jesus, who, as he embodies the Law eternal, therewith also emancipates God's redemptive power in history. He transcends the law of ordinances and liberates the promise to Abraham, the primordial meaning of election, "that in Jesus Christ the blessing of Abraham might come upon the Gentiles" (Gal. 3:14). Embodying the unconditional Grace of God, Jesus is the Messiah and fulfills the eternal purpose of God—the renovation of world history. It is the paradox of the Cross, in 1 Corinthians 1:18-25, which supplants the ancient paradox of election of Deuteronomy with the inclusiveness of absolute grace, with indiscriminate election of all men through Jesus Christ *who believe* (Rom. 10:3-4). It is in this sense alone that Paul can allow particularism to be the viator of universal grace. The chosen people was the bearer of God's promise to Abraham: now, however, implemented through Christ and by faith in him (Rom. 4:16-25). The vicarious people have become the vicarious Lord.

Paul's gospel, therefore, was ecumenical not because the Law eternal—i.e., God's righteousness (Rom. 3:21)—had been done away with but because it had been fulfilled. Neither was it ecumenical simply because, as Dodd suggested, justification is by faith apart from the works of the law.[55] Paul's gospel broke the centripetal inertia of Judaism, for in the death and resurrection of Jesus Christ there was the final *Apocalypsis*, the unveiled mystery bodied forth, of the absolutely un-conditional grace of God for those who receive it. This was the causal Reality; it was a consequence that justification was by faith and that Paul knew nothing in which to glory save in the Cross and nothing to rejoice in save a new creation *ex nihilo*.

Herewith, the veil of the Temple had been rent from top to bottom, as Mark was to affirm (15:38). The apparent injustice of the owner of the vineyard in Jesus' parable of the hired laborers is vindicated by unconditional grace (Matt. 20:14-15). It becomes evident why "the first may be last and the last first" in the view of Jesus[56] and how it is, as Luke has it, that "men will come from the east and west, and from north and south, and sit at the table in the kingdom of God" (13:29-30). And finally, the unveiled mystery has a bearing upon Jesus' injunction to be mindful of the Father in heaven, who "makes his sun to rise on the evil and the good, and sends rain on the just and the unjust" (Matt. 5:45).

With the dissemination of the Pauline *kerygma*, the hitherto controlling centripetal dynamic of Judaism, resident in early Christianity, gave way to a centrifugal thrust. By the final quarter of the first century, attended by historical circumstances, Christianity had become predominantly a Gentile movement in the Mediterranean world. Without this thrust, as Goodspeed judged, the early Church might have remained "just another sect of Judaism"[57]; or it might have been, as B. W. Bacon argued with impressive cogency, a "messianic Judaism."[58] While prognoses are secondary to actualities, it is true that there is little or no extant documentation of the Apostolic Age to demonstrate otherwise, the overwhelming bearing of the Pauline letters to confirm it, and the primitive "Catholicism" of Luke–Acts to mute the conflict of issues of the age itself.

VII

CONCLUSION

From the ancient history of ecumenism many observations and conclusions are possible; only two can be mentioned, and those briefly. The first is that what has been described as the centripetal dynamic of God's election is hardly distinguishable from the "Satanic" temptation, for yielding to which Jesus rebukes Peter in Matt. 16:23. Election carries with it the temptation of Satan. It attended Jesus' own vocation (Luke 22:28) and is represented in his course from the wilderness following his baptism by John, to the agony of Gethsemane.

In this connection it is heartening to have the word of a representative of present-day Judaism affirming that "election is but a means to an end. As, through Abraham, all the peoples of the earth might be blessed," yet it is disappointing to be reminded by yet another spokesmen that the messianic expectation of Judaism entails belief that "the special position of the people Israel never disappears."[59] The issue, however, is not confined to Judeo-Christian ecumenism; rather, it serves to underline the centripetal inertia endemic among the historic branches of Christendom itself. While I do not believe it true, as Sandmel suggests, that for Paul the Church was "but a new particularism," it can hardly be denied that it soon tended to become so, with echoes, perhaps, becoming audible in 1 Peter 2:9-10 and with permutations of the ancient tradition of *primacy* and defensive concerns for *apostolicity* discernible in the New Testament itself. Evidently again we need to hear the twofold testimony of St. Paul, as our second and final observation: "Let him who boasts, boast of the Lord" (1 Cor. 1:31). And there is also his ultimate caution to all heirs of the election in Christ and stewards of the mysteries: "But we have this treasure in earthen vessels, to show that the transcendent power belongs to God and not to us" (2 Cor. 4:7).

In the end, for St. Paul, the only elect One is Jesus Christ. Election resides, as it was fulfilled, in Him. All other election is derivative and is appropriated only by faith as new "life from the dead" (Rom. 11:15). Respecting all precedence, Paul's final word is: "For God has consigned all men to disobedience, that he might have mercy upon all" (Rom. 11:32). For these reasons ecumenism is possible and all particularism irrelevant.

NOTES

1. Kurt Wilhelm, "The Idea of Humanity in Judaism," in *Studies in Rationalism, Judaism, and Universalism*, ed. Raphael Loewe (London: Routledge & Kegan Paul, 1966), p. 292. Cf. Samuel Sandmel, *The Genius of Paul* (New York: Farrar, Straus and Cudahy, 1970), p. 20. That pure universalism "did not exist in Jewish thought, not even in the heights of the Exilic period," is Sandmel's view in acknowledgment of the paradox.

2. Df. Deut. 6:4-7; 7:6-7; 9:5; 10:14-15; 26:5-9; 28:1-5.

3. Samuel H. Bergman, "Israel and the *Oikoumēne*," in Raphael Loewe, ed., *Studies.*, p. 47. See also note 30 below.

4. Anderson, *Creation Versus Chaos* (New York: Association Press, 1967), p. 37: "From the Exodus, Israel looked back to the creation, confessing that the God who was active at the beginning of her history was likewise active at the beginning of the world's history "; Buber, *The Prophetic Faith*, trans. C. Witton-Davies (New York: Harper, 1960), pp. 31-36.

5. Deut. 7:6. Cf. Gerhard von Rad, *Genesis: A Commentary*

(London: SCM Press, 1961), pp. 16-18. The Abraham tradition is joined to the Exodus-Sinai tradition in Israel's "corporate confession of faith" of Deut. 26:5-9. Won Rad also sees the Yahwist editor as interpreting the "primeval history" (i.e., Creation) in terms of the Exodus "creation" of Israel as a people. The Yahwist becomes a true prophet, "for he proclaims the distant goal of the sacred history effected by God in Israel to be the bridging of the cleft between God and all mankind" (p. 23). Anderson, *Creation*, p. 37, speaks of the Exodus as Israel's creation *ex nihilo*.

6. H. H. Rowley, *The Biblical Doctrine of Election* (London: Lutterworth, 1952), p. 44.

7. Ibid., p. 45.

8. Gerhard von Rad, *Genesis*; see note 5 above.

9. Rudolf Bultmann, *Primitive Christianity*, trans. R. H. Fuller (London: Thames and Hudson, 1956), p. 21.

10. Wilhelm, "Idea of Humanity," pp. 298-300, holds that indeed Isa. 60:3 means, "Jerusalem will be the metropolis of all humanity; but the idea that the Gentiles will then find it possible to profess Judaism plays no crucial part in this picture." He entertains the view of Maimonides, *viz.*, "mankind coming to the light, and not the light to Mankind." Evidently, then, the revelation of God does not necessarily entail the unity of the people of God in Wilhelm's view. Israel seems to remain an "intermediary."

11. John Skinner, *Prophecy and Religion* (Cambridge: At the University Press, 1926), p. 268.

12. Ibid., p. 309.

13. Compare Mic. 5:4 and 4:1-4 with Isa. 2:2-5; 11:2-9.

14. W. O. E. Oesterley and T. H. Robinson, *Hebrew Religion* (New York: Macmillan, 1937), p. 316. Cf. Ferdinand Hahn, *Mission in the New Testament*, trans. Frank Clarke (Naperville, Ill.: A. R. Allenson, 1963), pp. 19-20. Hahn believes of II Isaiah that there is "absence of any idea of going out to the nations. Israel is God's witness solely by reason of its existence and of God's salvation which is given to it." He concludes: "We may therefore say that in the Old Testament there is no mission in the real sense." He notes that while Israel's role is "entirely passive," there is the universalistic view of God's salvation and lordship over the nations.

15. Oesterly and Robinson, *op. cit.*, p. 316.

16. W. D. Davies, *Paul and Rabbinic Judaism* (London: S.P.C.K., 1948), pp. 61, 62. Cf. the consensus in the following authors: G. F. Moore, *Judaism in the First Centuries of the Christian Era* (Cambridge: Harvard University Press, 1962), 326 ff.; Charles Guignebert, *The Jewish World in the Time of Jesus* (London: Routledge & Kegan Paul, 1951), p. 154; R. H. Pfeiffer, *History of New Testament Times* (London: A. & C. Black, 1949), pp. 51f.

17. Davies, *op. cit.*, p. 62.

18. Ibid., p. 63. Cf. Matt. 23:16. Pfeiffer observes that the monotheism of II Isaiah implies the universal worship of Yahweh, but that the accentuation of the Temple cultus in post-exilic times together with the ascendency of Torah served to divide Jews from Gentiles (. . . *New Testament Times*, pp. 7, 46, 51).

19. Joachim Jeremias, *Jesus' Promise to the Nations*, trans. S. H. Hooke (London: SCM Press, 1958), p. 12.

20. Ibid., p. 17.

21. Ibid.

22. It is remarkable that Bergman recognizes even today "the centripetal force which, directed inward, emphasizes what is particular and divisive" as antithetical to "the centrifugal force, directed outward and universalistic" in bearing, but urges that "neither of the two contrasting tendencies may be repressed without what is characteristically peculiar to the Jewish religion being lost." ("Israel and the Oikoumēne," p. 48.)

23. Cf. *He That Cometh*, trans. G. W. Anderson (New York: Abingdon, 1954), pp. 280f. As Mowinckel says, "Even in Deutero-Isaiah, universalism is limited by Jewish nationalism" (p. 148).

24. Ibid., p. 4.

25. Ibid., p. 449.

26. Ibid., pp. 148-49. Cf. Rabbi Wilhelm's belief ("Idea of Humanity," p. 292) that "traditional" and "modern Jewish messianic" views look to a divinely instituted kingdom "of this world," of justice and moral order; yet "with this aspect of the messianic expectation, belief in the special position of the people of Israel never disappears."

27. Oesterley and Robinson, *Hebrew Religion*, p. 417.

28. H. H. Rowley, *Biblical Election*, p. 161.

29. Ibid., p. 149.

30. Cf. James Hope Moulton and George Milligan, *Vocabulary of the*

Greek New Testament (London: Hodder and Stoughton, 1963). *Oikoumēne* appears fifteen times in the New Testament and in every case signifies the world of mankind as distinguished from the natural world or cosmos. The primary meaning is the "inhabited world" and may denote also the Roman Empire. Important instances include Matt. 24:14, Mark 14:9, Luke 4:5 and 21:26, Acts 11:28 and 24:5, Revelation 16:14. The adjective *oikoumenikôs* does not occur in the New Testament.

31. Cf. Acts 2:22-39.

32. Cf. J. A. Robinson, *Epistle to the Ephesians* (London: Macmillan, 1955), p. 11, and Johannes Weiss, *History of Primitive Christianity*, trans. and ed. Frederick G. Grant (New York: Wilson-Erickson, 1937), 2:661.

33. Cf. M. S. Enslin, *Reapproaching Paul* (Philadelphia: Westminster Press, 1972), pp. 97—98, and C. K. Barrett, *Luke the Historian in Recent Study* (London: Epworth Press, 1961), pp. 61-63.

34. See D. Davies, *The Setting of the Sermon on the Mount* (Cambridge: At the University Press, 1966). That the early Christians would be concerned with the role of Torah in the messianic age, as Davies urges, cannot be denied on his wholly cogent premise that the early "Christians believed that Jesus of Nazareth was the messiah of Jewish expectations" (p. 109). Important for understanding the lively presence of Judaistic Christianity is Davis' analogy drawn from the Exodus-Sinai background: that "the event [Exodus] was an act of grace, but it is accompanied in the Old Testament by a demand, the Law" (p. 119).

35. Rom. 1:16. Cf. Rom. 2:9-10, where the recompense falls first upon the Jew as, likewise, the reward of righteousness. For Acts the priority of the Jews as candidates for reception of the Gospel has acquired dogmatic status. In 1 Cor. 1:24 no priority is accorded; parity prevails.

36. Jeremias, *Jesus' Promise*, p. 70.

37. Enslin (*Reapproaching Paul*, pp. 108-11) convincingly presents the view that Romans was composed en route to Jerusalem as Paul's *confessio fidei* in face of impending uncertainties attaching to his personal visit. See Rom. 15:30-32. See also T. W. Manson, "St. Paul's Letter to the Romans—and Others," *Bulletin of John Rylands Library*, 31 (1948): 224-40.

38. Gal. 3:6-18; Rom. 4:13-18. Cf. John 4:22.

39. Isa. 49.6. In the context of Rom. 15:7-9, Paul finds Old Testament support for the indecision of the Gentiles from Pss. 18:49; 117:1; Deut. 32:43, and Isa. 11:10. Isaiah is referred to by Paul twenty times in Romans, and there are an additional eight references to the Servant passages.

40. Cf. the author's article, "Christology or Ecclesiology? A Critical Examination of the Christology of John Knox," *Religion and Life*, 27:4 (1958), and John Knox's reply in *The Church and the Reality of Christ* (New York: Harper & Row, 1962), pp. 29-31.

41. M. Kähler, *The So-Called Historical Jesus and the Historical Biblical Christ*, trans. and ed. Carl E. Braaten (Philadelphia: Fortress Press, 1964), pp. 84-86.

42. Mowinckel, *He That Cometh*, p. 449.

43. John 4:22. John's use of the preposition "from" in the words ὅτι ἡ σωτηρία ἐν τῶν Ιουδαίων ἐστίν is fully intended. There is little doubt that John has reason for making this Jesus' own word and that the entire incident confronts, as it seeks to interpret, the long-debated issue in the early Church.

44. See Benjamin W. Bacon, *The Gospel of Mark* (New Haven: Yale University Press, 1925), p. 262. Bacon's main thesis still prevails, and Vincent Taylor's demurrers, however carefully based, are not decisive in my view, since he retains those factors that vindicate the general correctness of Bacon's claim. See Taylor's *The Gospel According to Mark* (London: Macmillan, 1953), pp. 126-29.

45. T. W. Manson, *The Sayings of Jesus* (London: SCM Press, 1950), p. 20.

46. Jeremias, *Jesus' Promise*, p. 39.

47. Cf. 2 Cor. 3:7-18 as of primary importance.

48. Wilhelm, "Idea of Humanity," p. 291.

49. 1 Cor. 3:16−17, 6:19; 2 Cor. 6:16 and John 4:21−22.

50. Acts 21:17−36 is to be consulted and confirms the judgment of Enslin, *Reapproaching Paul*, p. 113. The Lucan author takes no notice of Paul's gifts for the poor of the Jerusalem church. Cf. Rom. 15:30-31 and Acts 20:17-38.

51. Cf. Gal. 2:20; 2 Cor. 5:14; Rom. 6:2-8.

52. Cf. C. H. Dodd, *Epistle of Paul to the Romans* (London: Hodder and Stoughton, 1932), pp. 64-65, in regard to the "double meaning."

of the law in Paul's thought. Cf. Col. 2:15.

53. For Paul, Christ inaugurates the new Exodus and the new covenant *ex nihilo*.

54. S. Sandmel, *The Genius of Paul*, p. 159.

55. Dodd, *op. cit.*, p. 63.

56. Cf. Matt. 20:16, 19:30; Mark 9:35, 10:31; Luke 13:30.

57. Edgar S. Goodspeed, *Paul* (Philadelphia: J. C. Winston, 1947), p. 56.

58. B. W. Bacon, *The Story of St. Paul* (Boston: Houghton Mifflin Co., 1904), p. 4. Cf. A. D. Nock, *St. Paul* (New York: Harper, 1963), p. 19.

59. S. H. Bergman, "Israel and the Oikoumēne," p. 51, and respectively, Wilhelm, "The Idea of Humanity in Judaism," p. 292 in Loewe (ed.), *Studies*.

CHURCH HISTORY IN CONTEXT:
THE CASE OF PHILIP SCHAFF

Klaus Penzel

This essay is an attempt to scrutinize the position of Philip Schaff (1819-93) as a church historian. The Swiss-German immigrant scholar, author of the monumental *History of the Christian Church* and *Creeds of Christendom*, editor of the *Schaff-Herzog Encyclopedia*, founder of the American Society of Church History in 1888, and ecumenical torch-bearer, should need no lengthy introduction. But two prefatory remarks are called for in order to indicate the nature, scope, and direction of the discussion to follow:

1. Anyone who searches the literature about Schaff will no doubt be surprised to discover the variety of descriptive labels that have been used to characterize his position as a church historian. German scholars seem to be inclined to associate him firmly with the school of August Neander. In 1882, for instance, the theological faculty of the University of Berlin hailed his *History of the Christian Church* as "the most notable monument of universal historical learning produced by the school of Neander."[1] More recently, Peter

The author is Professor of Church History, Perkins School of Theology, Southern Methodist University.

Meinhold again introduced Schaff simply as "the pupil of Neander."[2] On the other hand, in this country a recent essay bestowed upon Schaff the large honor of designating him "America's greatest follower of Ranke,"[3] and still another recent essay credited him with having operated "with a modified Hegelian perspective."[4] But, certainly, the name of Ferdinand Christian Baur must also be invoked, for Schaff himself declared that as a student at Tübingen he had gained from Baur "my first idea of historical development or of a constant and progressive flow of thought in the successive ages of the Church."[5] That so many labels can be applied to Schaff might be taken as an indication of the eclectic nature of his scholarship—which is true enough, though it is almost equally correct to state simply that Schaff had what Goethe considered "important"; "a soul which loves the truth, and receives it wherever it finds it."[6] But if Schaff can be associated with such diverse positions as those of Hegel, Ranke, Neander, and Baur, then any study of his church-historical work would seem to necessitate, first of all, a brief conceptual analysis of those cultural currents, and their major representatives, which together are usually credited with the rise of the historical consciousness in nineteenth-century German culture.

2. Shortly before his eightieth birthday, Friedrich Meinecke, the greatest twentieth-century representative of the German Historical School, wrote to a younger colleague as follows:

> In my quiet reading I am now very much interested in F. C. Baur's *History of the Christian Church*. I really should try to get to know the man in order to bring into view for myself Hegel's influence upon historical thinking. But besides Hegel there is also some authentic historicism alive in him, particularly in his History of Church Historiography, where also Ranke's influence is noticeable. But Baur himself is a powerful thinker. There are therefore still

some high mountains left for me, along the slopes of which one can
at least still take a stroll.[7]

Besides these tantalizingly brief remarks there are, unfortunately, no further references to Baur in Meinecke's published
correspondence. But my purpose in quoting Meinecke's
reference to Baur is simply to justify, and to explain still
further, the nature of my own excursion along the slopes of
another high mountain—Schaff's church history—which
stands out so clearly in the impressive mountain range of
nineteenth-century Protestant church historiography, though
closer to Neander and Baur at its beginning than to Harnack
and Troeltsch at its end.

Since no more is here intended than "to take a stroll"
through Schaff's work, I feel justified in limiting myself—
somewhat arbitrarily, no doubt—to two of Schaff's first
American publications: *What Is Church History?* (1846) and
History of the Apostolic Church, with its remarkable opening
section entitled "General Introduction to Church History"
(1853). I feel further justified in arranging our stroll in just
such a way that as we proceed we shall not only take a closer
look at Schaff's position as a church historian, against the
background of the early nineteenth-century rise of historical
consciousness in Germany, but we shall assess also Schaff's
contemporary significance by confronting some of the
questions and challenges that, ever since the early nineteenth
century, history has posited for theology.

I

In the late 1830s, when Schaff began his course of studies at
the University of Tübingen, one of the most extraordinary
periods in the history of German culture was drawing to its
close. One only needs to remember that Beethoven had died

in 1827, Hegel in 1831, Goethe in 1832, and Schleiermacher
in 1834. It appears to be nearly impossible to find for this
age a designation on which all could agree. It is the Age of
Goethe, the Age of German Idealism, the Age of the
Romantic Movement, the towering culmination of what
Meinecke has simply called "the German movement" (from
Leibniz to Goethe), acclaiming it the German mind's "second
great achievement after the Reformation."[8] In the setting of
this exciting age, especially under the impact of its romantic
and idealistic currents, there emerged a new philosophical
understanding of the nature and processes of history and a
further refinement of the critical tools of historical research.[9]

A brief word is in order here about the perfecting of the
critical methods of historical research. It was Barthold Georg
Niebuhr's great merit to have firmly wedded historical
research once and for all to the methods of textual criticism
which classical philology had already begun to employ so
successfully in the study of its sources. The lasting significance
of this achievement, as has been suggested,[10] is perhaps best
summarized in an adaptation of a Kantian statement. Thus,
as the natural sciences are "scientific" only to the extent that
they apply mathematics, so the historical sciences were from
now on to be regarded as being "scientific" only to the
extent that they use philology in the critical analysis and
reconstruction of the textual witnesses of the past. Niebuhr
even expected the Germans to accept " a national mission in
philology."[11] (But the romantic poet Novalis had already
singled out the introduction of philology into Protestant
theology for the critical study of the biblical texts, for which
he blamed Luther, as the probable cause of that theology's
inherent malaise.[12])

My concern here, however, is primarily with the philosophical understanding of history that issued forth from the
complex world of German romantic-idealistic thought. If we

accept Meinecke as our guide (as I would suggest), then we can reduce the nearly labyrinthian variety of seminal new thoughts to just two—the great concepts of "individuality" and of "identity"—for they can together be said to have produced the revolutionary new picture of the world that arose in early nineteenth-century German culture, in sharp contrast to Enlightenment thought. Meinecke's summary view is offered in almost rhapsodic terms.

> The whole world now appeared to be filled with individuality, each individuality, whether personal or supra-personal, governed by its own characteristic principle of life, and both Nature and History constituting what Friedrich Schlegel called an "abyss of individuality." . . . Individuality everywhere, the identity of mind and nature, and through this identity an invisible but strong bond unifying the otherwise boundless diversity and abundance of individual phenomena—these were the new and powerful ideas which now burst forth in Germany in so many different ways.[13]

In a similar vein, A. O. Lovejoy defined the shift from the Enlightenment to the early nineteenth century, a shift brought about by "the Romantic revolution" with its rediscovery of the "principle of plenitude," as "the substitution of what may be called diversitarianism for uniformitarianism as the ruling preconception in most normative provinces of thought."[14]

The student of cultural history, especially of the history of historical scholarship in its various cultural settings, is at this point confronted by a host of issues that invite further discussion. But here we need to add only a brief word about the two powerful concepts of identity and individuality, their major representatives and larger significance.

Obviously, the concept of *identity* was at the heart of the German idealistic philosophy, with its culmination in Hegel's thought; the concept of *individuality*, on the other hand, was the romantic movement's contribution, which likely found

its major explication in Schleiermacher's thought and certainly became the most prominent theoretical foundation
stone of the Historical School, from Niebuhr to Ranke, and
even beyond the nineteenth century, to historians like
Meinecke. It is, of course, well known that Hegel's philosophy, erected on the twin pillars of the Absolute Spirit and
the dialectical method, embodied the revolutionary notion of
the progressive development of truth. Truth, Hegel believed,
is something moving, developing, fluid; it makes its way only
through sharp conflicts and hard contrasts. Hegel's philosophy was, therefore, bound to contribute to historical
thinking the powerful concept of dialectical development, a
development in which an underlying identity—call it the
Absolute Spirit, God, an idea, or a spiritual force—comes to
actualize itself in the myriad individual phenomena of
history. This, roughly, is the meaning that Hegel must be
thought to have had in mind when he announced in the
opening paragraphs of his *Philosophy of History:*

> The only thought which philosophy brings with it [viz., to the
> treatment of history], is the simple concept of *reason*: that reason
> rules the world, and, that therefore, in world history, too, things
> have come about rationally.[15]

Turning to Schleiermacher, we must first of all acknowledge that he employed primarily, though in various com-
binations, the romantic-idealistic concepts of identity, individuality, and organism (or organic growth).[16] But when he
turned his attention to history, he by no means conceived it
as being subject to the laws of the Hegelian dialectic, but
rather as a process of individualization in which the Absolute,
or a spiritual force, unfolds and actualizes itself concretely.
Schleiermacher's joyous exclamation—"Is really the whole
world anything else but the individualization of the identity
[of the Absolute] ?"[17]—could easily be paraphrased to read:

"What else is the whole Christian world, with its multiplicity of distinct historical phenomena, but the individualization of the Christian spirit?" It is therefore Schleiermacher who has correctly been credited with having been the first to introduce a combination of the concepts of individuality and organic growth—an understanding of history as an evolutionary, organic, individualizing process—into the study of church history.[18]

With the critical apparatus of historical scholarship being perfected, and with German romanticism and idealism providing the conceptual tools and the metaphysical undergirding (even a "theology of history") for a new and deepened understanding of the nature and processes of history—how, then, was the historian's task to be defined more specifically? For an answer we should turn briefly to Wilhelm von Humboldt's programmatic essay "On the Historian's Task" (1820). The author's initial definition reads as follows: "The historian's task is to present what actually happened. The more purely and completely he achieves this, the more perfectly has he solved his problem."[19] But then Humboldt tells us that this goal, here at first stated in what appear to be purely "empiricist" or "positivistic" terms, will be reached only if the historian is ready to employ conjointly "two methods" in his research:

> [T]he first is the exact, impartial, critical investigation of events; the second is the connecting of the events explored and the intuitive understanding of them which could not be reached by the first means. To follow only the first path is to miss the essence of truth itself; to neglect this path, however, by overemphasizing the second one is to risk falsification of truth in its details.[20]

Humboldt even went so far as to claim that it is "beyond doubt that there is a point at which the historian is directed to a realm beyond the world of events in order to perceive their true configuration,"[21] as he also firmly maintained that

"Universal history cannot be understood without a divine world governance."[22] He then concluded: "In its final, yet simplest, solution the historian's task is the presentation of the struggle of an idea to realize itself in actuality." But we should note Humboldt's belief that the historian must intuitively grasp the idea in the events, for the idea is "not *directly* perceptible in everything that happens."[23]

It could easily be shown how this particular approach to the study of history came to permeate the whole age, how, in the first half of the nineteenth century, it was to define for most German scholars the nature and scope of the "historical-critical method" and, consequently, the "scientific" character of all historiography. Schleiermacher, for instance, assigned to the church historian the task of viewing "every historical mass" as both "one indivisible being and doing in the process of becoming" and "a compound of innumerable individual moments," and then concluded: "Genuinely historical observation consists in the combination of both."[24] But Humboldt could have asked for no finer echo of his own views than is to be found in the final paragraph of Baur's *The Epochs of Church Historiography*, in which the author, speaking of the historian's "double task" of perceiving the "universal" and the "particular" in history, finally stated programmatically:

> In proportion as the historian must, on the one hand, become absorbed as deeply as possible in the particular, individual, concrete aspects of historical phenomena, in order to attain the complete reality of historical life, so on the other hand he must also raise himself to the heights of the universal Idea, in order to grasp the particular from the universal and to see in it only the particularity of the universal. The task of historiography is completed only in the union of these mutually complementary methods, which make up the two aspects of the same process—moving from the particular to the universal and from the universal to the particular.[25]

Kant had still been able to assert that "Historical knowledge is *cognitio ex datis*; rational knowledge is *cognitio ex principiis.*"[26] To the later generations of German romanticism and idealism this statement appeared to be not only another manifestation of the unfortunate Kantian dualism of history and metaphysics, but also a typical expression of the fundamental shortcoming of all purely "empiricist" historiography, whether of the Enlightenment or any later period. Now it was believed that the true historian will employ both "empiricism" and "speculation"—that is, critical attention to the historical detail and a philosophical approach to history centered on "ideas"—as the necessary components of historical research. And when stated in this generality, it is equally applicable to Humboldt and Ranke, Schleiermacher and Hegel, Baur and Neander. All these men had once again, after the Enlightenment's "secularization" of the historical process, "sacralized" history, in consequence of their common belief that history is ultimately, in one sense or another, the revelation of God himself. All of them believed, though each in his own fashion, "that there existed an automatic harmony between empirical fact and metaphysical truth."[27]

It is, therefore, patently wrong to call Ranke an "empiricist" or "positivist," even though he had set for all historical studies the great goal of discovering "what actually happened";[28] as it is equally wrong to impute to Hegel a perverse desire to distort the individual facts of history by pressing them arbitrarily into the Procrustean bed of the *a priori* laws of his philosophical system. To be sure, each side, in the heat of controversy, helped to prepare the ground for a distorted assessment of the other side's position. But having said this, I hasten to add that, nevertheless, deep differences remained. The idealistic philosopher concentrated more on the "universal," the "idea"; the Historical School more on the "particular," the "event," the "individual personality." Hegel inclined toward a "pantheism of history," while Ranke retained for himself a Christian theism that allowed him to

perceive God in history "like a holy hieroglyph."[29] Even
more importantly, Hegel believed that he could perceive the
idea *directly* in the events, that only the conceptual thought
of the idealistic philosopher is ultimately capable of comprehending all reality, all truth, and therefore that in the end
the idealistic philosopher can be expected to construe in his
own mind a total picture of the world independently of all
empirically observed and verified data (though, of course, it
should never be found to contradict them).

On the other hand, all historians, with Ranke taking the
lead, reaffirmed Humboldt's axiomatic statement that the
ideas, necessary as they are for an understanding of the
historical process, cannot be perceived directly in history, but
can only be intuited dimly, by means of, and after, the most
careful critical analysis of the texts and other material
witnesses of the past.

Finally, differences also show forth when the question is
asked: And to whom should be given the crown for having
made the major contribution to the rise of the historical
consciousness in the nineteenth century, to the evolution, in
Nietzsche's telling phrase, of that century's "sixth sense"?[30]
R. G. Collingwood was convinced that the historical movement that began with Herder culminated in Hegel's philosophy of history,[31] while Meinecke, as was to be expected,
assures us that a continuation of his classical study *The
Origin of Historicism* (the brilliant final chapter is on Goethe)
would have taken him from Niebuhr, Humboldt, the roman-
ticists, and Schleiermacher, to Ranke—without neglecting,
however, the contributions made by idealistic philosophers.[32] But, all controversy, present and past, aside, few
will want to deny that the romantic-idealistic conception of
history represented true progress over Enlightenment historiography at exactly those two points that Collingwood
identified as still needing to be remedied:

first, the horizon of history had to be widened through a more sympathetic investigation of those past ages which the Enlightenment had treated as unenlightened or barbaric and left in obscurity; and secondly, the concept of human nature as something uniform and unchanging had to be attacked.[33]

Indeed, the romantic-idealistic philosophy of history had not only helped to extend the historical horizon to include, at least in theory, all mankind and all history, but its individualizing, empathetic approach to all life had made it possible also for the historian to explore all history with a sympathetic, unbiased concern for the individual characteristics of every historical phenomenon, of whatever time and place, seeking and seeing everywhere forms of human life that are unique, unrepeatable, and valuable in themselves. According to Meinecke, the imperishable core of nineteenth-century German historicism was its replacement of the Enlightenment's "generalizing view" of human life by an "individualizing view."[34] At the same time, the metaphysical assumptions, in particular the romantic-idealistic concept of development—whether conceived organically, as in romantic thought, or dialectically, as in idealistic philosophy—had enabled the historian to tie the strong bond of unity around all the myriad individual historical manifestations that were being unearthed by his scholarly labors. He found himself, therefore, not yet trapped in the quicksand of that historical relativism which came to prevail widely in later decades and with which German historicism as such is now often being identified.

In this all too brief summary of very complex cultural developments, I have tried to allude to some of the aspects of nineteenth-century German historicism that George G. Iggers recently has singled out as being "invaluable for all scholarly historiography":

—the ideal of objectivity, the critical apparatus of historical scholarship, the concern of the historian to understand a historical situation within its own terms and at the same time his recognition that historical reality, involving life, spontaneity, and meaning, requires an empathetic approach different from that suited to the study of nature.[35]

How contemporary theology should respond to the "theology of history" that played so prominent a role in the opening chapters of nineteenth-century German historicism is an important question that should elicit further serious consideration in another context.

Here we now ask: What effects did these German developments have on the writing of church history in the first half of the nineteenth century? Obviously, neither Neander nor Baur (nor Schaff, of course) can be fully understood without some knowledge of this larger background that I have just tried to sketch. Indeed, Neander and Baur represented the same antagonism, but also the same common ties, in the writing of church history that, on another plane, had characterized the relation between Schleiermacher and Hegel. And both Neander and Baur were nurtured in various ways by the Historical School of Niebuhr, Humboldt, and Ranke. It was Schaff's good fortune to study under both Baur at Tübingen and Neander at Berlin. At Tübingen, Schaff had found faculty and students arraigned in two hostile camps that he dubbed the "critical" and the "evangelical." By enlarging on this distinction, we can now identify Germany's two greatest church historians in the first half of the nineteenth century as follows: Baur as the head of the "critical" (and "idealistic") camp, and Neander as the head of the "evangelical" (and "romantic") camp.

The "critical" camp of German church historians, though their number was still small, was gathered, then, around the commanding figure of Ferdinand Christian Baur. No doubt he was the major voice of an historical theology that had as its primary goal the search for the historical truth. It was committed to remaining free of all restrictive dogmatic presuppositions, and was dedicated to the strictest application of the critical tools of historical scholarship to the study of the origin and history of Christianity. In pursuing these goals, especially in his research into the history of dogma, Baur employed brilliantly the categories of Hegel's philosophy. Speaking almost for his entire age, he early in his career had stated: "Without philosophy, history remains for me eternally dead and dumb."[36] Later, after having come under Hegel's sway, he occasionally could designate his historiographical procedure simply as "the critical, or if you want, the speculative method."[37]

Baur's "critical" and "speculative" approach to the study of the Christian past led to remarkable results. But none, perhaps, was more important, and controversial, than the insistence on treating the biblical source of Christianity historically—that is, as a part of the natural flow of events and not as a divine miracle interrupting the historical sequence. He was convinced that all historical scholarship must endeavor

> to penetrate with all the means at its disposal into that which still confronts it as a solid, closed mass . . . in order to melt and dissolve this mass and to draw it into the general flux of historical becoming, a flux in which, in the endless concatenation of causes and effects, one event is always the presupposition of another, in which all together are mutually supported and maintained; and what alone must remain forever incomprehensible is that which could in advance make the claim to stand in the midst of history outside of all historical continuity.[38]

When his researches finally led him to confront the miracle of the resurrection of Jesus, his characteristic response was as follows:

What the Resurrection is in itself lies outside the sphere of historical investigation. The historical consideration has only to hold to the fact that for the faith of the disciples the resurrection of Jesus became the strongest and most incontestable certainty. Christianity acquired only in this faith the firm foundation of its historical development. For history, the necessary presupposition of everything that follows is not the factuality of the resurrection of Jesus itself, but the belief in the same.[39]

Two comments by others deserve to be quoted here. Lord Acton remarked: "Whether or not the belief is true, he refuses to inquire. In the most characteristic passage ever written by a German historian, he declares that it is a question beyond the scope of history."[40] And Klaus Scholder invites us to ponder his statement: "This solution which is no solution . . . has remained to date the only possibility to write church history as universal history."[41]

August Neander reigned at the same time supreme as the head of the "evangelical" camp of German church historians. A Jew converted to Christianity, he introduced the spirit and aims of the Awakening—that early nineteenth-century German revival movement—into the study of church history. But Neander, who had been trained under the rationalistic church historian Gottlieb Jacob Planck at Göttingen, had also opened himself to the historical temper of his time; later, he had embraced wholeheartedly Schleiermacher's view of the nature of Christianity as "life," as he had also absorbed Schleiermacher's romantic concept of individuality, which thereupon became all-powerful in his church history. Thoroughly researched monographs, in which he described lovingly and brilliantly the religious life of great individuals— Emperor Julian (1812), Bernard of Clairvaux (1813), John Chrysostom (1822), Tertullian (1824)—had first made him famous. Baur himself expressed appreciation of this side of Neander's work: "With all the claims of their individuality, they confront the historian, who rejoices in their free-

dom."[42] Hence the much admired "liberality" and "catholicity," but also the all-pervasive "edifying" character of
Neander's church history.

Neander, whose well-known motto was *Pectus est, quod
theologum facit*, was, indeed, the great practitioner of a
"pectoral" approach to the study of church history. He did
not believe that the church historian's primary task was to
search, free of all restrictive dogmatic presuppositions, for
the historical truth; rather, he desired at all times to write
church history "as a living witness of the divine power of
Christianity; as a school of Christian experience; a voice,
sounding through the ages, of instruction, of doctrine, and of
reproof, for all who are disposed to listen."[43] Neander
became therefore primarily the ardent, erudite student of the
history of Christian piety; following faithfully in the foot-
steps of pietistic church historiography, he endeavored to
describe primarily the historical fortunes of the "invisible
church," or the "Kingdom of God," looking everywhere in
history for what were to him the edifying manifestations of
the inexhaustible riches of Christ's life in his followers.

Not surprisingly, Neander also adhered, as Baur noted
disapprovingly, "to a strictly supernaturalistic conception of
the origin and nature of Christianity."[44] Neander thought of
biblical Christianity as the "century of miracles,"[45] to which
the critical methods of historical research should be applied
only insofar as they would help to confirm, rather than
destroy, the traditional supernaturalistic interpretation of
Christian origins. If, as in his *Life of Jesus*, he tried
half-heartedly to mediate between a "miraculous" and a
"non-miraculous" interpretation of primitive Christianity, he
would please neither side: to most of his contemporaries he
then appeared as one who had gone either too far or not far
enough. Still, Neander had a powerful, liberating effect on
those who came under his influence, by teaching them the

capacity to appreciate the diverse manifestations of Christian life in history, and also by showing them that everyone of these individual historical phenomena was a part of a unitive, evolutionary pattern of development.[46] It is understandable that in the nineteenth century and since, many have acclaimed Neander as "the father of modern church history."

My rather cursory survey of the German scene calls finally for a brief reference to David Friedrich Strauss, author of the sensational *Life of Jesus* (1835), the Tübingen School's most controversial member. Two of the book's outstanding features account for the stunning effect it had on contemporary and later thought. First, Strauss ruthlessly exposed for the first time the ambiguous character of Hegel's grand synthesis of Christian faith, idealistic philosophy, and history. Concentrating on the christological implications of Hegel's philosophy of religion, by cleverly employing Hegel's own philosophical categories, he showed that Hegel's philosophy should be viewed as one of Christianity's worst enemies, the deadlier because advanced under the disguise of a philosophical theology.

Secondly, Strauss brilliantly demolished the dominant rationalistic and supernaturalistic interpretations of the New Testament record of Christ's life by running both interpretations smoothly through the mill of the Hegelian dialectic and then proving, from their contradictions, that one canceled out the other. Though Strauss never doubted the historicity of Jesus, his own interpretation substituted for the Christ of Christian dogma (the God-Man who is a divine miracle, without analogy anywhere in human history) the Christ of myth: an ordinary human being to whom, after his death, the high-flung notions of Christian supernaturalism had been attached. Baur, who agreed with Strauss's critical approach to the New Testament but faulted him for having failed to engage in the literary criticism of the New

Testament writings, later wrote: "One must have lived at the time when Strauss's book appeared to have any idea of the commotion it provoked."[47]

Why this commotion? According to a recent study of mid-nineteenth-century German theology, Strauss had "radically put in question the historical object of faith, Jesus Christ," as a few years later Ludwig Feuerbach was to "put in question the metaphysical object," when he made God out to be an illusion produced by a projection of human consciousness.[48] Thus, there were now lying on the table for all to see those two problems that, according to Karl Barth, were to provide "the deeply disturbing background to the history of theology in all the ensuing decades."[49] A third problem, then posed by Karl Marx, was to disturb theology only in our own century.

If these were some of the most prominent features of the German cultural and theological scene at the time when Schaff was finishing his course of studies at the University of Berlin, how, then, was he to respond? One possible response might be as follows: to do church history in the shadow of Schleiermacher and Hegel, by grafting Baur onto Neander—just as Baur, in Lord Acton's apt characterization, "grafted Hegel on Ranke,"[50] and by ignoring Strauss. In sum, this kind of response is precisely Schaff's position as church historian.

II

In a sense, this part of my essay is no more than an extended "footnote" to the general assessment of Schaff as church historian previously offered. Even a quick perusal of Schaff's two books, *What Is Church History?* and *History of the Apostolic Church*, reveals how wholly receptive Schaff had been in Germany to the romantic-idealistic philosophy of history. History, he now told his American readers, is no longer regarded as "a mere, inorganic mass of names, dates, and facts,"[51] no longer as a blind game of "capricious chance"[52]—as in Enlightenment historiography—but is interpreted as "spirit and life, therefore process, motion, development."[53] Moreover, only that approach to the study of the past will assure the writing of true or "scientific" history which is guided by the assumption (Humboldt's assumption!) that "History is neither all body nor all soul, but an inseparable union of both, therefore both the body and the soul, the fact and the idea, in their mutual vital relation, must be recognized and brought into view."[54] The "organic-genetic" method, in Schaff's preferred terminology, of German romanticism and idealism must replace the "pragmatic" and purely "empiricist" method of the Enlightenment's approach to the study of the past. Furthermore, those two books leave no doubt about the strong influence on Schaff, at least initially, of Hegel's philosophy of history, especially its principle of dialectical development that Schaff had first encountered in Baur's lectures at Tübingen. Hegel and Baur were right in regarding history as "a self-evolution of the absolute spirit and hence supremely rational throughout"[55]; and this meant to Schaff that even church history follows consistently the laws of the Hegelian dialectic.

Nevertheless, Schaff's general endorsement of Hegel's philosophy of history was tempered considerably by certain qualifications and serious reservations. For, in keeping with his innate eclecticism, he combined from the very first Hegel's dialectical method with the organological method of German romanticism, with Schleiermacher's and Neander's interpretation of the history of Christianity as a self-unfolding organic process in which Christ's life becomes "individualized" in his followers. For this and other reasons he took strong exceptions to Hegel on two grounds. First, in Hegel's philosophy the individual is wrongly regarded as "the blind organ of the world-spirit; evil is held to be a necessary medium for reaching the good, and thus the idea of guilt and moral accountability is necessarily lost." Second, in Hegel's own hands, the dialectical method tends wrongly toward a dissolution of historical life with its individual diversity "into mere abstractions, the endlessly diversified fullness of history shrinks into a few logical forms, and living personalities are transformed into ideal shadows." In other words, Schaff joined the majority of contemporary German theologians and the members of the Historical School in rejecting what all of them took to be the "pantheistic" and "panlogistic" features of the Hegelian system. It follows that he spoke of Hegel's "pantheism" and "panlogism" as the "fatal rock" of his philosophy, and that he considered his philosophy "in itself no safe conductor through the halls of Church History."[5][6]

The most drastic proof of the dangers inherent in Hegel's philosophy, however, was to Schaff the work done by Baur's Tübingen School in the history of the early Church. Schaff was repelled by Strauss's *Life of Jesus*; but he was no less strongly opposed to Baur's own application of Hegelian categories, as well as of the modern methods of textual criticism, to the study of the Apostolic and post-Apostolic periods: their labors seemed to him to be aiming at no less than the destruction of the very foundations of Christianity. Schaff was so vividly conscious of his antagonism to this side of the Tübingen School that—in the heat of argument, no doubt—he claimed in 1853 that the work of Baur and his followers—"the Gnostics of German Protestantism"—would figure "hereafter only in the history of human aberrations and heresies."[5][7]

If, however, the romantic-idealistic philosophy of history was essentially correct, and alone capable of providing the conceptual tools for an adequate understanding of the historical process in general, and of the nature and history of Christianity in particular, what then was to be its right, its proper application? Schaff replied:

> The right application of the theory of development depends altogether on having beforehand a right view of positive Christianity, and being rooted and grounded in it, not only in thought, but also in heart and experience.[58]

What did Schaff mean? First of all, this meant to Schaff, as these two and all later publications show quite clearly, a traditional Christian supernaturalism which the Awakening had revived and anchored firmly in the experience of "conversion," of "rebirth," all assaults of the modern intellect against this position notwithstanding. (Schaff, we should remember, had been "awakened" at the age of sixteen and had been in constant touch with members of the Awakening throughout his German years of study.)

Schaff was firmly convinced that the truth-claims of Christianity—for instance, those regarding its divine origin and nature—are demonstrated sufficiently and adequately by Christianity's power to convert the sinner even now and to give him the Spirit-induced experience of Christ's presence, which is his salvation. In short, he had turned the Awakening's experience of spiritual rebirth into an epistemological principle that itself was no longer subject to any higher authority. In the final analysis, Schaff had made the Awakening's "religious experience" for the church historian the prerequisite for understanding the nature of Christianity itself, as he had also made it the final authority for deciding on the extent of the mediation that was to be both permissible and mandatory between the traditional Christian point of view and the "sciences" of his time, especially Schleiermacher's philosophical theology, Hegel's speculative philosophy, and the methods of historical research as worked out by Niebuhr, Humboldt, and Ranke.

It is this whole point of view which, above all, stamped Schaff as Neander's pupil. Neander had stated it quite clearly, and in a similar vein, that "Certainly, our understanding of history will depend on the conception which we have formed to ourselves of Christianity itself," though he was conscious of a "necessary circle of cognition" at this point: for while history cannot be understood without knowledge of "what constitutes its working principle," it is only the study of history itself "which furnishes us the proper test by which to ascertain whether its principle has been rightly apprehended."[59] Nevertheless, Schaff took certain exceptions even to Neander's position. For Neander, as was well known to his contemporaries, opposed most grimly, in the combined strength of the piety of the Awakening and the romantic principle of "individuality," Hegel's philosophy and the orthodoxy of a resurgent Lutheran confessionalism; but precisely those two tendencies, provided they were properly understood and applied, Schaff found necessary to graft onto Neander.

I have already tried to demonstrate the considerable impact Hegel, and Baur, had on Schaff. Now I merely need to add that during Schaff's last year in Germany the rising tide of Lutheran confessionalism carried him beyond Neander's pietistic conception of the "invisible church" and made him embrace a more orthodox, even "Catholic," doctrine of the church as the Body of Christ, the *Christus prolongatus*. Schaff now conceived of the historical, visible church as the continuation of Christ's life, Christ's sole habitation, and God's sole organ of salvation on earth—indeed, as theantropic in nature, like the Christ of the Chalcedonian dogma. And we should now note that is was this particular theory of the church, with its strong roots in romantic thought and its rather close resemblance to Roman Catholic ecclesiology, which Schaff then, finally, declared to be "the *spiritus rector*, the conducting genius of the church historian," which he then held to be "indispensable" for a right understanding of church history (though he, too, acknowledged Neander's "necessary circle of cognition" when he remarked that the relation between this particular theory of the church and church history "is one of reciprocal light and confirmation"[60]).

In short, it was at this very point at which Schaff revealed one of the most characteristic principles of his church historiography—that a particular conception of the church is to be a primary factor in determining the nature and task of church history as an intellectual discipline—that he also found himself, in the indicated, limited sense, at variance with Neander's position. Nevertheless, how dependent Schaff was upon Neander in general is clearly shown in his *History of the Apostolic Church*, the original German version of which he had dedicated in 1851 to the memory of his Berlin teacher. This book can be understood as a conservative rebuttal to the Tübingen School's radical criticism of the traditional interpretation of the Apostolic Church and to its equally radical reconstruction of New Testament Christianity.

Today, we might be inclined to single out as one of the book's most striking features Schaff's refusal to engage in any kind of literary criticism of the New Testament writings, or, for that matter, to discuss Strauss's *Life of Jesus.* Schaff simply gave short shrift to Strauss by maintaining: "We cannot enter into the confused and confusing hypotheses of modern hypercritics; the less, since by their wild extravagances and their mutual contradictions they have already refuted themselves."[61] Schaff chose to ignore the problem raised by Strauss. And not even in Schaff's second attempt at writing his *History of the Christian Church* (1859/67), but only in the third and final version of 1882ff., almost thirty years later, did he finally offer an extended discussion of the Tübingen School's textual criticism of the New Testament writings—only to reject even then all of its most radical findings.

What accounts for this thoroughly negative reaction? Perhaps the most important reason is to be found in the Neander School's identification of the essence of Christianity not only with Christ, or the canonical Scriptures, but with the Apostolic Age as such, the "century of miracles." This age, though human and historical in its appearance, was believed to stand outside all history (just as the experience of spiritual rebirth, with its human aspects, was believed to be an essentially supernatural reality and therefore beyond the grasp of human comprehension). Hence Schaff maintained, like Neander, that the romantic-idealistic principle of development and the critical methods of historical research can be applied only to the historical stream of Christianity, but not to its supernatural source, the Apostolic Age. To touch this age with the profane hands of historical criticism and philosophical categories in ways that would obstruct the traditional view of the miraculous beginnings of Christianity is no less than the sin against "the right view of positive Christianity."

Baur, of course, retorted by pointing to what he conceived to be the weak link in Neander's historiographical scheme: "How can the same principle work first supernaturally, then naturally? And how meaningless it is to talk, nevertheless, of a process of development!"[62] He further maintained that the Neander School's "miraculous" interpretation of New Testament Christianity showed a close affinity to the Roman Catholic conception of church history, for Roman Catholicism "cannot be without the miracle, it lives in the conception of the miracle." By contrast, Baur thought of his own church historiography as embodying a truly Protestant conception of church history.[63] But the last word should be left to Neander and to Schaff.

Neander showed himself unimpressed by arguments like Baur's. Indeed, he was certain that the very notion of the final cessation of miracles sometime in the second century marked his own church history as distinctly Protestant over against the Roman Catholic belief in the "succession of miracles" throughout all the centuries of church history.[64] As to Schaff, his habitual retort was that true Protestantism (as he understood it) has more in common with Roman Catholicism than with many so-called Protestants, such as Baur and Strauss. And he was able to explain the transition from the Apostolic Age to church history proper as follows:

> The hand of God has drawn a bold line of demarcation between the century of miracles and the succeeding ages, to show by the abrupt transition and the striking contrast, the difference between the work of God and the work of man, and to impress us the more deeply with the supernatural origin of Christianity and the incomparable value of the New Testament.

—though he had to concede that

> The stream of divine life in its passage from the mountain of inspiration to the valley of tradition is for a short time lost to our view, and seems to run underground. Hence the close of the first and the beginning of the second centuries, or the age of the Apostolic Fathers, is often regarded as a period of critical conjecture and doctrinal and ecclesiastical controversy rather than of historical narration.[65]

Here my brief sketch of Schaff's position could end, though I need to add that Schaff never doubted that he had succeeded as a church historian in doing full justice to a Protestant view of Christianity, the romantic-idealistic philosophy of history, and the critical methods of modern historical research. Philip Schaff—a "pupil of Neander"? Most certainly. Influenced by Baur and operating with a "modified Hegelian perspective"? Indeed so. "America's greatest follower of Ranke"? That depends, for to attempt an answer would necessitate taking a closer look not only at Ranke but also at Ranke's other American followers, and it is probably as well that H. W. Bowden dropped this label in his most recent study, *Church History in the Age of Science*.

But it is Bowden's instructive study that invites one further refinement of my assessment of Schaff's position. Bowden tried to measure Schaff against an understanding of science that came to prevail, as he believes, in the United States roughly since the 1880s. "Iconoclasm," "empiricism," and "naturalism" are listed as its most distinctive features.[66] My own attempt, however, as must be obvious, has been to scrutinize Schaff's position in the context of another understanding of "science" and "scientific" church historiography, which prevailed in Germany during the nineteenth century's first half. Many have remarked on that century's very complex and important development from one conception of science to the other, from—as some have dubbed it—"idealism" to "realism," from "speculation" to "specialization." Lord Acton put it this way:

> When the euthanasia of metaphysic . . . was setting in about 1850, physical science emerged as its rival, and history [did Lord Acton mean "positivistic" history?] as its heir. The philosophers themselves turned into historians and beat their speculations into facts.[67]

Bowden's study has shown convincingly, I believe, that

Schaff refused to beat his "speculations" (whether of the romantic-idealistic thought world or of Christian dogma) into the "facts" that would pass muster before the late nineteenth-century tribunal of an "iconoclastic," "empirical," "naturalistic" science. To be sure, further developments did occur in his position, but they took, interestingly enough, the form of reverting to the ruling conception of Neander's church historiography—that of the "invisible church" or the "kingdom of God"—and of a gradual evaporation of Hegelian categories and terminology. In this present essay, however, I have merely tried to show that Schaff had acquired his own understanding of the "scientific" nature of church history, and of all history, in an earlier cultural context, and had acquired it so firmly that he retained most of its basic elements to the end of his life, even in so different a cultural setting as that of the late nineteenth-century American university. But whichever way we look at Schaff, we are likely to find that a critical study of the founder of the American Society of Church History can be of value even today, certainly to all of us who also face the necessity of defining the nature of church history and the task of the church historian.

III

The great modern confrontation between criticism and faith, history and dogma, the historian and the believer, presents one of the most complex issues—with innumerable ramifications all of which would need to be explored—that theology in our time is facing.[68] It was Gotthold Ephraim Lessing, toward the end of the eighteenth century, who had already caught a first glimpse of that "ugly, broad ditch" which the rise of historical consciousness was to open up in modern times between history and much traditional philosophy and theology. Lessing thought he had learned that "accidental truths of history can never become the proof of necessary truths of reason."[69] If, as has been suggested,[70] we substitute the phrase "eternal truths of faith" for "necessary truths of reason," then we, too, already have caught a first glimpse of that problematic to which I should like to direct attention in this final section. But this problematic, in which criticism and faith, history and dogma, and historical and dogmatic theology seem to be placed in irreconcilable opposition to each other, can be defined more clearly and stated even more provocatively.

On the one hand, there is Baur's claim:

> Christianity is and remains an historically given religion. . . . It entered the general connexion of historical events at a definite point in time and can only be comprehended on the basis of certain writings which are the documentary witnesses of its origin.[71]

Ernst Troeltsch believed that in Baur's historical-critical theology, though primarily in consequence of his Hegelianism,

> an autonomous dogmatics is entirely unneccessary, that the whole power and fullness of Christianity becomes visible and effective in its historical development, that church history becomes God's incarnation and the explication of Christ, and that therefore all theology and Christology become superfluous.[72]

Troeltsch himself agreed with Baur's insistence on the purely historical character of Christianity, even though this agreement caused him much distress, as any student of his laborious wrestling with the *Historicism and Its Problems* knows. Christianity, Troeltsch maintained, "is in every moment of its history a purely historical phenomenon, subject to all the limitations to which an individual historical

phenomenon is exposed, just like the other great religions."
And since "the historical and the relative are identical," he
concluded that Christianity can no longer claim to be the
"absolute religion."[73]

But even more disturbing, to the believer, is the conclusion
to which historical thinking led Franz Overbeck, one of
Baur's later followers: "To place Christianity under the
category of the historical means to concede that it is of this
world, and in it, like all life, has only lived in order to die."[74]
Finally, there is the deeply troublesome awareness that an
historical orientation toward all life, with its relativistic
implications, is in the end bound to issue in an "anarchy of
values," as Ernst Troeltsch and Wilhelm Dilthey came to
suspect;[75] that, in particular, a historical approach to the
study of the Christian religion will make illusionary the
traditional Christian claim of a final and absolute norm
underlying the historical diversity of Christianity. Arthur C.
McGiffert, a student of Harnack, drawing together his
insights into the nature of church history, asserted that
"Christianity has not been one thing but many and often
contradictory things"; and he came to believe that "there is
no such thing as Christianity in general—though there are
many particular Christianities."[76] No doubt these are voices
epitomizing the "Crisis of Historicism."[77]

On the other hand, there is Cardinal Manning's statement,
which Harnack viewed as "frivolous": "One must overcome
history by dogma."[78] There is the condemnation of "historicism" as stated in the papal encyclical *Humani generis:*
"Concentrating its attention only on the events of human
life, it subverts the foundations of any absolute truth or law,
as regards both philosophical matters and Christian dogma."
As Jaroslav Pelikan explains, condemned here is

[historicism's] immanentism, which rules out the role of supernatural intervention and divine revelation in human affairs, and the consequent relativism, which treats all statements of either philosophical or theological doctrine as historically conditioned and therefore incapable of having binding force for all time.[79]

There is, finally, on the Protestant side, Karl Barth's "laughter." In discussing Strauss's work, Barth found it centered in the attempt to "master revelation in the same way as history in general is mastered"; but, as Barth continued, Strauss's futile labors only went to prove that "something absolute as a part of the world and of human history as such is a sword of lath."[80] Since, then, human history as such and revelation, the historical-critical method (as applied, for instance, by Baur and Strauss), and the Christian faith (as understood by Barth) refuse to be correlated, Barth concluded with finality: "Proper theology begins just at the point where the difficulties disclosed by Strauss ... are seen and laughed at."[81] Earlier, in the Preface to the first edition of his celebrated *The Epistle to the Romans*, Barth had already declared that if he had to choose between the nineteenth century's historical-critical method and the orthodox doctrine of Inspiration, he would "without hesitation adopt the latter, which has a broader, deeper, more important justification."[82]

Several initial comments on Barth's position may be in order. For one thing, having ranked Barth with a Roman Catholic cardinal and a papal encyclical now may appear to be particularly appropriate, for, as Barth's second statement would seem to show, there is even today still much truth, at least for some Protestant theologians, to the orthodox Protestant notion: *"Breviter, quod illis est Papa, nobis est scriptura."* Again, Barth's "laughter" cannot but bring to mind such bitter words as those that Dilthey once spoke to his friend Count York, a highly cultivated, devout Lutheran (words which may yet come to haunt our anti-historical

and anti-liberal systematic theologians): "He did not even
wish to gain salvation through a faith that could not stand up
to thought."[83] I take it that his reference was to historical
thought. Then there is, finally, the remark that this century's
large-scale turning away from the nineteenth century's
historical orientation is nowhere more clearly discernible
than "in the simultaneously anti-liberal and anti-historical
revolution of Protestant theology with which Karl Barth has
overcome, against Harnack, the triumph of David Friedrich
Strauss and the distress of Ernst Troeltsch."[84] According to
Barth, when modern Protestantism embraced the historical-
critical method, it took a decisive step in the wrong direction.

  With Lessing's "ugly, broad ditch" thus staring us in the
face, are we then forced to conclude that the historical-
critical method and a religious orientation cannot possibly
co-exist in the same person, or can do so only on terms that,
on closer scrutiny, one side or the other is bound to reject?
Schaff and many other church historians ever since would
have denied the need for such an unhappy conclusion. Thus,
we might now summarize Schaff's own response to the
problematic of historical criticism and Christian faith with
some such formulation as this: The method to be employed
in the study of church history is "determined, on the one
hand, by the generally recognized principles of historical
research and presentation; on the other hand by the special
demands of a theological discipline." From this it follows
that the church historian must utilize "the latest verified
findings and approved scientific methods," while maintaining
simultaneously a religious orientation toward his materials—a
religious orientation that, however, by no means impairs the
full application of the scientific method in his study of
church history. For the church historian knows that "theology and history, if truly scientific, can never be at variance,

since both are devoted to the acquisition of truth, which is *one*."

Lest this particular combination of historical and meta-historical standards be thought to resemble too closely, for comfort, the hoped-for harmony of the Messianic age when the wolf and the lamb shall dwell together peacefully, we should add that an uneasy awareness persists that the application of the historical-critical method to the study of church history "can sometimes lead to tensions" between the faith and dogmas of the Church and the results of historical research and may thus "confront the church historian with difficult decisions." Nevertheless, the basic position remains the same and can be summarized once more as follows:

> The study and description of the life of the Church through the centuries proceed according to the same laws of historical criticism as in every genuine historical science. On the other hand, church history differs from the purely natural science and works according to its own principles which have been drawn from revelation. The right connection of both elements does not take place in such a manner that the theological principles determine or even change the historical results, but they will be related to the purposes of the founder of the Church, that is, they will be interpreted and evaluated theologically according to the principles of revelation.

I hope I shall be forgiven for having just employed a literary device that smacks of deception. The foregoing quotations were not drawn from Schaff's own writings—though they could easily have been, for similar statements abound in Schaff—but from the most recent standard church history texts written by German Roman Catholic scholars: Biehlmeyer-Tüchle, Jedin, and Lortz.[85] I have employed this device if for no other reason than to emphasize once more my point—Baur's, but also Schaff's, point!—that in the great

modern confrontation between history and dogma many
Protestants and Roman Catholics will discover a close kinship
to each other, in their common attempts at upholding "the
eternal truths of faith" (however much they may still differ
in their understanding of them) over against the real or
imagined threat posed by "the accidental and relative truths
of history." I might add that the same point is made quite
well in Bowden's *Church History in the Age of Science*, in
which the Roman Catholic church historian John Lea
(1824-92) is called Schaff's "ideological and chronological
contemporary"; for, as Bowden goes on to show, "a
theological substratum undergirded the work" of both, even
though it is obviously true that "they differed as to the
identifiable locus of God's activity" in history.[86]

Over against these various attempts, by Schaff and others,
at mediating between historical criticism and Christian dogma
with such apparent ease and unshakable self-confidence (and,
in Schaff's case, in the problematic strength of that
"theology of history" that was the common property of
theologians, philosophers, and historians alike in early nineteenth-century German culture), we need to sharpen the
contrast once more by availing ourselves of Peter Gay's
helpful distinction between "criticism" and "myth."[87] Gay
understands "critical thinking" as "disenchanted thinking."
Thus, in holding nothing sacred, it moves freely through
every subject and asks questions of all." "Mythical thinking,"
on the other hand, is "incapable of this sort of penetration,"
for even at its highest level it "retains at least a shred of the
miraculous—of that which must remain untouched by
profane hands." Gay goes on to assert that "history based on
critical thinking is superior to history based on myth"; for
"as long as myth pervades the historian's mind, there are
areas in which he will be unhistorical—*which* area depends, of
course, on his myth."

Admittedly, Gay's preference for critical thinking over mythical thinking is a value judgment with which I happen to agree, certainly to the extent that I consider Baur's "critical" church history, whatever its shortcomings and however large a dose of indigestible Hegelianism it had absorbed, superior to Neander's and Schaff's "supernaturalistic" and hence "mythical" church history. I also find directly applicable to our study Gay's further assertion that

> religious men, devout Christians, have written great histories, and have made significant contributions to the techniques of history. . . . Yet even these masters were shackled by their piety: they could be scrupulous, accurate, inventive, scientific only within a certain framework.

Gay's examples are the Benedictines of St. Maur, the Bollandists, and even Ranke, while I would list, in our context, Neander and Schaff, even though Neander, in obvious contrast to Schaff, was sadly deficient in style and in the organization and presentation of his materials.

Where, then, do I finally come out? I acknowledge the superiority of "critical thinking" over "mythical thinking," of history over dogma. I agree with Baur's insistence that we must apply the historical-critical method radically and consistently to our understanding of Christianity, its origin, history, and nature; that we must search for the truth with the available tools of historical scholarship, irrespective of any restrictive dogmatic presuppositions and regardless of the cost; and that, with it all, we must continuously aspire at becoming, and at remaining, members in good standing of what has so felicitously been called the "invisible Tübingen School."[88] But in the face of these assumptions, what is to be the fate of theology, of church dogma? Are we to agree with a recent study of Baur the author of which laments:

"Apart from history, theology would belong nowhere! One can be dismayed by this, but then, who knows any better?"[89]

Baur's bequest to modern theology may, indeed, have been a theological impasse that has to date remained characteristic of theology's confrontation with history—notwithstanding Schaff, those Roman Catholic church historians whom I cited earlier, and, perhaps, even most of us who, as church historians, if we are unable to bridge Lessing's "ugly, broad ditch" on the quiet Sundays of theoretical reflections, seem to be doing it quite happily during working days in the practice of our craft. Wisdom's last word would then be an appropriate paraphrase of Ranke's wistful remark about the troubled relations between history and philosophy in his own time:

> Thus, our paths as historians lead us to the problems of philosophy [or theology]. If philosophy [or theology] were what it should be and history were perfectly clear and complete, the two disciplines would be in complete agreement.[90]

In the end, then, we seem to be left with a distant, unattainable goal, a hope to be realized only eschatologically, as even Schaff conceded when he remarked that we shall "see church history in a perfect light only when we stand on the mount of Christ's second coming, and of his triumphant Zion"[91]—though, admittedly, the view he already had by standing on Schleiermacher's and Hegel's shoulders appeared at least to him to be, after all, remarkably similar to the one we shall have later on, when the returning Christ will have brought history to its end.

Still, there is one more voice, that of Gerhard Ebeling, which can perhaps provide some further light and point us in a right direction. A true contemporary member of the "invisible Tübingen School," Ebeling has opted forcefully for modern Protestantism's full acceptance of the historical-critical method. He has encouraged us "to go ahead with the critical examination of our foundations, to let everything burn that will burn and without reservations await what proves itself unburnable, genuine, true"—in short, to choose "the path into vulnerability, into the fires of criticism."[92] According to Ebeling, when nineteenth-century Protestantism embraced the historical-critical method, it made the right decision, for it then merely reconfirmed, though in a quite different historical setting, the Reformers' decision in the sixteenth century. Ebeling believes that the Reformation principle of *sola fide* must be understood as destroying "all secretly docetic views of revelation which evade the historicalness of revelation by making it a history *sui generis*, a sacred area from which the critical historical method must be anxiously debarred,"[93] as he, likewise, asserts that a contemporary systematic theology which absorbs

> the whole outlook of the critical historical method. . . will achieve the critical destruction of all supposed assurances [*sola fide*!], but above all . . . will be kept strictly to its proper concern—namely, the historic revelation in Jesus Christ [*solus Christus*!] —in full awareness of the historicalness of its own systematic theological labours.

Ebeling pleads with us, therefore, to explore fully the true theological import of the many remarkable results that the previous century's historical-critical theology brought forth; and since he believes that this, unfortunately, has not yet been done, he turns the tables on the systematic theologians by suggesting that it is "not historical, but systematic theology that makes plain the crisis which has arisen in Protestant theology."[94]

It is in the light of these convictions that Ebeling has provided also a new understanding of the task and nature of church history, the substance of which is already indicated in the title of his trail-blazing essay: "Church History Is the History of the Exposition of Scripture."[9][5] Ebeling's provocative proposal for re-defining the nature of church history deserves, especially in our context, our most careful attention, since it continues Schaff's forceful insistence that the concept of the church is to be a decisive factor in constituting church history as an intellectual discipline. In Ebeling's understanding, however, the object of church history is no longer the "kingdom of God" in its course through history (as in Pietism), nor the organic growth of the church as the "Body of Christ" (as in romanticism), nor the dialectic development of the "Idea" of the church in time and space (as in idealism)—three concepts that came to co-exist, an an uneasy alliance, in Schaff's own eclectic mind—but the church as the *"creatura verbi"* (Martin Luther), as the *"congregatio sanctorum, in qua evangelium pure docetur et recte administrantur sacramenta"* (*Augsburg Confession*, art. 7).

I find Ebeling's definition—whatever its shortcomings—of the task and nature of church history suggestive and fruitful. For it would seem to allow the church historian simultaneously to honor and employ fully the critical methods of historical scholarship, to continue in the Christian—albeit the Protestant Reformation—tradition, and to turn a deaf ear, deservedly, to all those voices of despair that in our own time would find no proper place for church history as an academic discipline between the Scylla of critical history and the Charybdis of Christian theology: e.g., those that try to justify, as a last, desperate resort, church history's existence as a branch of the phenomenology of religion, or those seeking to salvage from the alleged modern wreckage of church history its two disjointed halves by proposing the curious distinction between "church history" (which clings stubbornly to Christian theology) and "history of Christianity" (which has been thrown up against, and is firmly embracing, critical history).[96] Church historians ought to test Ebeling's definition of their discipline, circumventing its weaknesses, building on its strengths, and in so doing laying the theoretical foundations on which they might stand more securely in the daily practice of their craft. It is a position such as this—in Van A. Harvey's words, a "radical historical confessionalism"[97]—from which I myself should like to proceed.

NOTES

Note: Translations from the German are my own, unless indicated otherwise.—K. P.

1. Quoted in D. S. Schaff, *The Life of Philip Schaff* (New York: Charles Scribner's Sons, 1897), p. 467.

2. In *Geschichte der kirchlichen Historiographie* (Freiburg/Munich: Karl Alber, 1967), 2:161.

3. H. W. Bowden, "Science and the Idea of Church History, An American Debate," *Church History* 36.3 (1967): 317.

4. W. K. B. Stoever, "Henry Boynton Smith and the German Theology of History," *Union Seminary Quarterly Review* 24. 1 (1968): 69.

5. Quoted in D. S. Schaff, *Philip Schaff*, p. 20.

6. J. W. von Goethe, *Conversations with Eckermann* (Washington and London: M. Walter Dunne, 1901), p. 289 (December 16, 1828).

7. *Ausgewählter Briefwechsel* (vol. 6 of Meinecke's *Werke*), ed. L. Dehio and P. Classen (Stuttgart: K. F. Koehler, 1962), pp. 402f.

8. In *Die Entstehung des Historismus* (vol. 3 of Meinecke's *Werke*), ed. C. Hinrichs (Munich: R. Oldenbourg, 1965), p. 2.

9. The literature pertaining to the rise of the historical consciousness in early nineteenth-century German culture, and to the history of church historiography—in particular to Baur, Neander, and Schaff—is too vast to be listed here in detail. Many books and articles that I have found particularly informative, however, are indicated in the footnotes.

10. By Erich Rothacker, in *Mensch und Geschichte* (Bonn: Athenäum-Verlag, 1950), p. 10.

11. B. G. Niebuhr, *Kleine historische und philologische Schriften*, 1 (Bonn: E. Weber, 1828): 337.

12. Novalis [Pseud. of F. von Hardenberg], *Die Christenheit oder Europa; Ein Fragment* (1799), ed. O. Heuschele (Stuttgart: P. Reclam, 1961), p. 29.

13. In *Die Idee der Staatsräson*, vol. 1 of Meinecke's *Werke*), ed. W. Hofer (Munich: R. Oldenbourg, 1960), p. 425. Translation is that of Steven Lukes, "The Meanings of 'Individualism,'" *Journal of the History of Ideas* 32.1 (1971): 56.

14. In *The Great Chain of Being* (New York: Harper Torchbooks, 1960), pp. 297 and 294, respectively.

15. G. W. F. Hegel, *Die Vernunft in der Geschichte*, vol. 18 A of *Sämmtliche Werke*, 5th ed., ed. J. Hoffmeister (Hamburg: F. Meiner, 1955), p. 28.

16. Cf. K. M. Beckmann, *Unitas Ecclesiae* (Gütersloh: G. Mohn, 1967), pp. 37-64, esp. p. 56. Important is Meinecke's essay, "Zur Entstehungsgeschichte des Historismus und des Schleiermacherschen Individualitätsgedankens," in *Zur Theorie und Philosophie der Geschichte*, vol. 4 of *Werke*, ed. E. Kessel (Stuttgart: K. F. Koehler, 1965), pp. 341-57..

17. From a letter dated December 14, 1803, in Wilhelm Dilthey, ed., *Aus Schleiermacher's Leben, In Briefen*, 4 (Berlin: G. Reimers, 1863): 94.

18. Wilhelm Maurer, "Das Prinzip des Organischen in der evangelischen Kirchengeschichtsschreibung des 19. Jahrhunderts," *Kerygma und Dogma* 8.4 (1962): 271.

19. In W. von Humboldt, *History and Theory* 6.1 (1967): 57.

20. Ibid., p. 59.

21. Ibid., p. 68.

22. Ibid., p. 67.

23. Ibid., pp. 70f. (my italics).

24. In his *Brief Outline of the Study of Theology*, trans. T. N. Tice (Richmond, Va.: John Knox Press, 1966), p. 60 (§150).

25. P. C. Hodgson, ed. and trans., *Ferdinand Christian Baur: On the Writing of Church History*, Library of Protestant Thought (New York: Oxford University Press, 1968), p. 257.

26. Immanuel Kant, *Critique of Pure Reason*, trans. N. K. Smith (New York: St. Martin's Press, 1965), p. 655.

27. G. G. Iggers, *The German Conception of History* (Middletown, Conn.: Wesleyan University Press, 1968), p. 279.

28. L. von Ranke's "wie es eigentlich gewesen" should always be pondered in its context: cf. his Preface to *Geschichten der romanischen und germanischen Völker*, vol. 33 of *Sämmtliche Werke*, 3 ed. (Leipzig: Duncker und Humblot, 1885), p. vii. Iggers' essay, "The Image of Ranke in American and German Historical Thought," *History and Theory* 2.1 (1962): 17-39, brings out the remarkable fact that Ranke's numerous and ardent American admirers, as well as his foes—in contrast to the Germans—consistently misunderstood the German master as the leading "positivist" historian.

29. L. von Ranke, *Zur eigenen Lebensgeschichte*, ed. A. Dove (vols. 53/54 of *Sämmtliche Werke*, 1890), p. 89.

30. Friedrich Nietzsche, *Beyond Good and Evil*, trans. H. Zimmern, vol. 12 of *The Complete Works*, ed. O. Levy (New York: Russell & Russell, 1964), p. 167.

31. In Collingwood's *The Idea of History* (New York: Oxford University Press, Galaxy Books, 1956), p. 113.

32. Meinecke, "Zur Entstehungsgeschichte des Historismus," p. 344.

33. In *The Idea of History*, p. 86.

34. In *Die Entstehung des Historismus*, p. 2.

35. In *The German Conception of History*, p. 278.

36. F. C. Baur, *Symbolik oder Mythologie, oder die Natur-religionen des Altertums*, 1 (Stuttgart: J. B. Metzler, 1824): xi.

37. Baur, *Lehrbuch der christlichen Dogmengeschichte* (Tübingen: L. F. Fues, 1858), p. viii.

38. Quoted in Hodgson (ed.), *Baur: On the Writing of Church History*, p. 253.

39. Baur, *Das Christentum und die christliche Kirche der drei ersten Jahrhunderte* (Tübingen: L. F. Fues, 1853), p. 39.

40. [John Emerich]Lord Acton, "German Schools of History," in *Historical Essays and Studies* (London: Macmillan & Co., 1908), p. 369.

41. In "Ferdinand Christian Baur als Historiker," *Evangelische Theologie* 21. 10 (1961): 456.

42. Quoted in *Baur: On the Writing of Church History*, p. 211.

43. August Neander, *General History of the Christian Religion and Church*, trans. J. Torrey, vol. 1 (2d ed.; Boston: Crocker & Brewster, 1851), from Preface to 1st edition.

44. Quoted in *Baur: On the Writing of Church History*, p. 213.

45. The phrase had apparently been coined by the Swiss historian Johannes von Müller. Cf. P. Schaff, *History of the Apostolic Church*, trans. E. D. Yeomans (New York: Charles Scribner's Sons, 1853), p. 675.

46. J. H. Nichols has shown well the liberating effect of Neander's church history in the case of Schaff's Mercersburg colleague John W. Nevin, whose church history teacher at Princeton had used "Mosheim for facts and Milner for piety" and had judged everything "polemically from Princeton's orthodox point of view." See *Romanticism in American Theology: Nevin and Schaff at Mercersburg* (Chicago: The University of Chicago Press, 1961), p. 43.

47. *Kirchengeschichte des 19. Jahrhunderts*, ed. Edouard Zeller (Tübingen: L. F. Fues, 1862), p. 363.

48. Claude Welch, ed. and trans., *God and Incarnation in Mid-Nineteenth Century German Theology*, Library of Protestant Thought (New York: Oxford University Press, 1965), p. 9.

49. In *Protestant Thought: From Rousseau to Ritschl*, trans. B. Cozens, rev. by H. H. Hartwell (New York: Harper & Row, 1959), p. 382.

50. In "German Schools of History," p. 368.

51. In *History of the Apostolic Church*, p. 90.

52. Ibid., p. 108.

53. Ibid., p. 90.

54. Ibid., p. 34.

55. Schaff, *What Is Church History?* trans. J. W. Nevin (Philadelphia: J. B. Lippincott & Co., 1846), p. 76.

56. Ibid., pp. 76ff.

57. Schaff, *History of the Apostolic Church*, p. 113.

58. Ibid., p. 91 (Schaff's italics).

59. Neander, *General History of the Christian Religion and Church*, p. 1.

60. Schaff, *What Is Church History?*, p. 37.

61. In *History of the Apostolic Church*, p. 592.

62. Quoted in *Baur: On the Writing of Church History*, p. 214.

63. Baur, *Die Tübinger Schule und ihre Stellung zur Gegenwart* (2d ed.; Tübingen: L. F. Fues, 1860), pp. 44f.

64. Neander,, *Katholizismus und Protestantismus*, ed. H. Messner (Berlin: Wiegandt und Grieben, 1863), p. 192.

65. *History of the Christian Church*, vol. 2 (5th ed.; New York: Charles Scribner's Sons, 1889): 7.

66. H. W. Bowden, *Church History in the Age of Science: Historiographical Patterms in the United States 1876-1918* (Chapel Hill: University of North Carolina Press, 1971), p. xiii.

67. In "German Schools of History," p. 386.

68. The pages of *Church History* over the past thirty years, for instance, show well the extent to which American church historians have been vexed by the question, and the many valuable contributions they have offered in trying to define more precisely the nature of their discipline, in relation to both critical history and Christian theology: e.g., J. H. Nichols, "Church History and Secular History," 13 (June 1944): 87-99, and "The Art of Church History," 20 (March 1951): 3-9; L. J. Trinterud, "The Task of the American Church Historian," 25 (March 1956): 3-15; S. E. Mead, "Church History Explained," 32 (March 1963): 17-31; and, finally, A. C. Outler, "Theodosius' Horse: Reflections on the Predicament of the Church Historian," 34 (September 1965): 251-61. Unfortunately, space does not permit me to relate my own understanding of the nature of church history to these earlier essays.

69. "On the Proof of the Spirit and of Power," in *Lessing's Theological Writings*, ed. and trans. H. Chadwick (Stanford, Calif.: Stanford University Press, 1957), pp. 55 and 53, respectively.

70. By P. C. Hodgson, in *The Formation of Historical Theology: A*

Study of Ferdinand Christian Baur (New York: Harper & Row, 1966), p. 271.

71. Baur, *Der Kritiker und der Fanatiker in der Person des Herrn Heinrich W. J. Thiersch. Zur Charakteristik der neuesten Theologie* (Stuttgart: Becher's Verlag, 1846), p. 3.

72. In "Adolf von Harnack und Ferdinand Christian Baur," *Festgabe für Adolf von Harnack*, ed. K. Holl (Tübingen: J. C. B. Mohr [P. Siebeck], 1921), p. 284.

73. In *The Absoluteness of Christianity and the History of Religions*, trans. D. Reid (Richmond, Va.: John Knox Press, 1971), p. 85.

74. In *Christentum und Kultur*, ed. C. A. Bernoulli (Basel: Benno Schwabe, 1919), p. 7.

75. Troeltsch, "Protestantisches Christentum und Kirche in der Neuzeit," in Paul Hinneberg, ed., *Die Kultur der Gegenwart*, p. 1, sect. 4.1 (2d ed.; Berlin and Leipzig: B. G. Teubner, 1909), p. 609; Dilthey, "Rede zum 70. Geburtstag" (1903), vol. 5 of *Gesammelte Schriften* (3d ed.; Stuttgart: B. G. Teubner—Göttingen: Vandenhoeck und Ruprecht, 1961), p. 9.

76. In *Christianity as History and Faith*, ed. A. C. McGiffert, Jr. (New York: Charles Scribner's Sons, 1934), pp. 12f.

77. For a suggestive discussion of the role of Troeltsch and of Dilthey in the "Crisis of Historicism," see Iggers, *The German Conception of History*, chaps. 6 and 7.

78. Both quotations from Wilhelm Pauck, *The Heritage of the Reformation*, rev. and enl. ed. (Glencoe, Ill.: The Free Press, 1961), p. 347.

79. Quotation and comment in Jaroslav Pelikan, *Historical Theology* (Philadelphia: Westminster Press—New York: Corpus Instrumentorum, 1971), p. 155.

80. In *Protestant Thought: From Rousseau to Ritschl*, p. 383.

81. Ibid., p. 389.

82. *The Epistle to the Romans*, 6th ed., trans. E. C. Hoskyns (London: Oxford University Press, 1933), p. 1.

83. Quoted in H. Holborn, "Wilhelm Dilthey and the Critique of Historical Reason," *Journal of the History of Ideas* 11.1 (1950): 98.

84. H. Heimpel. "Geschichte und Geschichtswissenschaft," *Vierteljahreshefte für Zeitgeschichte*, 5 (1957): 2.

85. K. Biehlmeyer, *Church History*, rev. ed. H. Tüchle (13th ed; trans. V. O. Mills; Westminster, Md.: Newman Press, 1958), 1: 2f.; Herbert Jedin and J. P. Dolan, eds., *Handbook of Church History*, 1 (New York: Herder and Herder, 1965): 3; Joseph Lortz, *Geschichte der Kirche in ideengeschichtlicher Betrachtung*, 21st ed.; 1 (Münster: Aschendorff, 1962): 6. As for Schaff, see, for instance, his *History of the Apostolic Church*, pp. 34f.

86. Bowden, *Church History in the Age of Science*, pp. 69 and 92, respectively. It could easily be shown, if space permitted, (1) that Schaff himself had drawn heavily upon the Roman Catholic Johann Adam Möhler, as Möhler in turn acknowledged Neander's strong influence upon his thinking, and as all three opposed Baur; and (2) that even today most German Catholic church historians stand firmly with Möhler's theory of church history. It would be interesting to explore more fully these various cross currents, as well as the close parallelism that I (and others) seem to detect between the nineteenth-century confrontation of Baur and Neander (and Möhler and Schaff) and the twentieth-century confrontation of Bultmann and Barth, and their respective schools.

87. In *A Loss of Mastery: Puritan Historians in Colonial America* (Berkeley and Los Angeles: University of California Press, 1966); all quotations from pp. 121f.

88. By E. W. Schneider, in *Ferdinand Christian Baur in seiner Bedeutung für die Theologie* (Munich: J. F. Lehmann, 1909), p. 327.

89. Heinz Liebing, "Historical-Critical Theology. In Commemoration of the One Hundredth Anniversary of the Death of Ferdinand Christian Baur, December 2, 1960," (trans. P. C. Hodgson), in Ernst Käsemann *et al.*, *Distinctive Protestant and Catholic Themes Reconsidered* (New York: Harper & Row, 1967), p. 68.

90. From Ranke's lecture of 1831, "Uber die Idee der Universalhistorie," trans. from Iggers, *The German Conception of History*, p. 80.

91. Schaff, *History of the Apostolic Church*, p. 676.

92. See "The Significance of the Critical Historical Method for Church and Theology in Protestantism," in Ebeling's *Word and Faith*, trans. J. W. Leitch (Philadelphia: Fortress Press, 1963), pp. 51f.

93. Ibid., p. 56.

94. Ibid., p. 59.

95. This essay, first published in 1947, is now available in English in Ebeling, *The Word of God and Tradition*, trans. S. H. Hooke (Philadelphia: Fortress Press, 1968), pp. 11-31.

96. For the first view, see J. C. Brauer, ed., *Reinterpretation in American Church History*, vol. 5 of *Essays in Divinity*; Chicago and London: University of Chicago Press, 1968), pp. 20ff.; for the second, see W. A. Clebsch, "History and Salvation: An Essay in Distinctions," in *The Study of Religion in Colleges and Universities*, ed. Paul Ramsey and J. F. Wilson (Princeton: Princeton University Press, 1970), pp. 40-72.

97. In his *The Historian and the Believer* (New York: Macmillan Co., 1966), p. 288.

ON REVELATION

Schubert M. Ogden

I

According to Rudolf Bultmann, the idea of revelation in the New Testament

> contains not only the idea that the salvation of man rests on revelation as God's wondrous action, and only on it, so that without it man would be and remain in death, but also the idea that revelation has occurred decisively in the sending of Jesus Christ and becomes present from moment to moment in word and faith.[1]

On the assumption that this remains a sound, if succinct, summary of the results of contemporary exegesis, the thesis of the present essay is twofold: (1) that an adequate Christian systematic theology must continue to acknowledge the necessity of revelation in two different, though closely related, senses of the word; but (2) that, for various reasons, it can no longer rationalize this necessity in the ways that have hitherto been typical of Christian witness and theology. The nature of the argument to be developed in support of

The author is Professor of Theology, Perkins School of Theology, Southern Methodist University.

this thesis, as well as its limitations, may be further clarified by brief comments on both parts of this initial formulation.

Although the task of systematic theology differs from that of historical theology (including exegesis), the primary test of the appropriateness of a systematic statement can only be its congruence with the witness of faith of the New Testament. Of course, simply to specify this test is a good deal easier than to apply it. We now recognize not only the historicity of exegesis, and the ongoing evolution in both its methods and its results, but also the irreducible pluralism of motifs as well as of forms of expression already documented by the canon itself. In fact, we can hardly deny that "*the* witness of faith of the New Testament" is rather the object of theological interpretation than its datum and that, therefore, all attempts to test the appropriateness of systematic statements are bound to be circular. Furthermore, on the position taken here, appropriateness in this sense neither is nor can be the only criterion of systematic adequacy.

Congruence with the canonical witness, although a necessary test of systematic statements, is nevertheless not sufficient. Insofar as such statements also claim, as they do, to be meaningful and true, and thus solicit the assent of every human mind, they perforce render themselves subject to the further criterion of understandability. Here, too, naturally, the test of the criterion is much more easily stated than applied. To determine whether such general criteria of meaning and truth as one must invoke to apply it are in fact what they purport to be, involves one in yet another "hermeneutical circle," a circle from which there likewise is no escape. But we need not dwell on this further difficulty, since it is only incidental to the immediate point, which is simply that congruence with the witness of Scripture is not only a difficult test to apply to systematic statements, but is also an insufficient test, since by itself it can establish nothing whatever as to their meaning or truth. Nevertheless, the claim stands that the appropriateness of systematic statements is as necessary to their adequacy as is their understandability and that the primary test of their appropriateness is their agreement with the scriptural witness. Accordingly, any account of the meaning of "revelation" that is to be systematically adequate must pass this primary test. Although this would not suffice to establish its adequacy, failure of the test would be quite sufficient to establish the contrary.

As for the second part of the formulation, the pertinent comment is that systematic theology as such is, above all, a matter precisely of rationalization. If theological reflection has anything distinctive to contribute, it lies less in its conclusions than in its arguments, less in the claims it advances than in the reasons it gives for them. Correspondingly, the burden of theological criticism is always to assess conventional rationalizations, thereby eliminating those that can no longer be maintained and, so far as possible, indicating others whereby the claims of the Christian witness may still be vindicated. From what has been said, it will be evident that the relevant rationalizations are of two basic kinds: those pertaining to the appropriateness of systematic statements, and thus to establishing their agreement with the witness of the New Testament; and those pertaining to their understandability, and thus to vindicating their meaning and truth in accordance with completely general criteria, themselves critically established.

Obviously, there are severe limits to pursuing either kind of rationalization in a single essay, especially on a topic as fundamental as revelation. Consequently, the exegetical side of the present argument is not to be developed beyond indicating what I take to be a sufficiently responsible interpretation of the New Testament witness to be worthy of serious consideration. And so, too, with the other side of the argument, which must be left even less developed. For, so far from trying to establish my own understanding of revelation as also meaningful and true, I must be content merely to formulate as clearly as I can what one would need to rationalize in order so to establish it.

II

The argument may appropriately begin with the first of the two ideas that Bultmann holds to be included in the New Testament idea of revelation—namely, that man's salvation so entirely depends on the saving action of God that without the revelation by which that action occurs the only future of man would be death. I take it that there is little question that this complex idea is, in fact, an essential component of the New Testament understanding of revelation. On this understanding, not only is every man as such utterly dependent on the prevenient action of God for his authentic life, but that action takes place precisely as a revelation, as a manifestation of God himself to a being capable of receiving and responding to such a manifestation. But, if this is correct, an essential step toward a systematic account of the meaning of "revelation" is to consider just what is implied by this understanding. For, clearly, no such account could be complete which failed to include what the New Testament itself necessarily presupposes in understanding revelation as it does. Our first question, therefore, is this: What is implied as to the sense or senses of the word "revelation" by the New Testament's own basic presuppositions in using it?

The answer, I shall argue, is that "revelation" in one sense of the word properly designates the original event that is constitutive not only of Christian existence but also of human existence in general or simply as such. To see the reasons for this, consider, first, the understanding of God that the New Testament presupposes. Despite the fact that the language in which it typically speaks of God is that either of myth or of a merely categorial metaphysics, there is abundant evidence that the God to whom it bears witness is only inadequately represented by all such language. When Paul confesses, for instance, that for Christians "there is one God, the Father, from whom are all things and for whom we exist" (1 Cor. 8:6), or, in ascribing glory to God, attests that "from him and through him and to him are all things" (Rom. 11:36), any merely mythical or categorial understanding of God is clearly transcended. And what we find in Paul is documented by New Testament theology more generally. The theism it presupposes is, in intention if not in symbol and concept, a truly radical or transcendental theism. God is implicitly understood to be not merely one being among others, even the greatest, but, in the phrase of the later theological tradition, "the Being of all beings"—the one strictly transcendental individual whose individuality is constitutive of reality as such.

To this extent, at least, the classical theistic tradition has always been justified in insisting that the existence of God, as intended in the New Testament, must be conceived as necessary existence. As the ultimate ground and end of "*all* things," and thus of any other existence that is so much as even conceivable, God can exist only necessarily, being the necessary condition even of the possibility of whatever comes to exist. Implied by such necessary existence, however, is that God also is and must be strictly ubiquitous or omnipresent. Precisely as transcendent, as the one transcendental individual distinct from all others, God is and must be immanent in all things as their primal ground, even as they are all immanent in him as their final end. But, in that case, if anything whatever is experienced or understood, even as barely possible, God, too, must be somehow experienced or understood as its necessary ground and end.

And this brings us to the second reason for the answer to our question: the understanding of man which is also presupposed by the New Testament's uses of the word "revelation." Here, too, of course, one must insist on a distinction between the intention of New Testament anthropology and the symbols and concepts in which that intention is only imperfectly expressed. But, allowing for this distinction, one may say that man, as the New Testament intends to speak of him, is a being who not only exists and experiences but also understands—who does not simply live his life in the manner of his fellow creatures, but is both given and required to lead his life by means of his own understanding of himself in relation to his world. In fact, it is just such self-understanding at its most fundamental level which, in the New Testament view, is the constitutive event of human existence. Man is or becomes man only because or insofar as he relates himself understandingly, and thus in freedom and responsibility, to both his own existence and the world around him.

Yet this is not all. The New Testament expressly affirms that man simply as man is also understandingly related to God, if only in the inauthentic mode of misunderstanding God's gift and demand, and regardless of the extent to which such understanding as man has is adequately reflected upon and expressed. So, according to the Prologue of the Fourth Gospel, the Word that was in the beginning with God, and was God, was also the source of life and as such "the light of men," indeed, "the true light that enlightens every man" (John 1:1, 4, 9). Or, again, Paul insists that all men are "without excuse" for their ingratitude and idolatry, since "what can be known about God is plain to them, because God has manifested it to them" (Rom. 1:19f.). Or, finally, there is the speech in Acts 17:22ff., in which Paul is represented as saying to the Athenians,

> What therefore you worship as unknown, this I proclaim to you. The God who made the world and everything in it . . . made from one every nation of men to live on all the face of the earth, having determined allotted periods and the boundaries of their habitation, that they should seek God, and perchance might feel after him and find him, though he is not far from each one of us; for "In him we live and move and are."

Recalling the understanding of God that the New Testament presupposes, we should have no difficulty seeing the reason for these typical affirmations. For, if God does and must exist necessarily, and thus must somehow be understood if anything at all is understood, the constitutive event of human existence as the event of self-understanding can only include an understanding of God. Man is or becomes man only because or insofar as, in understanding himself and his world, he also relates himself understandingly to God's gift and demand. Consequently, whatever the New Testament's own uses of "revelation," there can be no question that, given the presuppositions of its use with respect to man as well as God, God himself is present to every man simply as such in the event in which, being present to himself and his world, man is *eo ipso* present to God.

Of course, the New Testament itself speaks of this original presentation of God to man precisely as "revelation."[2] But, important as it is to recognize this, the argument I have developed is not just from some ἅπαξ λεγόμενου, some particular New Testament use of "revelation," but from what is necessarily presupposed by *all* its uses—namely, that the only God who is revealed to man is such that he must be universally understood and that the only man who is the recipient of God's revelation is such that he can and must understand. The value of this argument, I believe, is to disclose the deeper reasons for the New Testament's own speaking of revelation as in one sense universal because it is the original event of every human life. So far from merely reflecting the then current apologetic situation (as shaped, say, by Hellenistic Judaism or Stoic natural theology), such speaking was the necessary implication of the understanding of God and man that was fundamental to the entire New Testament witness.

If this is correct, however, there also is no great difficulty in rationalizing the appropriateness to Scripture of theology's characteristic acknowledgment throughout most of its long history of something like a "natural revelation"—or, as I prefer to say, following Schleiermacher, "original revelation."[3] The warrant for such acknowledgment (including the teaching of the First Vatican Council that "God, the beginning and end of all things, can be certainly known by the natural light of human reason from created things"[4]) is by no means only that Scripture itself expressly makes it but that it is also strictly entailed by the New Testament's most fundamental presuppositions concerning man and God.

On the other hand, the criticism to be made of the relatively few theologies that have denied original revelation in this sense is not merely that it is a strange kind of loyalty to Scripture to deny for its sake what it itself plainly affirms, as Emil Brunner rightly urged in his famous controversy with Karl Barth.[5] The more serious criticism is that any such denial, however unintentional, is in the way of denying one or the other of the New Testament's own most basic presuppositions. For, if the argument I have developed is sound, the denial of original revelation necessarily entails the following dilemma: Either God is not really God as the New Testament understands him, or else man is not really man in accordance with the same understanding. Thus, when Barth, in utterly denying original revelation, nevertheless allowed that "man is man and not a cat," he was by implication denying that God is the God to whom the New Testament itself intends to bear witness.[6]

III

Yet, if there are the best of reasons for acknowledging that revelation in one sense of the word is the original presentation of God to every human understanding, clearly this is not the only, or even the primary, sense of "revelation" in the New Testament. As Bultmann rightly emphasizes, what the New Testament itself says about revelation includes the further idea that it has occurred decisively in the special event of Jesus Christ, and that it again and again takes place in the present in the witness and faith of which that event is the principle as well as the origin. Consequently, from the New Testament down to our own time, the primary sense of "revelation" in Christian theology has not been "original revelation," but what I call "special revelation," and, more exactly, "decisive revelation," which is to say, the re-presentation of God to men that has taken place and continues to take place through the particular strand of human history of which Jesus of Nazareth is the center. So true is this, in fact, that even theologians who have acknowledged that revelation is in some sense universal have usually intended something very different from the original revelation that I find it imperative to acknowledge.

Thus, while Paul Tillich, for instance, expressly speaks of "universal revelation," he characteristically asserts or implies that special revelation of some sort or other is the only revelation there is. This is evident from his analysis of revelation as the self-manifestation of ultimate mystery in a special miraculous event received in an ecstatic experience. "Mystery," "miracle," and "ecstasy"—these, according to Tillich, are the essential marks of revelation; and from this it follows that one properly speaks of revelation only insofar as one can also speak of a "medium" (or "bearer") of revelation in the form of some natural or historical event accompanied by human language. But this is to say, in effect, that one can speak only of special revelation; and so Tillich is only consistent when he takes "universal revelation" to refer not even to the universal occurrence of special revelation but only to its occurrence well beyond the bounds of "final revelation" and to the "universal possibility" of its occurrence.[7]

The point of this reference to Tillich is not critical but simply to underscore that it is precisely the sense of revelation as special revelation, or decisive revelation, by which the usual systematic treatments of the topic are all determined, including even revisionary ones. To employ the distinction used in recent Roman Catholic theology, I could say that what is generally meant by "revelation" in theological treatises is not "transcendental revelation" but "categorial (or predicamental) revelation."[8] It is the revelation constitutive of all specifically Christian existence, as distinct from the existence of man in general or simply as such.

The further and more important point, however, is that revelation in this sense has been universally claimed to be necessary by Christian theology. Even where the necessity of original revelation has been disputed or obscured, special revelation has not only consistently been acknowledged but acknowledged as something that simply had and has to take place. One reason for this, obviously, is that, being constitutive of all Christian faith and witness, as well as of their theological interpretation, the re-presentation of God in Jesus Christ has to be acknowledged as *sine qua non* because it is the strictly necessary condition of the possibility of Christian existence as such. But it is just as obvious that this minimal necessity is by no means the only necessity that theologians have typically claimed for special revelation, even if such other reasons as they have given for their claim are open to serious objections. The second question we need to ask, therefore, is how this traditional claim is to be rationalized. By what reasons, if any, can we continue to acknowledge not only that God is revealed decisively in Jesus Christ but also that this revelation is necessary?

One type of answer that we can no longer accept, I believe, might be developed as follows: Granted that there is, indeed, an original revelation of God to every human understanding, this revelation, being purely "natural," is in no way self-sufficient. Since, on any account, there is more to revelation and authentic faith in God than merely understanding that and what God is, even with full reflectiveness, all "natural revelation," as well as all "natural theology," does and must point beyond itself. Seeing, then, that the more to which it points is just what is manifested in the particular history of which Jesus of Nazareth is the center, we both may and must affirm that this history constitutes a properly "supernatural" revelation which is therefore revelation in a special—indeed decisive—sense.

This, I take it, is the kind of answer to our question that would most likely be given to it by anyone oriented mainly to the great central tradition of Christian theology. In the particular form it has received from the representatives of orthodoxy, Protestant and Catholic alike, it is characterized not only by the systematic distinction between "nature and grace," "the natural and the supernatural," but also by the tacit assumption that revelation and faith are primarily a matter of acquiring knowledge. Thus, special revelation is held to be necessary, in the last analysis, because it is only through it that the distinctive truths of Christianity, or the "mysteries of faith," are so represented to the human intellect as to be even possibly the objects of its attention and belief.

The decisive objection to this orthodox form of the answer is that the New Testament itself in no way warrants the assumption that God's revelation in Jesus Christ consists primarily in communicating supernatural knowledge. Although there are passages in the New Testament, just as in the Old, where revelation is indeed spoken of in some such way, Scripture does not characteristically appeal to revelation as providing special knowledge of God's existence and nature. This is sufficiently evident from the fact (rightly stressed by Bultmann) that it is entirely innocent of any particular theological problem in somehow relating to our natural and rational knowledge what we know through revelation.[9] But there is no need to labor the objection, what with the consensus that has now come to exist that orthodoxy's distinctive understanding of revelation can no longer claim the sanction of the New Testament. Not only Protestant neo-orthodoxy but, increasingly, progressive Roman Catholic theology as well, provide abundant evidence that any understanding of revelation as primarily the communication of supernatural knowledge has now been overcome.[10]

Still, it would be wrong to suppose that the same is true of the understanding of special revelation as in a proper sense supernatural. Despite their abandonment of the notion that such revelation itself consists in supernatural truths, most theologians continue to think and speak of it as a supernatural occurrence, which grounds a knowledge of God and ourselves beyond any that nature and reason as such could provide. In fact, stressing, as they do, that, on the New Testament idea of revelation as event, it is God's wondrous act of salvation, they find more than sufficient reason to insist on its character precisely as supernatural. But to this modified understanding, also, there are serious objections, so far as it is taken to answer our question as to the reasons for affirming the necessity of special revelation.

This is especially so of the form of the understanding which has recently been worked out by progressive Catholic theologians. Not the least motive of their work has been to see to it that the problem of revelation as it was acutely posed by the Catholic Modernists is at last given a more adequate solution than any previously available in the official teaching and theology of the Church.[11] Thus, while they have been careful, as the Modernists were not, to maintain the distinction between nature and grace, the natural and the supernatural, they have also made the point that strictly supernatural grace and, therefore, revelation are themselves constitutive of every human existence. Rahner makes this point in his quasi-Heideggerian way by arguing that grace and revelation (specifically, "transcendental revelation") are a "supernatural existential": as supernatural, they must be referred to a second, strictly gratuitous act of God's love in addition to his love in creation, even though, as existential, they are also a constitutive factor of the existence of man as such. But the objection to this kind of understanding revelation of himself in Jesus Christ should be necessary. Even if there is a more to revelation and faith that is strictly supernatural, if this more belongs, or, in the case of faith, *can* belong, to man quite apart from Christian revelation, it can hardly serve to explain the necessity of that revelation.

Rahner himself, of course, is sensitive to this objection and usually tries to meet it by arguing that the grace and revelation given to every man transcendentally are precisely and only the grace and revelation of Christ's incarnation, on which they are entirely dependent as on their final end. But one hardly knows what to make of this argument, seeing that

Rahner is just as emphatic that the mystery of the Incarnation itself has its ultimate ground and end in the *Urgeheimnis* of God's decision to communicate himself in love to every human being. Considering that, in Rahner's view, all the *mysteria sticte dicta* of Trinity, Incarnation, and grace are revealed implicitly in every man's encounter with this primal mystery, we have ample reason to conclude that the only sense, finally, in which he can consistently claim that specifically Christian revelation is necessary is in whatever sense this may be claimed for the full and adequate explication of that primal encounter.[12]

Even if Catholic theologians could consistently claim more than this, however, they would still be faced with a more serious objection, which also applies to the understanding typical of much Protestant neo-orthodoxy. This is the objection that the whole distinction between nature and grace, the natural and the supernatural, must be regarded with profound suspicion from the standpoint of the New Testament, as well as of Scripture generally. To some extent, of course, Protestant theology has always been critical of this distinction as understood and employed by Catholic theologians. Lutheran and Reformed orthodoxy alike rejected the doctrine that man's "original righteousness" is a supernatural *donum superadditum*, on the ground that its implication that man's natural state was imperfect clearly conflicts with Gen. 1:31.[13] And yet their own understanding that man's original gifts were natural did not preclude speaking of God's revelation in Jesus Christ as supernatural. For even these natural gifts themselves must be called supernatural, insofar as they are "above the nature *corrupted by sin* and are not restored except by supernatural grace."[14] Consistent with this traditional Protestant position, then, neo-orthodox theologians who have acknowledged something like a "natural revelation" have continued to think in terms of the distinction between "nature and grace." This is most obvious in the case of Brunner, whose use of the distinction is explicit; but a somewhat similar, if significantly qualified, position is taken also by Reinhold Niebuhr in his Gifford Lectures.[15]

Although, on this position, revelation itself is by no means the communication of supernatural truths, something more is revealed in Christ than is revealed to man originally or "naturally." In formal terms, this more is typically conceived by analogy with our knowledge of another human person, where we do not really come to know the person himself, as distinct from merely knowing about him, until he interprets himself to us through his own personal word. But this strictly formal conception is characteristically entangled with the claim that there is also a material difference between all that man can know of God naturally or rationally and what is made known to him in Christ alone. While natural revelation may indeed confront him with the God of power and law, thereby establishing his responsibility, it is solely in Christ that he meets the God of love and grace, and thus can live by faith and no longer merely by works.

It is, however, just this claim that special revelation has a different content from original revelation that the New Testament sharply calls into question. This is sufficiently evident from the reflection that, since a merely partial divine revelation can at most establish a merely partial human responsibility, it cannot possibly be what Paul intends to assert in Rom. 1:18ff. And what does he mean there by the "power" of God, which he asserts that God has manifested to every man, if not the very thing of which he speaks when he says in a preceding verse that the gospel is "the power of God for salvation to everyone who has faith, to the Jew first and also to the Greek" (vs. 16), or witnesses elsewhere that "Christ crucified" is precisely "Christ the power of God and the wisdom of God" (1 Cor. 1:23-24)?

The answer, I believe, is clear and, together with all the other evidence that Bultmann has carefully reviewed, fully justifies the conclusion he draws from it:

> There is no other light shining in Jesus than has always already shined in the creation. Man learns to understand himself in the light of the revelation of redemption no differently than he always already should have understood himself in face of the revelation in creation and law—namely, as God's creature who is limited by God and stands under God's claim, which opens up to him the way to death or to life. If the revelation in Jesus means salvation as an understanding of oneself in him, then the revelation in creation meant nothing other than this understanding of oneself in God in the knowledge of one's own creatureliness.[16]

Furthermore, in the systematic aspect of his work, Bultmann develops an alternative account of the distinctive "more" of revelation and faith beyond such knowledge of the existence and nature of God as is originally available to man. Appealing to the analogy of human friendship, he argues that the more I come to know when I actually find a friend is "nothing more *about* friendship," but simply that

> I now know my friend and also know myself anew, in the sense that, in understanding my friend, my concrete life in its work and its joy, its struggle and its pain, is qualified in a new way. In knowing my friend in the *event* of friendship, the events of my life become new—"new" in a sense that is valid only for me and visible only to me, that indeed only *becomes* visible in the now and thus must always become visible *anew*.[17]

By means of this analogy, conceptually clarified by Heidegger's distinction between *Existenzialität* and *Existenz*, Bultmann interprets the more of special revelation and faith as precisely their event—as consisting, therefore, not in *what* is revealed and believed in but in the fact *that* revelation and faith take place in my own existence. Thus he shows how the traditional distinction between nature and grace not only should but can be dispensed with, even while acknowledging that there is indeed more to revelation and authentic faith than what man can originally know of the nature and existence of God.

> The revelation of God brings no knowledge about the mysteries of other worlds; in fact, it communicates nothing even about God that any reflective person could not know by himself—namely, that man can receive his life by God's grace only in radical solitariness before him. No revelation needs to tell me what God's grace *means*. One thing alone it tells me, and with that it tells me everything: "This grace holds good for *thee*!" And because it tells me this in the words, "Thy sin is forgiven thee!" it opens my eyes to the fact that the first and last sin of man is to want to be himself by his own power.[18]

And yet, as is well known, Bultmann himself takes the position that God's decisive revelation in Christ is necessary not only to Christian existence but also to any human existence that is to actualize its authentic possibility. This is so, Bultmann argues, because, in spite of God's original revelation to men in the understanding of their own creatureliness, they do not really understand themselves as creatures and thereby honor God and give thanks to him. Their response to his revelation is not at all the authentic response of faith but rather the inauthentic response of sin—the attempt to secure the ultimate meaning of their existence by what they themselves are and have and do, instead of living, finally, by God's grace alone. So, while it is indeed necessary to acknowledge original revelation, it is also necessary to speak of it as now lying in the past, as something that, as men actually exist in the present, they have quite forgotten or suppressed. Having thus already lost their authentic possibility, then, men can have no hope of actualizing it unless God himself, by his own prevenient action, restores it to them. But, since it is just this that God has in fact done in sending Jesus Christ and establishing the Christian proclamation, it is this event as it takes place ever anew through word and sacraments that is God's decisive revelation not only to Christians but to all mankind as well.

This, clearly, is a different answer to our question from any of the family of answers that we have previously considered. It also seems clear, to me at least, that it is notably more appropriate to the underlying intention of the New Testament witness.[19] Yet even to it there are sufficiently serious objections that it can no longer be accepted just as it is.

The crux of these objections can be brought out by relying on a line of reasoning similar to that by which progressive Catholic theologians like Rahner attempt to show that supernatural grace and revelation are constitutive of every human existence, and that this is a fact whether or not one explicitly knows it and regardless of his acceptance of specifically Christian revelation. The ground of this fact (these theologians argue) is God's will that men universally shall be saved, which follows from his primal decision to communicate himself in love, which itself lies behind (although it need not have lain behind) even his creation of the world. Because God has graciously decided that all things shall be perfected in him, he wills to be present and, in fact, is present to every human being, so that even in the state of sin none of us is ever without the possibility of authentic faith.

But now, like any deduction, this reasoning can be reversed, with the following significant result: if any human being is ever simply without the possibility of authentic faith, even if he himself has already forfeited it by his own sin, then God either does not will the authenticity of every man or else is powerless to make it possible. In short, by this reasoning, the implication of Bultmann's position is that God is *not* the God

who "desires all men to be saved and to come to the knowledge of the truth," as well as "the living God, who is the
Savior of all men, especially of those who believe" (1 Tim.
2:4, 4:10).

That this reasoning in no way depends on the distinctive
premises of the Catholic version of classical Christian theism
should be clear enough. But what may well be emphasized is
that it is, if anything, even more to the point, given
Bultmann's own very different premises. He himself expressly
allows that one can support the view that "God does not
exist without the world, the Creator without the creation"
by appealing to John 1:1-3:

> to the remarkable statement that in the beginning was the Word,
> and that the Word of the Creator, through which everything has
> come to be. This is the Word which was in the beginning with God,
> indeed, was God.[20]

But, then, as we have seen, Bultmann also rejects the Catholic
understanding of the "double gratuity," according to which
grace, properly speaking, is due to a strictly supernatural act
of God above and beyond his love in creation. Consequently,
on his own premises, creation and redemption alike must be
said to be natural to God in the sense that God neither would
nor could be who he essentially is, were he not freely to
create worlds and freely to redeem them by his love. To say
that, however, is to have even less reason to maintain that
any human being could ever be without the possibility of
authentic faith—so far, at least, as having that possibility is
dependent on the action of God. On the other hand, to
maintain this is even more obviously to call into question
either God's goodness or his power.

Nor can this form of the problem of evil be in the least
dealt with along the lines of the so-called free-will defense.
To be sure, the actualization of authenticity can only be

man's own free decision, which, on Bultmann's view, certainly, does not follow necessarily from God's grace. Even God's revelation in Christ but restores the *possibility* of authentic faith, thereby leaving open the possibility of man's either continuing in sin or relapsing into it. Likewise, the extent to which man objectifies his existence and becomes explicitly conscious of his possibilities is also a function of human freedom, and thus a historical variable whose values include everything from ignorance and falsehood to the knowledge and truth that are given us in Christ and in the particular history of which he is the center. But what is at issue here is neither the actualization of man's authenticity nor its full and adequate objectification—both of which clearly are dependent, in part, on his own free choice—but rather the possibility of authentic faith, and that only insofar as it depends on the prevenient action of God himself. In the nature of the case, therefore, any appeal to man's freedom and his misuse of it is simply irrelevant to the problem and cannot even begin to solve it.

I conclude, therefore, that the dilemma that Bultmann's position involves is inescapable. Either God is after all not who he is assumed to be, or else there is no human being who is ever simply without God's grace to save, and hence without the possibility of authentic faith. To hold, however, as I do, that it is the second alternative alone that is appropriate to the New Testament witness does not imply that there is no sense at all in which a man may be said to have no authentic possibility. There are, in fact, three senses in which this may quite properly be said: (1) in the sense that the man in question is either not yet or no longer a human being in the relevant meaning of the words; (2) in the sense that, although he in fact is a human being, and thus has the possibility of authentic faith, he nevertheless is not explicitly aware of the fact, and so has it only implicitly; or (3) in the sense that, although he is in fact always given this possibility by God in the gift of his humanity, he himself not only has forfeited it in the past by his own decision for inauthenticity but, despite God's unceasing renewal of the gift, is also engaged in forfeiting it anew in the present.[21] And yet it should already be clear from this that, and why, accepting the second alternative also entails neither a superficial understanding of sin nor a simple identification of faith with theistic belief. Sin may be conceived as radically as you please, and the alternative still accepted, provided only that grace as well be conceived in a radical way. And so, too, one may say that authentic faith in God is indeed more than explicit belief in him, even while insisting that it is and remains every man's possibility. For Bultmann's own insistence still stands, that faith is by no means merely a human capacity or disposition that may be more or less fully developed. Indeed, faith is not possible at all but for the prevenient action of God, and it never becomes actual except as event—as man's ever new response in the moment to God's ever new act of grace.

But, if even the second answer to our question can no longer be fully accepted, how are we to answer it? Can no reason be given for the necessity of Christian revelation beyond the minimal necessity that, as we noted at the outset, can obviously be claimed for it? Is the conclusion to which we are led simply that God's revelation in Jesus Christ is indeed necessary to Christian existence but on no account necessary to human existence as such?

As this question is usually understood, the only answer, I believe, must be affirmative. I am convinced that none of the rationalizations of Christian revelation as necessary even to the possibility of man's authenticity can continue to be maintained—and that, not because they all fail to meet certain criteria of meaning and truth but because, as I have tried to indicate, they do not pass the primary test of agreeing with the scriptural witness. Precisely when one takes the claims of that witness in the full length and breadth of their intended meaning, he is led to conclude that the only necessary, but also sufficient, condition of the possibility of authentic faith is that original presentation of God to man which is the constitutive event of all human existence, and hence an event that never fails to take place as soon and as long as there is any distinctively human being at all.

But if the conventional rationalizations of revelation are thereby eliminated as untenable, it may be that the usual understanding of our question is not the only way of understanding it. Perhaps if we can ask it in a different way, more can be claimed concerning the necessity of special revelation, and hence of decisive revelation, than we have so far found reason to claim.

That this is possible does, in fact, seem to be the case. Granted that original revelation, and thus the possibility of authentic faith, is constitutive of every human existence as such, it by no means follows that men universally are explicitly aware, with full and adequate consciousness, of this fact and all that it involves. For, as we observed earlier, the extent to which any man objectifies his existence by means of explicit concepts and symbols is a function of human freedom, both his own and that of his fellows, and thus is a historical variable allowing for an indefinite range of possible values.

To be sure, the apparent universality of religion in some form throughout all human culture is evidence that men generally have somehow understood reflectively as well as existentially the gift and demand of God's original self-presentation to their existence. In becoming acculturated within his particular tradition, the individual has normally also been formed religiously by learning to objectify the ultimate mystery of his existence in traditional concepts and symbols. But the wide variety of religious forms, of beliefs, rites, and organizations, leaves no question that man is naturally religious only in something like the sense in which he is naturally social or moral. Such religion as he has, as distinct from the faith of which it is the objectification, is not natural but historical, and so available to him only as one religion among others, as one more or less reflective response to God's original revelation.

Both facts, however—the variety of religion as well as its universality—attest to the existence also of special revelation and to man's urgent need for it. At the base of every religion, as its origin and principle, is some particular occasion of insight, of reflective grasp through concept and symbol, of the mystery manifested in original revelation. Thus, not only Christianity but all religions exist only on the basis of, and themselves serve to constitute, some event of special revelation, which as the objectification of our existence in its gift and demand claims to be decisive for it. Nor is there any difficulty in seeing the reasons for this claim. For, in this matter, as in all others, man cannot merely live his life but has to lead it as well, and to this end needs to lay hold of his understanding of himself and of the reality encompassing him in explicit thought and speech. Even his understanding of himself before God is a reflective as well as an existential problem, since it is only insofar as it is fully and adequately objectified that he can become completely clear and certain as to God's gift and demand. Consequently, insofar as the God who is presented to him in all his experience and understanding is also re-presented to him through explicit concepts and symbols, he is confronted with a special revelation that may indeed claim to be decisive for his existence.

Moreover, in the religious sphere even more than in others, the problem of truth either is or becomes acute. Aside from the fact that the object of reflection here is in the nature of the case unique, and thus only improperly objectified by all our ordinary concepts and symbols, there are any number of ways in which it can be reflected, depending upon the particular aspect of man's existence that is taken as focusing the problem of faith. There is also the fact that in this sphere, above all, man's attempts at objectifying his experience are defeated in various ways by that inauthentic understanding of himself which is sin. Inevitably, then, there is the wide variety of religious insights and traditions, each with its claim to be true. But this only intensifies man's need for a special revelation of God's gift and demand that will be decisive—that will objectify his existence in a full and adequate way and thereby guide his decision amidst all the claims and counterclaims to religious truth.

It is along these rather different lines, I suggest, that our question as to the necessity of Christian revelation can very well be asked. Although such revelation cannot be necessary to the *constitution* of human existence, it can very well be necessary to the *objectification* of existence, in the sense of its full and adequate understanding at the level of explicit thought and speech. Insofar, then, as such objectification is in turn necessary, if not to the being of man, then to his becoming, it is by no means only Christians for whom the re-presentation of God in Jesus Christ can in a sense be claimed to be necessary. Of course, the qualification is essential, since Christian revelation is necessary to man as such in a different sense from original revelation. Whereas original revelation, we may say, is *immediately* and *proximately* necessary to man's authenticity, decisive revelation is only *mediately* and *remotely* necessary to it, being necessary in the first instance not to the constitution of his possibility, but to its full and adequate explication.[22] Even so, if man needs, as he does, just such an explication, he also has need of God's revelation in Jesus Christ—and that simply as a man, and so quite apart from the decision for specifically Christian existence.

This can be claimed, naturally, only on the assumption that Christian revelation is, in fact, what it purports to be—namely, the full and adequate objectification of human existence in its authentic possibility. But, if this assumption is true, the necessity that can be claimed for this revelation is more than a merely minimal necessity. For it is man as such, not merely the Christian, who can live only by the word—the inner word of God's love in the depth of his existence and, therefore, the outer word in his history, the veritable incarnation of that love.

IV

There remains the task of responding to an objection that will almost certainly be made to this argument. On the understanding of revelation that I have been indicating, the special revelation affirmed to be decisive by the Christian witness of faith is simply the full and adequate explication of God's original revelation to human existence. Thus, whatever may be claimed concerning the necessity of this revelation, it can in no way be necessary to the very possibility of man's authenticity. Not only is there no other light shining in Jesus than has always already shined in the creation, but no saving act of God occurs in him other than that which never fails to occur as soon and as long as there is any distinctively human being. If this is what the understanding comes to, however, there are those who will see it simply as falling back on what Kierkegaard spoke of as "the Socratic point of view," according to which Christian revelation can be nothing more than an occasion of "recollection" (ἀνάμνησις).[2 3] Our third and final question, therefore, is whether this is in fact the case. Does decisive revelation function merely as a midwife at the birth in time of the eternal truths of theism, or does it reveal something new to man?

We may observe, to begin with, that Kierkegaard's formulation of the alternatives in this connection is on the face of it inexhaustive.[24] As he presents them, there are two basically different understandings of existence between which one must choose: the Socratic understanding, according to which *no* event is constitutive of man's authentic possibility, because he already possesses it implicitly prior to any event; and Kierkegaard's own understanding, according to which *some* event is thus constitutive, because it is in it alone that man is given the possibility that he does not already possess, not even implicitly. But these, obviously, are not the only alternatives logically allowed for by the very disjunction on which Kierkegaard relies. There remains, if only as "a project of thought," a third understanding, according to which *every* event is constitutive of man's possibility, because, while it is in no way his eternal possession, it is given to him at least implicitly in every event that is constitutive of his existence.

There are good reasons, naturally, why Kierkegaard should have neglected this third alternative. Like so many others, he was bent on so rationalizing Christian revelation that it could be claimed to be necessary even to the possibility of man's authenticity, in that, as he himself put it, man's "eternal happiness" is based upon "historical knowledge." Nevertheless, since his understanding of existence is clearly not the only way in which one might make "an advance upon Socrates," rejection of his understanding need in no way be a retreat to "the Socratic point of view."

The pertinence of this observation, of course, is that it is the very alternative Kierkegaard neglected that has been pursued in the present argument. According to the understanding I have tried to indicate, Christian revelation is by no means merely the explication of the eternal truths of theism. For, while it is indeed nothing other than the full and adequate objectification of original revelation, original revelation itself is always and only an event—an event occurring in time, and so nothing merely eternal. To be sure, original revelation is not simply one event among others but, rather, the unique event which, being constitutive of man's existence, always occurs insofar as he exists at all. It is the event in which God's ever new presentation of himself to the world in love not only takes place but is also received and somehow responded to understandingly as gift and demand.

To this extent, then, man indeed possesses, if only implicitly, certain eternal truths of which Christian revelation is merely the explication—such truths as that God exists and is a loving God and therefore so acts toward the world as ever and again to embrace it with his love. As we noted earlier in the argument, however, there is more to revelation than man's possession of such truths, even in the form of explicit belief. Original revelation itself is precisely event—the event of God's self-presentation in every moment not only as God but as *my God*, as the concrete ground and end of my own unique existence and of just this particular world of which I am here and now a part. Because this is so, however, decisive revelation by no means functions merely as a midwife at the birth of explicit theism. As the objectification of God's original revelation in every present, it is the re-presentation of his love itself as the ever new gift and demand of my existence.

In sum: *What* Christian revelation reveals to man is nothing new, since such truths as it makes explicit must already be known to him implicitly in every moment of his existence. But *that* this revelation occurs does reveal something new to him in that, as itself event, it is the occurrence in his history of the transcendent event of God's love. As Bultmann says of the proclamation of Jesus,

> *What* he says he does not say as anything new or unheard of; but *that* he says it, that he says it *now*, is what is decisive and what

makes the situation of all who hear it into a new and decisive situation.[25]

This is not to say, naturally, that the content of Christian revelation is somehow unimportant or unnecessary. It is to say simply that what makes it revelation is also the fact of its occurrence and that it is with respect to this fact that it is the decisive revelation of something new: God's "new creation" in Christ, and so man's authentic possibility of "faith working through love" (2 Cor. 5:17; Gal. 6:15, 5:6).

NOTES

1. "Offenbarung: IV. Im NT," *Religion in Geschichte und Gegenwart*, 4 (2d ed.; Tübingen: J. C. B. Mohr, 1930): 663f. See also Bultmann's more extended discussion in *Der Begriff der Offenbarung im Neuen Testament* (Tübingen: J. C. B. Mohr, 1929); trans. Schubert M. Ogden in *Existence and Faith: Shorter Writings of Rudolf Bultmann* (New York: Meridian Books, 1960), pp. 58-91.

2. This is evident, for example, from the fact, uniformly obscured in the commonly used translations, that Paul uses the very same verb φανερῶν in Rom. 1:19: "What can be known about God is plain to them because God has manifested (ἐφανέρωσεν) it to them," as in Rom. 3:21:

> But now the righteousness of God has been manifested (πεφανέρωται) apart from the law, although the law and the prophets bear witness to it, the righteousness of God through faith in Jesus Christ for all who believe.

3. See Friedrich Schleiermacher, *Der christliche Glaube, nach den Grundsätzen der evangelischen Kirche im Zusammenhange dargestellt* (7th ed.; Berlin: Walter de Gruyter & Co., 1960), 1:30; trans. H. R. Macintosh *et al.* in *The Christian Faith* (Edinburgh: T. & T. Clark, 1928), pp. 17f.:

The feeling of absolute dependence becomes a clear self-consciousness only because this idea [i.e., of God] simultaneously comes into being. To this extent, one can indeed say that God is given to us in feeling in an original way; and if one speaks of an original revelation of God to man or in man, what will always be meant is that, along with the absolute dependence that belongs to all finite being no less than to man, there is also given to him the immediate self-consciousness of it which becomes the consciousness of God. In whatever measure this actually comes forth in a personality in the course of time, in just that measure we ascribe piety to the individual.

Granted that Schleiermacher here, as elsewhere, seems to think of "piety" after the model of *Bildung*, and thus as a human capacity or disposition that may be more or less fully developed, he nevertheless makes two points that are essential for any systematic understanding of revelation: (1) that authentic and inauthentic faith alike presuppose revelation; and (2) that the revelation they presuppose is the "original revelation" constituted by man's not only being absolutely dependent on God for his being and meaning but also understanding existentially the fact of his dependence.

4. Heinrich Denzinger, ed., *Enchiridion Symbolorum Definitionum et Declaratorum de Rebus Fidei et Morum* (33d ed.; Freiburg: Herder Verlag, 1965), p. 588 (§3004).

5. *Natur und Gnade: Zum Gespräch mit Karl Barth* (Zürich: Zwingli Verlag, 1934), p. 12; trans. Peter Fraenkel in John Baillie, ed., *Natural Theology* (London: Geoffrey Bles, 1946), p. 25.

6. *Nein! Antwort an Emil Brunner* (Munich: Christian Kaiser Verlag, 1934), p. 25; trans. P. Fraenkel in Baillie, ed., *Natural Theology*, p. 88.

7. See *Systematic Theology*, 1 (Chicago: University of Chicago Press, 1951): 106-59, especially pp. 138ff., 142. How opposed Tillich is to the whole concept of original revelation is clear from his rejection of any notion of an "inner word" or an "inner revelation" as being a mystical, idealist, spiritualist notion that leads only too easily to rationalism. "Against the doctrine of the inner word," he contends, "Christian theology must maintain the doctrine of the word as a medium of revelation, symbolically the doctrine of the Word of God" (pp. 125f.).

8. See, e.g., Karl Rahner and Joseph Ratzinger, *Offenbarung und Überlieferung* (Freiburg: Herder Verlag, 1965), pp. 11-24; trans. W. J. O'Hara in *Revelation and Tradition* (New York: Herder & Herder, 1966), pp. 9-25; also Bernard J. F. Lonergan, *Method in Theology* (New York: Herder & Herder, 1972), p. 119, where the distinction drawn between "the inner word that is God's gift of his love" and "the outer word of the religious tradition" clearly serves to say the same thing in different terms.

9. See *Religion in Geschichte und Gegenwart*, 2d ed., 4:661.

10. See John Baillie, *The Idea of Revelation in Recent Thought* (New York: Columbia University Press, 1956); also Gregory Baum, " 'The Religions' in Recent Roman Catholic Theology," *The Journal of Religious Thought*, 26.2 (1969): 41-56. According to Baum, "what is most characteristic of the progressive movement" is "a modified understanding of divine revelation," which "has been developed by Catholic theologians in the 20th century and officially acknowledged in the teaching documents of the Vatican Council II" (p. 43).

11. Rahner is quite explicit about this (*Offenbarung*, pp. 11ff.; trans., pp. 9ff.); and Baum, to my mind rightly, links the modified understanding of revelation with the assertion going back to Maurice Blondel that "divine revelation happens in some way in the lives of all "men" (" 'The Religions' in Catholic Theology," p. 44).

12. In some passages Rahner seems almost to give up the attempt to rationalize his position. Thus, in a recent article, "Secular Life and the Sacraments," *The Tablet*, 225. 6822 and 6823 (1971): 236ff. and 267f., he concludes:

It may be that theological reflection is faced here with truths which cannot easily be brought together—the truth [sic], namely, that grace is always at work from within and nevertheless also comes from without through the particular time-bound intervention of the sacramental sign.

13. See Heinrich Schmid, *The Doctrinal Theology of the Evangelical Lutheran Church*, trans. Charles A. Hay and Henry E. Jacobs (3d ed.; Minneapolis: Augsburg Publishing House, 1961), p. 230; also Heinrich Heppe, *Die Dogmatik der evangelisch-reformierten Kirche dargestellt und aus den Quellen belegt*, ed. Ernst Bizer (2d ed.; Neukirchen:

Neukirchener Verlag, 1958), pp. 190f.; trans. G. T. Thomson in *Reformed Dogmatics* (London: George Allen & Unwin, 1950), p. 239. See also Paul Tillich, *A History of Christian Thought*, ed. Carl Braaten (New York: Harper & Row, 1968), pp. 125f., 192ff.

14. Heppe, *Die Dogmatik*, p. 191, quoting J. H. Hottinger (trans., p. 239).

15. *The Nature and Destiny of Man: A Christian Interpretation* (New York: Charles Scribner's Sons, 1941 and 1943), esp. 1:125—49. The principal qualification of Niebuhr's position, aside from the absence of any specific designation of "special" or "historical" revelation as "supernatural," is introduced by his doctrine that "a 'hidden Christ' operates in history" (2:109, n. 6). Thus, while he holds that "the longing, though not the assurance, of forgiveness and reconciliation is a part of [man's] common experience [= general revelation]," he can also affirm that there may be "experiences of repentance," and hence "the knowledge of divine love," even though "they may not be consciously related to Biblical revelation" (1:143, 257; see also 2:123, 208). In fact there are passages in which Niebuhr seems to conceive special revelation as nothing but the objectification of what is originally revealed to man as such. "It is in Christ," he says, "that the vague sense of the divine, which human life never loses, is crystallized into a revelation of a divine mercy and judgment" (2:109).

16. *Der Begriff der Offenbarung im Neuen Testament*, pp. 38f.; trans., p. 86.

17. "Die Geschichtlichkeit des Daseins und der Glaube," *Zeitschrift für Theologie und Kirche*, 11 (1930): 351; trans. Schubert M. Ogden in *Existence and Faith*, pp. 99f.

18. *Glauben und Verstehen,* 2 (Tübingen: J. C. B. Mohr, 1952): 272; trans. James C. G. Greig in *Essays, Philosophical and Theological* (London: SCM Press, 1955), p. 302. The failure to make clear that Bultmann's strictly Heideggerian distinction between the abstract structure of human existence and its concrete event is in no way the Catholic distinction between nature and grace is the most serious weakness in Gotthold Hasenhüttl, *Der Glaubensvollzug: Eine Begegnung mit Rudolf Bultmann aus katholischem Glaubensverständnis* (Essen: Ludgerus Verlag Hubert Wingen KG, 1963).

19. Much the same could be said of the position developed earlier by

Wilhelm Herrmann, *Der Begriff der Offenbarung* (Giessen: J. Ricker-
sche Buchhandlung, 1887), and the later position of H. Richard
Niebuhr, *The Meaning of Revelation* (New York: Macmillan Co., 1941).
In fact it could be argued that, when the distinctive qualifications of
Niebuhr's position are taken into account, this position, even more than
his brother's, points toward the alternative understanding of revelation
that I am concerned to indicate.

20. *Glauben und Verstehen*, 4 (Tübingen: J. C. B. Mohr, 1965): 125;
trans. Robert W. Funk in *Journal for Theology and the Church*, 2 (New
York: Harper & Row, 1965): 93.

21. Cf. Søren Kierkegaard, *Philosophical Fragments: Or a Fragment
of Philosophy*, trans. David F. Swenson and Howard V. Hong (rev. ed.;
Princeton: Princeton University Press, 1962), pp. 18f. Significantly,
Kierkegaard recognizes that "the condition for understanding the
Truth," being "an essential condition," is necessarily such that "the
learner" can neither be deprived of it nor remain in a state of
deprivation "without his own responsibility." Consequently, "the
learner himself has forfeited the condition, *and is engaged in forfeiting
it*" (italics added).

22. Cf. Edward H. Sugden, ed., *Wesley's Standard Sermons* (London:
Epworth Press, 1921), 2:451f., 456f. Wesley's own use of this
distinction, of course, is to clarify the different senses in which not
only faith but also good works are necessary to "the scripture way of
salvation." But the evident counterpart of his answer to this question is
just the sort of answer to our question of the necessity of revelation for
which I am arguing. For the analogy here is strict: as faith is to good
works, so the original presentation of God is to his decisive re-presentation in Jesus Christ.

23. Kierkegaard, *Philosophical Fragments, passim*.

24. See William Russell Pregeant, *The Meaning of Matthew's
Christology: A Hermeneutical Investigation in Conversation with the
Theology of Schubert M. Ogden* (Ann Arbor: University Microfilms,
1971), pp. 8ff.

25. *Glauben und Verstehen*, 1 (2d ed.; Tübingen: J. C. B. Mohr,
1954): 204; trans. Louise Pettibone Smith in *Faith and Understanding*,
1, ed. Robert W. Funk (New York: Harper & Row, 1969): 237.

A SELECT BIBLIOGRAPHY OF ALBERT C. OUTLER*

*Compiled by Wanda W. Smith, with
Kate C. Warnick and Carlotta S. Outler*

BOOKS

Psychotherapy and the Christian Message. New York: Harper & Bros.,
1954.

Augustine: Confessions and Enchiridion. Vol. 7. Library of Christian
Classics. Philadelphia: Westminster Press, 1955.

The Christian Tradition and the Unity We Seek. New York: Oxford
University Press, 1957.

John Wesley. Library of Protestant Thought. New York: Oxford
University Press, 1964.

That the World May Believe: A Study of Christian Unity. New York:
Joint Commission on Education and Cultivation, Board of Missions
of the Methodist Church, 1966.

Methodist Observer at Vatican II. Westminster, Md.: Newman Press,
1967.

Who Trusts in God: Musings on the Meaning of Providence. New York:
Oxford University Press, 1968.

Evangelism in the Wesleyan Spirit. Nashville: Tidings, 1971.

CONTRIBUTIONS TO EDITED WORKS

"The Patristic Christian Ethos and Democracy." In *Science, Philosophy
and Religion*. 2d symposium. New York: Conference on Science,
Philosophy and Religion in Their Relation to the Democratic Way of
Life, 1943. Pp. 446-70.

*A virtually complete bibliography of the published writings of
Albert C. Outler may be found in the *Perkins Journal* 27.3 (Spring
1974): 42-51.

"The Reformation and Classical Protestantism." In *The Vitality of the Christian Tradition*, ed. George F. Thomas. London and New York: Harper & Bros., 1944. Pp. 116-48.

"The Person and Work of Christ in the Thought of Saint Augustine." In *A Companion to the Study of Saint Augustine*, ed. Roy W. Battenhouse. New York: Oxford University Press, 1955. Pp. 343-70.

"Some concepts of Human Rights and Obligations in Classical Protestantism." In *Natural Law and Natural Rights*, ed. Arthur L. Harding. Dallas: Southern Methodist University Press, 1955. Pp. 3-28.

"Freud and the Domestication of Tragedy." In *The Tragic Vision and the Christian Faith*, ed. Nathan Scott. New York: Association Press, 1957. Pp. 264-80.

"Our Common History as Christians." In *The Nature of the Unity We Seek*, ed. Paul Minear. St. Louis: Bethany Press, 1958. Pp. 79-89.

"The Church Unity We Have." In *Christian Unity in North America; A Symposium*, ed. J. Robert Nelson. St. Louis Bethany Press, 1958. Pp. 73-80.

"Anxiety and Grace: An Augustine Perspective." In *Constructive Aspects of Anxiety*, ed. Seward Hiltner and Karl Menninger. New York: Abingdon Press, 1963. Pp. 89-102.

"H. Shelton Smith: An Appreciative Memoir." In *A Miscellany of American Christianity: Essays in Honor of H. Shelton Smith*, ed. Stuart C. Henry. Durham, N. C.: Duke University Press, 1963. Pp. 3-21.

"Do Methodists Have a Doctrine of the Church?" In *The Doctrine of the Church*, ed. Dow Kirkpatrick. New York: Abingdon Press, 1964. Pp. 11-28.

"Scripture, Tradition and Ecumenism." In *Scripture and Ecumenism*, ed. Leonard J. Swidler. Pittsburgh: Duquesne University Press, 1965. Pp. 9-22.

"Vatican II and Protestant Theology in America." In *Vatican II: An Interfaith Appraisal*, ed. John H. Miller. Notre Dame, Ind.: University of Notre Dame Press, 1966. Pp. 619-25.

"A Response" (to the *Dogmatic Constitution on the Church*). In *The Documents of Vatican II*, ed. Walter M. Abbott and Joseph Gallagher.

New York: Guild Press—American Press—Association Press, 1966. Pp. 102-6.

"Die höhere Autorität." In *Die Autorität der Freiheit*, ed. Johann Christoph Hampe. Munich: Kösel-Verlag, 1967. Vol. 1, pp. 51-55.

"Reformation Roman-Style." In *American Participation in the Second Vatican Council*, ed. Vincent Arthur Yzermans. New York: Sheed & Ward, 1967. Pp. 313-18.

"The Current Theological Scene: A View from the Beach at Ebb-Tide." In *Proceedings of the Eleventh World Methodist Conference*, ed. Lee F. Tuttle and Max W. Woodward. London: Epworth Press, 1967. Pp. 157-67.

"An Uncommon Ecumenist." In *One of a Kind: Essays in Tribute to Gustave Weigel*. Wilkes-Barre: Dimension Books, 1967. Pp. 43-49.

"Theologische Akzente." In *Der Methodismus*, ed. C. Ernest Sommer. Vol. 6, *Die Kirchen der Welt*. Stuttgart: Evangelisches Verlagswerk, 1968. Pp. 84—102.

"Methodism's Theological Heritage: A Study in Perspective." In *Methodism's Destiny in the Ecumenical Age*, ed. Paul M. Minus, Jr. New York: Abingdon Press, 1969. Pp. 44-70.

"The Mingling of Ministries." In *Digest of the Proceedings of the Eighth Meeting of the Consultation on Church Union, Atlanta, Georgia, March 17-20, 1969*, ed. Paul A. Crow, Jr. (Princeton, 1969), 8:106-18.

"The Ordinal." In *Companion to the Book of Worship*, ed. William F. Dunkle, Jr., and Joseph D. Quillian, Jr. New York and Nashville: Abingdon Press, 1970. Pp. 103-33.

"The Interpretation of the Gospels Today: Some Questions about Aims and Warrants." In *Jesus and Man's Hope*, ed. Donald G. Miller and Dikran Y. Hadidian. Pittsburgh: Pittsburgh Theological Seminary, 1971. Pp. 47-57.

"Discursive Truth and Evangelical Truth." In *Colleges and Commitments*, ed. Lloyd J. Averill and William W. Jellema. Philadelphia: Westminster Press, 1971. Pp. 102-6.

"How Can We Arrive at a Theological and Practical Mutual Recognition of Ministries? A Methodist Reply." In *Concilium* 74, ed. Hans Küng and Walter Kasper. New York: Herder and Herder, 1972.

"Doctrine and Dogma." In *Encyclopaedia Britannica*, 15th ed., 1974. Pp. 927-29.

"God's Providence and the World's Anguish." In *The Mystery of Suffering and Death*, ed. Michael J. Taylor. Staten Island, N. Y.: Alba House, 1973. Pp. 3-23.

INTRODUCTIONS TO WORKS BY OTHER AUTHORS

Foreword to Early Ashby Johnson, *The Crucial Task of Theology*. Richmond, Va.: John Knox Press, 1958. Pp. 7-11.

Foreword to George A. Hadjiantoniou, *Protestant Patriarch: The Life of Cyril Lucaris (1572–1638), Patriarch of Constantinople*. Richmond, Va.: John Knox Press, 1961. Pp. 5-6.

Foreword to Eugene Carl Bianchi, *John XXIII and American Protestants*. Washington and Cleveland: Corpus Books, 1968. Pp. 5-13.

ARTICLES IN JOURNALS

"Origen and the *Regulae Fidei*." *Church History* 8. 3 (1939): 212-21.

"The Historical Approach to Theology." *Duke School of Religion Bulletin* 5.1 (1940): 3-8.

"The 'Platonism' of Clement of Alexandria." *Journal of Religion* 20.3 (1940): 217-40.

"The Problem of Religious Community in Protestantism." *Journal of Religious Thought* 1.2 (1944): 117-27.

"*In* the World Yet Not *of* the World." *Christendom* 10.1 (1945): 44-55.

"A Christian Context for Counseling." *Journal of Pastoral Care* 2.1, (1948): 1-12.

"Colleges, Faculties and Religion: An Appraisal of the Program of Faculty Consultation on Religion in Higher Education, 1945–58." *Educational Record* 30.1 (1949): 45-58.

"For Us Men and Our Salvation." *Religion in Life* 20.2 (1951): 31-35. 483–91.

"Christian Faith and Psychotherapy." *Religion in Life* 21.4. (1952): 483-91.

"A Way Forward from Lund." *Ecumenical Review* 5. 1 (1952): 59-63.

"The Ecumenical Movement: Prospects of Evanston." *Perkins Journal* 7.3 (1954), pp. 14-16.

"Theological Foundations for Christian Higher Education." *The Christian Scholar* 37, Supp. (1954): 202-13.

"Backgrounds and Patterns in Contemporary Theology." *Perkins Journal* 8. 3 (1955): 4-10.

"The Incipience of Faith." Dudleian Lecture for the Academic Year 1955–56, Harvard University, delivered at Andover Chapel, April 10, 1956. *Harvard Divinity Bulletin* 22. 7 (1957): 43-60.

"Augustine and the Transvaluation of the Classical Tradition." *Classical Journal* 54. 5 (1959): 213-20.

"Ordeal of a Happy Dilettante." *Christian Century* 77.5 (1960): 127-29.

"Towards a Re-Appraisal of John Wesley as a Theologian." *Perkins Journal* 14.2 (1961): 5-14.

"Protestant Churches Meeting the Communist Challenge." *Perkins Journal* 15. 1 (1961): 33-40.

"The Test of Orthodoxy." *Theology Today* 19. 3 (1962): 427-29.

"The Shaping of the Mind of Latin Christendom." *Perkins Journal* 16. 2-3 (1963): 5-8.

"From Disputation to Dialogue." *Ecumenical Review* 16. 1 (1963): 14-23.

"Vatican II—Between Acts." *Perkins Journal* 18. 3 (1965): 13-21.

"Liberty Deferred: A Crisis at Vatican II." *Southwest Review* 50. 3 (1965): 209-22.

"Theodosius' Horse: Reflections on the Predicament of the Church Historian." Presidential Address, American Society of Church History, December 29, 1964. *Church History* 34. 3 (1965): 251-61.

"The New Ecumenical Situation: A Bibliographical Essay." *Perkins Journal* 19. 1-2 (1965–66): 26-31.

"*Veni, Creator Spiritus*—The Doctrine of the Holy Spirit." *Perkins Journal* 19. 3 (1966): 31-40.

"Vatican II, A Synoptic View." *London Quarterly and Holborn Review* 192. 3 (1967): 188-99.

"Methods and Aims in the Study of the Development of Catholic Christianity." *Anglican Theological Review* 50. 2 (1968): 117-30.

"Visions and Dreams: The Unfinished Business of an Unfinished Church." A Sermon for the Uniting Conference of the United

Methodist Church, April 23, 1968. *The Daily Christian Advocate* 1. 3 (1968): 133-35.

"Iconoclasm and the Integrity of Faith." *Theology Today* 25. 3 (1968): 295-313.

"The Jewish-Christian Dialogue: Its Ecumenical Setting." *Perkins Journal* 24. 1 (1970): 22-29.

"Does Our Abortion Stand Reflect the Church's Position?" *The Christian Advocate* 15. 17 (1971): 7-8, 18.

"Pastoral Care in the Wesleyan Spirit." *Perkins Journal* 25. 1 (1971): 4-11.

"Revelation and Reflection: Comment in Favor of an Apophatic Theology." *Perkins Journal* 26. 2 (1973): 14-20.

"History as Ecumenical Resource: The Protestant Discovery of 'Tradition.' " Presidential Address, American Catholic Historical Association, December 28, 1972. *Catholic Historical Review* 59. 1 (1973): 1-15.

"The Beginnings of Personhood: Theological Considerations." *Perkins Journal* 27.1 (1973): 28-34.